Japan's Emerging Youth Policy

From the 1960s onwards, Japan's rapid economic growth coincided with remarkably smooth transitions from school to work and with internationally low levels of youth unemployment. However, this changed dramatically in the 1990s and, by the 2000s, youth employment came to be recognized as a serious concern requiring an immediate response. What shape did this response take?

Japan's Emerging Youth Policy is the first book to investigate in detail how the state, experts and the media, as well as youth workers, have reacted to the troubling rise of youth joblessness in early twenty-first-century Japan. The answer that emerges is as complex as it is fascinating, but comprises two essential elements. First, instead of institutional 'carrots and sticks' as seen in Europe, actors belonging to mainstream Japan have deployed controversial labels such as *NEET* ('Not in Education, Employment or Training') to steer inactive youth into low-wage jobs. However, a second, contrasting approach has been crafted by entrepreneurial youth support leaders, building on what the author refers to as 'communities of recognition'. As illustrated in this book using evidence from real sites of youth support, this approach puts an emphasis on 'exploring the user' (i.e. the support-receiver) whereby complex disadvantages, family relationships and local employment contexts are skilfully negotiated. It is this second dimension in Japan's response to youth exclusion that suggests sustainable, internationally attractive solutions to the employment dilemmas that virtually all post-industrial nations currently face but which none has yet seriously addressed.

Based on extensive fieldwork that draws on both sociological and policy science approaches, this book will be welcomed by students, scholars and practitioners in the fields of Japanese and East Asian studies, social innovation, comparative social policy, youth sociology, the sociology of social problems and social work.

Tuukka Toivonen is a Junior Research Fellow in Management at Green Templeton College, University of Oxford, UK (www.tuukkatoivonen.org).

The Nissan Institute/Routledge Japanese studies series

Series Editors:

Roger Goodman
*Nissan Professor of Modern Japanese Studies, University of Oxford,
Fellow, St Antony's College*

J.A.A. Stockwin
*Formerly Nissan Professor of Modern Japanese Studies and former
Director of the Nissan Institute of Japanese Studies, University of Oxford,
Emeritus Fellow, St Antony's College*

Other titles in the series:

Japan's Emerging Youth Policy

Getting young adults back to work

Tuukka Toivonen

Routledge
Taylor & Francis Group

LONDON AND NEW YORK

First published 2013
by Routledge
2 Park Square, Milton Park, Abingdon, Oxon, OX14 4RN

Simultaneously published in the USA and Canada
by Routledge
711 Third Avenue, New York, NY 10017

Routledge is an imprint of the Taylor & Francis Group, an informa business

British Library Cataloguing in Publication Data
A catalogue record for this book is available from the British Library

Library of Congress Cataloging in Publication Data
Toivonen, Tuukka H. I. (Tuukka Hannu Ilmari), 1979–
Japan's emerging youth policy : getting young adults back to work / Tuukka
Toivonen.
  p. cm. – (Nissan Institute/Routledge Japanese studies)
    Includes bibliographical references and index.
    1. Youth—Employment—Government policy—Japan. 2. Youth—
Employment—Japan. 3. Unemployment—Japan. 4. Youth—Japan—Social
conditions. I. Title.
    HD6276.J32T65 2012
    331.3'470952—dc23
                        2012013309

ISBN: 978-0-415-67053-1 (hbk)
ISBN: 978-0-203-09383-2 (ebk)

Typeset in Times New Roman
by Taylor & Francis Books

MIX
Paper from
responsible sources
FSC
www.fsc.org   FSC® C004839

Printed and bound by CPI Group (UK) Ltd, Croydon, CR0 4YY

This book is dedicated to Japan's youth support workers, the light at the end of the tunnel for many a wounded young soul.

Contents

List of figures and tables

Figures

Tables

List of appendices

Preface

'How to get youth back to work' was not always a central question on the minds of parents, policy-makers and rehabilitators in Japan. For with the country's economic miracle that so awed the world from the 1960s onwards came another wonder: exceptionally low incidence of youth unemployment. The unemployment rate for youth in their early twenties remained less than half of that in many Western countries, including the USA and the UK, throughout the 1970s and 1980s. We now know that these enviably low rates of exclusion from stable employment were not the outcome of high manufacturing-led growth alone – or even of life-time employment per se – but relied on a special, firmly institutionalized school-to-work transition system.[1] While hardly the most celebrated aspect of Japan's global success story, the analysts who first disentangled the underlying sociological machinery could scarcely hide their admiration for its efficiency and flow. In this era, a synergistic pact existed between the state, schools and companies, which cooperated closely to funnel the majority of youth from classrooms into employment of the permanent variety – a key marker of adulthood and normalcy for males especially.

The breakdown of this previously stable system of transitions from the 1990s onwards, in the context of highly specific life-course ideals and other cultural patterns that have been far slower to change, partly explains why young adults and their employment became a hotly debated issue in post-bubble Japan.[2] As elsewhere, with the deepening of post-industrialization, the issue of returning young adults to work emerged to confound many an ordinary family and decision-maker, and eventually it also came to be constructed as a major social problem through the media. Rather than post-industrialization or labour market deregulation per se – which are wider processes that affect not only Europe but also other East Asian countries[3] – it is precisely the remarkable stability and cohesion of its prior system of school-to-work transitions and long-term employment that may make Japan a particularly interesting case from a comparative perspective. Against the old status quo, recent changes appear radical to the point of challenging the very logic of Japan's labour market regime, with deep implications for youth as a demographic group, as a life-stage, and as a target for policy intervention.

The issue of youth worklessness came to be problematized in Japan in the mid-2000s under the influence of the transnational paradigm of 'activation' and under the specific guise of 'independence support'. To set the stage for this book's investigation of this process, it is necessary to venture briefly into Japan's changing discourses on the use of discipline in the socialization of children and youth at the outset. This is because Japanese efforts to return youth to employment have been rooted as much in a peculiar legacy of disciplinarian youth rehabilitation as they have been shaped by post-industrial pressures and international policy paradigms. Youth activation within Japan, as this book will illustrate in detail, grew out of the convergence of these initially distinct worlds.

The demise of disciplinarianism

How to effectively exercise discipline and impart 'correct' behaviours on youth remained, despite relatively smooth transitions into employment, fiercely debated topics in Japan's high-growth era. Basic education continued to rely heavily on various collective training techniques associated with the notion of 'group living' (*shūdan seikatsu*), which still remains relevant to socialization processes – and indeed to youth policy – today.[4] Notably, corporal punishment, while varying in severity and frequency, remained a routine practice at many institutions from the elementary level right up to high schools.[5] In the 1970s, among the most conspicuous targets of corrective action were delinquent youth (*hikō*), who were seen as a growing threat to social stability. In the 1980s, public attention turned increasingly to the problem of the so-called school-refusal and to the children who were said to engage in it (*tōkō kyohi*).[6] Such distinctive groups of 'problem youth' – of which these two are far from the only examples – were typically cast as immature, deviant or lacking in toughness, rather than as victims of complex circumstances or social structures.

No educator better personifies this earlier, more disciplinarian period and its eventual demise than Totsuka Hiroshi.[7] Following a career as a successful Olympic yachtsman, Totsuka decided in 1976 to dedicate his energies to the rehabilitation of problematic young people, mainly emotionally disturbed teenagers at first, whom parents and other educators had found impossible to manage. Enrolling their offspring in Totsuka's famously 'Spartan-style' (ascetic and harsh) training school – for them, a solution of last resort – parents hoped that, in the course of rigorous coaching and the effective administration of corporal punishment (*taibatsu*), the children would successfully re-adapt to, and learn to survive in, mainstream Japanese society.

Totsuka's original training regime, drawing on the notion that physical punishment was a wholly justifiable and even preferable practice if it served the purposes of education (*kyōiku*), was considered a success by not a few former participants and commentators in its heyday. Disturbing as recently released scenes of training, where students are being injured with oars and bamboo sticks, may seem,[8] such tactics were not so far-removed from dominant schooling and coaching ideals in the 1970s and early 1980s. Notably, corporal punishment even came to be portrayed then as an important educational solution and cornerstone of so-called managed education (*kanri kyōiku*) amid a public crisis over school violence. That the likes of Ishihara Shintarō, the long-term governor of Tokyo with a nationalist reputation, fell among Totsuka's supporters reflects the fact that Totsuka's philosophy was a firm part of mainstream educational attitudes in this era.

But Totsuka and his disciplinarian methods would not prevail. Following four fatal incidents in the early 1980s – one of which involved a student reportedly suffering 115 blows to the body from a variety of weapons, punches and kicks – he faced a lawsuit that would drag on for two decades. Once it finally concluded, Totsuka was ordered to serve a substantial prison sentence from 2003 to 2006. With important consequences for educational and rehabilitative practices, public attitudes towards the extreme application of discipline turned increasingly negative as the Totsuka trial was being fought. Instead of being seen as a solution to educational ills, corporal punishment – the symbol of disciplinarian practices – came to be reframed as a serious social problem in and of itself, making it harder and harder to justify the use of physical force for any positive educational or coaching purposes.

By the 2000s, the tide had turned entirely: with increasing attention being paid to the harmful effects of 'abuse' (*gyakutai*), the exercise of harsh discipline in the home, the school and even the company was being openly questioned and 'softer' forms of encouragement recommended instead. Of course, there is no evidence that violent practices had altogether disappeared, and there certainly was a perception even at the end of the decade that child abuse, for instance, had continued to increase.[9] But what we know for certain is that there emerged a far higher sensitivity to the disciplining of children and youth among the public, who now predominantly condemned the use of violence in this realm. The disciplinarian approach to socialization so openly advocated in the past by Totsuka and implicitly embraced by dominant segments of Japanese society had fallen into disrepute, becoming a minority position very difficult to defend before the mainstream media. The aging yacht school leader's increasingly confrontational, desperate encounters with reporters and news crews in the late 2000s provided a sharp reminder of this changed reality.

It is an interesting accident of history that, just as the idea of disciplinarian rehabilitation became discredited, the social reintegration of youth became a major national policy concern for the first time in affluent postwar Japan. By the early 2000s, at the very latest, it had become painfully apparent that the miraculously low unemployment rates that Japan had previously been praised for belonged to a reality that obtained no longer; that school-to-work transitions had become far less smooth an affair than in the past; and that the new employees of this 'post-bubble' era did not (or could not) always work in the same way as their parents had. While the underlying structural shifts were (at first) too subtle to capture the public's attention, Japanese middle-class society was shocked by the appearance of the so-called *freeters*, or young part-time workers without permanent contracts. The young part-time workers whom this label referred to were said to embody a new, more mobile and individualistic lifestyle that was diametrically opposed to the postwar model of an ideal worker, i.e. that of the full-time 'regular', or standard, employee (*seishain*). Yet *freeters* were still workers, even if they challenged normative standards and were branded as 'irregulars' (*hiseiki*). It was, indeed, with the further discovery, just a few years later, of a hitherto unknown non-working layer of young people, the so-called *NEETs*, that the crisis over youth and work really erupted.

With such an unexpected new reality coming into view just as established rehabilitation practices had become discredited, time was ripe for a fundamental rethinking of both youth and employment-related policy. This rethinking would to a certain extent be influenced by Totsuka's troubled disciplinarian legacy, but it would nevertheless give rise to a set of genuinely novel practices and competing paradigms, including an 'accommodating' approach to youth rehabilitation. These innovations and ideas unfolded primarily in what is in Japan variably referred to as the field of 'youth employment support' (*wakamono shūrō shien*), 'youth independence support' (*wakamono jiritsu shien*) or simply 'youth support' (*wakamono shien*). Engaging in one way or another with this emergent field, how did concerned groups of experts, parents, policy-makers and rehabilitators – as well as the mainstream media, always so willing to help construct controversial youth problems – propose to return young people back to work in an unstable era characterized by 'softer' educational approaches and post-industrial labour markets? It is the related processes of negotiation, unfolding throughout the 2000s, that occupy the very centre of the seven chapters that comprise this volume.

A book about emerging practices

This book is thus predominantly not a story about the deterioration of previously 'functional' institutions (e.g. school-to-work transition mechanisms), the unravelling of Japan's social security system or the decline of Japanese society in general. Several existing books on the sociology of Japan and related fields have already addressed such topics insightfully.[10] Instead, what this volume represents is an effort to articulate emerging youth policies and underlying practices that necessarily relate to the problems and structures of 'old' postwar Japan, but that reach towards new alternative models. As such, it hopes to transcend the conventional domains of youth and policy to provide a reminder of the continued capacity of diverse societal actors in Japan, when nudged by new opportunities, to creatively synthesize ideas that at first glance seem as compatible as oil and water, and to generate new social innovations at the grass-roots level. Although researched some years earlier, this work therefore offers certain insights pertaining to how changes may unfold in the years following the massive earthquake and tsunami of 11 March 2011 – a natural disaster and human tragedy of colossal scale followed by a nuclear crisis as well as ongoing social upheaval. While not discussed extensively in this volume, it is possible that the popular image of Japanese youth may transform as a consequence of young people's active participation in volunteering and rebuilding efforts, with implications for youth problem debates, policy-making processes and youth agency.[11]

This book is, it should now be clear, relevant also to those interested in studying the development of social entrepreneurship in contemporary Japan, for the reader will find important examples of social innovation, experimentation and 'scaling-up' of specific models in the chapters that follow.[12] It may very well be its coverage of the invention, within the field of youth support, of new combinations of work, employment and community that will in the long term prove the main contribution of the present volume. Although as of writing this 'Preface' in March 2012, Japan, much like other advanced nations, continues to struggle with an increasingly bankrupt employment system and outdated notions of what constitutes 'work', it is hoped that this book will demonstrate that the key elements of a more attractive social framework, in fact, already exist. Learning from proximate, observable prototypes – rather than, for example, from idealized images of the past or from equally idealized models from other countries – may well offer a most promising way forward when it comes to re-thinking the relationship between 'youth' and 'work' in Japan.

Acknowledgements

While it may bear my name as the sole author, I am proud to acknowledge that this book has grown out of the support and goodwill of an extraordinarily wide range of remarkably talented individuals and groups.

It gives me particular pleasure to recognize, at the outset, the invaluable guidance of Professor Genda Yūji, my foremost mentor in Japan. He demonstrated tremendous hospitality, not only in inviting me to visit the Institute of Social Science at Tokyo University from April 2007 to March 2008, but also in welcoming me as a full member of Genda Kenkyūshitsu. Genda-ken soon became my precious home base as I conducted fieldwork across Japan. It was very much with the help of Yūji that I could gain access, at several levels, to the fascinating, frequently puzzling world of Japanese youth support. This significantly accelerated the fieldwork process. Yūji's zest for intellectual exploration and originality was always palpable and continues to be a profound sense of inspiration. I sincerely hope that he will feel that my representation of the youth policy process as well as the world of youth support is reasonably accurate and balanced (and that he likes some of the new concepts and 'keywords' that I have proposed in this book!). I also remain thankful for the frank advice and vital logistical support of Miura-san, Satō-san and Takahashi-san at Genda-ken.

Of those directly involved in the management and development of youth support services, I would like to acknowledge the continued, invaluable support of Kudō Kei and Iwamoto Mami in particular. I remain indebted also to the leaders and staff at the Children's Life and Culture Association (CLCA) in Odawara, Hagurekumo in Toyama Prefecture, Fermata in Osaka, Rōkyō Sentā and New Start in Chiba, Chishingaku Juku and Kurume Zemināru in Fukuoka, Nihon Seishōnen Ikusei Kyōgikai in Okinawa, and the staff of each of the Youth Support Stations that I was allowed to visit. Watanabe-san and Yamanaka-san of the Japan Productivity Centre for Socio-Economic Development helped me get in touch with several of these groups and also arranged for me to observe national meetings between the government and youth support practitioners, and thus deserve heartfelt thanks as well.

Cooperating closely with the above-mentioned youth support leaders, Japan's youth workers are one of the most incredible group of people I had the opportunity to meet while conducting fieldwork. Their contribution to the research that led to this volume is fundamental. Any acknowledgement I can provide here is bound to be disproportionately modest in relation to the amount of time they spent explaining their craft and methodology to me. My dedication of this book to Japan's youth workers reflects the gratitude and respect that I feel for this special group that rarely gets the credit it deserves for changing the life of many a young individual for the better.

I would like to recognize explicitly the warm cooperation of the staff as well as of course the young users of my main field sites, K2 International and the Yokohama Youth Support Station. They not only responded patiently to my endless queries, but invited me to join them by becoming a volunteer staff member (despite the fact that I had no prior experience or training in youth work). I can only wish that my presence did not cause significant disruption and that I was able to make a positive contribution, however small, to these already diverse communities.

Among the several committed government officials whom I had the privilege to interview at the Cabinet Office and the Ministry of Health, Labour and Welfare (MHLW) of Japan, there was one gentleman who dispensed a degree of support far beyond what could reasonably be expected of any informant, whether in the public or private sectors. In addition to sharing rare insights regarding the policy-making process behind new youth inclusion measures, Handa Arimichi of the MHLW tutored me about the history of Japanese youth policy and acquainted me with a colourful range of individuals working in this area. Although rarely captured in purely academic accounts (including, I fear, my own), Mr Handa convinced me of the difference that personal commitment and zest can make within what may to outsiders seem monolithic bureaucratic institutions. It was also he who took me for a precious private visit to meet Mr Yamaguchi who had been in charge of programmes quite similar to today's Support Stations and Independence Camps in the 1960s and the 1970s.

A number of scholars have commented on various segments and earlier versions of this study. Albeit with the risk of missing several names, I acknowledge the consistently encouraging support of David Slater and David Willis, as well as the constructive feedback afforded by Takehiko Kariya, John Campbell, Hiroshi Ishida, Mark Rebick and Junya Tsutsui, not to forget Michiko Miyamoto (also an important fieldwork mentor) and Mei Kagawa who refereed the first journal article that emerged from this project and was published in Tokyo University's time-honoured *Sociologos*.

I sincerely thank professors Ito Peng of Toronto University and Peter Kemp at Oxford for reading the entire original manuscript and for affording insightful comments. I am not entirely sure whether my argument, elaborated at the end of this book, that Japanese youth policy is 'emerging' will satisfy their questions regarding the extent of 'change' in this policy realm, but I hope that it will at least inspire further conversations on this topic.

At Kyoto University, where I enjoyed a brief but highly productive stay in 2008, I became indebted to Professor Kyoko Inagaki, my generous host researcher, and also received valuable comments from Professors Toshimitsu Shinkawa and Emiko Ochiai. Professor Ochiai and her colleagues at the Department of Sociology further supported the writing of this book during my extremely pleasant second stay at Kyoto University in 2009 and 2010 as a Japan Society for the Promotion of Science postdoctoral fellow, an important institution which also deserves a very warm thanks for its generous financial support (which I benefited from during the editing process).

As my mother would know from personal experience, librarians are the indispensable but largely invisible facilitators of many an intellectual project, including this one. That is why I would like to express my appreciation to the particularly conscientious work of the staff of the Bodleian Japanese Library at the Nissan Institute at Oxford as well as to Gill Edwards of my own very dear Green Templeton College.

I also gratefully acknowledge the indispensable support of the Emil Aaltonen Foundation of Finland, the Matsushita International Foundation, the Sasakawa Fund and the Japan Foundation Endowment Committee, without which the research leading to this book would not have been financially feasible.

The constant encouragement and inspiration I have received from several close friends throughout the years has certainly been central to my development as a scholar. Danjo Obreschkow and the band deserve a very special thanks – their presence has given meaning and tremendous joy to what could have otherwise been a rather dull, work-centred existence. All those who supported me during fieldwork and my challenging final DPhil year have indeed enriched my life and, by extension, this book. They cannot be thanked enough, though I shall try. My colleagues at the Department of Social Policy and Intervention, especially those who cohabited the GRS room where the bulk of this book was originally written, have likewise been marvellous.

My two dedicated supervisors at Oxford, Professors Martin Seeleib-Kaiser and Roger Goodman, were a consistent source of intellectual inspiration and encouragement throughout my doctoral course at Oxford between 2006 and 2009. They have continued to provide enlightened mentorship and I have been especially happy to recently co-author new pieces of original research with both.

I should not miss this chance to thank the three anonymous reviewers for encouraging me to more forthrightly present my own critique of the phenomena investigated in this book. Without such encouragement, I probably would not have enjoyed writing the final chapter of this volume as much as I did. I also owe a great debt to Hannah Mack, Emma Hart, Dominic Corti and Ed Needle at Routledge for their conscientious, patient support throughout the publication process. Sheila Garrard's careful copy-editing work has made this book more readable than it would otherwise have been.

Last, but not least, this book and any other kind of progress I may have made over the past decades owe most to my family back in Finland. I thank my parents, sister and grandparents (who sadly passed away before they could see this book published) for the almost impossible degree of loving support they have afforded me as I have resided in, and travelled between, three far-flung countries. I am truly blessed that we have now been joined by my incredible partner Naho, who tolerated my many late nights working on this manuscript up to the magical moment when, after midnight one fateful Friday night, I was finally ready to press 'Send'.

Tuukka Toivonen,
March 2012,
Oxford

A note to the reader

Japanese terms, where used, are romanized, and English translations are provided where appropriate. Most of the time, Japanese terms are given in parenthesis following the English translations. However, Japanese terms that are based on English-language words, such as *parasaito shinguru*, are written in their English form but italicized, e.g. as *parasite single*, so as to not unduly confuse the reader. The word *freeter* is an exception here: I write it in this form in spite of the fact that it is a Japanese neologism, because this usage (*freeter* rather than *furītā*) has become commonplace in English-language publications.

Translations of Japanese terms into English, where no prior commonplace translation exists, are conducted by the present author and may thus differ from translations used by other writers. All Japanese words except names of people and of organizations or departments are italicized. Names of Japanese authors are given in Japanese fashion, i.e. surname first, as in Kosugi Reiko. To denote long vowels in Japanese words, macrons are used throughout, so that for example 'Oosawa' is written as Ōsawa and 'houritsu' as *hōritsu*.

I have puzzled somewhat over how to write some of the key categories that appear in this book. The most central one, referring to the target group of Japan's youth activation policies, is *NEET*, which I have decided to italicize to distinguish it from the British NEET category (which has to be viewed as a separate category with a different definition and connotations). I use the form *nīto* only in specific sections in Chapter 3 when explicitly discussing the indigenization of the British NEET label in Japan.

Abbreviations

ADHD	attention deficit hyperactivity disorder
ALMP	active labour market policy
CBT	cognitive behavioural therapy
CDSO	Career Development Support Office (Kyaria Keisei Shienshitsu) of the Ministry of Health, Labour and Welfare
CLCA	Children's Life and Culture Association (a youth support group in Odawara)
ISS	Institute of Social Science at Tokyo University (Shakai Kagaku Kenkyūjo); also known as Shaken
JILPT	Japan Institute for Labour Policy and Training (Nihon Rōdō Kenkyū Kenshūjo); formerly, Japan Institute of Labour, or JIL
JPCSED	Japan Productivity Centre for Socio-Economic Development (Shakai Keizai Seisansei Honbu)
KNKK	Koyō Nōryoku Kaihatsu Kikō (Employment and Skills Development Organization)
LDP	Liberal Democratic Party
METI	Ministry of Economy, Trade and Industry (Keizai Sangyōshō)
MEXT	Ministry of Education, Culture, Sports, Science and Technology (Monbu Kagakushō)
MHLW	Ministry of Health, Labour and Welfare (Kōsei Rōdōshō)
NEET	Not in Education, Employment or Training
NPO	A registered not-for-profit organization
OECD	Organisation for Economic Co-operation and Development
YIC	Youth Independence Camp (Wakamono Jiritsu Juku)
YSS	Youth Support Station (Wakamono Sapōto Sutēshon)
YYSS	Yokohama Youth Support Station.

1 Getting young adults back to work: A post-industrial dilemma in Japan

> The issue is not that NEETs do not work. They simply cannot work.
> –Genda Yūji (Genda and Maganuma 2004:244)

How did the state, interested experts and the media, as well as youth supporters respond to the sudden rise of worklessness among young adults in early twenty-first-century Japan? This is the driving puzzle around which the present volume is organized. The answer that emerges is complex, but it has two essential facets. First, we find that actors within the central government, affiliated experts and the mainstream media collaborated to deliver what may be called 'symbolic activation'. This was an arrangement whereby, instead of carrots and sticks, or handouts made conditional on participation in official activation measures, certain symbolic labels were deployed to direct formally inactive young adults back into the (low-wage) labour markets. Second, we discover that, in a striking challenge to state policy, youth supporters and their managers implemented practices that contrasted quite dramatically with, and highlighted alternatives to, the dominant (international) paradigm of activation. Under the guise of state-led independence support, what in fact took shape were new kinds of 'communities of recognition' as well as a youth work methodology of 'exploring the user' (i.e. the support-receiver). It is this second dimension in how Japan responded to youth joblessness that suggests promising long-term solutions to the post-industrial youth employment dilemma that virtually all advanced nations currently face but which none has yet seriously addressed.

This introductory chapter begins by setting out the essential socio-economic as well as ideological (and ideational) context to the emergence of youth activation in Japan. This necessarily requires a discussion on how other countries have responded in the face of similar problems, including the key policy ideas they have favoured. Because highly charged youth labels such as *freeter* and *NEET* came to play a central role in the domestic Japanese policy process, two further sections are dedicated to surveying these controversies. Set out next is the key argument that Japanese government-led efforts to get disengaged youth 'back to work' are best understood as constituting a system of symbolic activation. The present chapter concludes with a description of research design matters and the Japanese youth support field, followed by a synopsis of the entire book.

What kind of dilemma?

Though rarely phrased in these exact terms in public debate, what may be called 'the post-industrial dilemma' is a helpful starting point for understanding why pre-existing policies and practices around youth and employment are being thought about anew in advanced countries around the world, including Japan. By this dilemma I mean the challenge of maintaining socially acceptable levels of sufficiently paid employment in the face of lower GDP growth rates, borderless finance, international competition, technological transformation and complex labour market change. Youth, more than older cohorts, have had to cope in a post-industrial society where unemployment is on the rise (Figure 1.1) and where employment in agriculture and manufacturing has diminished to the point that the majority of jobs are to be found in the more

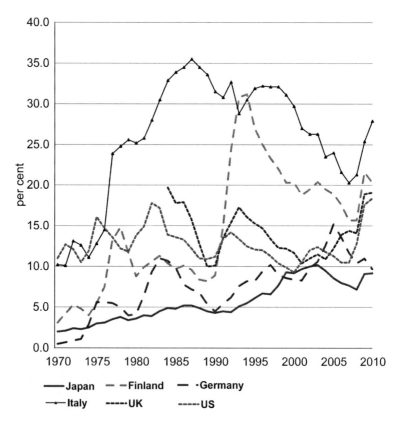

Figure 1.1 Youth unemployment trends, 1970–2010 (15- to 24-year-olds), %
Source: OECD StatExtracts (downloaded 22 March 2012)

fluid service sector (Figure 1.2). Indeed, the terms 'post-industrialism' (Bell 1973) and 'post-industrialization' are usually employed to denote the increasing centrality of the service sector following processes of deruralization and dein- dustrialization, though the concept is used quite variably by different authors (see, for example, Esping-Andersen 2009 regarding the impact of women's growing participation in paid work and Pierson 1998, who stresses the impli- cations of population aging). I use 'post-industrial' primarily to point to labour markets that are service sector-oriented and more fluid than those of an industrial era.

Although a post-industrial society need not in theory be perpetually marred by high unemployment, the dilemma of how to maintain politically acceptable levels of sufficiently paid employment – especially among young adults – remains currently a major issue for nearly all advanced nations. The roots of

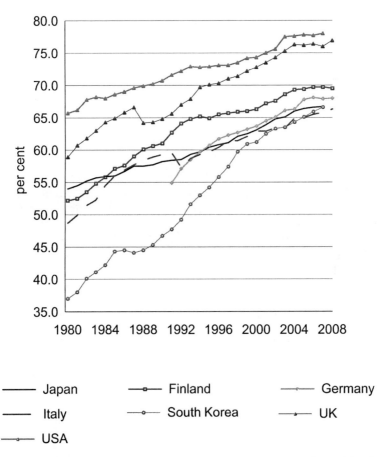

Figure 1.2 Trends in service-sector employment as a percentage share (%) of total employment in selected OECD countries
Source: World Bank (2010)

this dilemma are complex, but, due to the centrality of the service economy, where productivity growth (as conventionally measured) is limited and a high volume of relatively unskilled labour is demanded, it has been suggested that there may exist an unavoidable trade-off between 'either joblessness or a mass of inferior jobs' (Esping-Andersen 1999:111). We will later review key responses that have been proposed in the face of post-industrial changes in the West, but first let us take a more detailed look at the case of Japan. To begin with, when and how did the post-industrial employment dilemma appear there, specifically in relation to young people?

Changes in the labour markets, the organization of work and transitions

In terms of timing, it was the bursting of the real estate bubble at the beginning of the 1990s and the subsequent long recession that ushered in the most challenging and definitive period of post-industrialization in Japan (see Schoppa 2006; Peng 2004).[1] To cut a very long story short, this period had major impacts on Japan's youth labour markets, on the organization of work and on the (previously) institutionalized school-to-work transition system, as follows.

- *Youth labour market trends.* Strikingly, unemployment rates doubled, or more than doubled, for all age groups between 1990 and 2003, though those in their teens and twenties were particularly hard hit as they already suffered from higher than average unemployment at the beginning of this period (Figure 1.3). The consequences of early joblessness tend to be so severe in Japan that the worst-hit cohorts of new graduates would eventually come to be dubbed a 'Lost Generation'. Parallelling changes in levels of unemployment, the share of part-time work and other forms of irregular employment (*hiseiki koyō*) also doubled in the 1990s and the early 2000s following successive labour law changes that made it easier to hire non-standard workers in both the manufacturing and service sectors (Figure 1.4; Weathers 2001; Gottfried 2008:189). Notably, a particularly high share of 25–34-year-old female employees – over two-fifths – came to be employed as irregulars (Statistics Bureau 2011). This substantial deregulation of the labour markets meant that a large portion of Japanese youth came to live outside the constraints as well as the strong social protections of the life-time employment system (*shūshin koyō seido*) – a key pillar of economic independence and well-being in the postwar period (Goodman and Peng 1996) – with sharp consequences for inequality.[2]

  Underlying the quantitative surge in non-standard work was an ongoing process of post-industrialization whereby Japanese service employment increased by nearly ten percentage points between 1990 and 2007, to a total of 67 per cent of all workers. In the same period, employment in manufacturing decreased from 34 per cent to less than 28 per cent (World Bank 2010), suggesting a significant qualitative shift in the nature of employment opportunities.

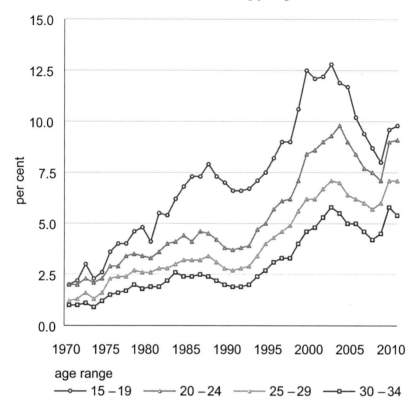

Figure 1.3 Youth unemployment trends in Japan (1970–2010), %
Source: Statistics Bureau (www.stat.go.jp/data/roudou/longtime/03roudou.htm#hyo_2);
long-term time series data, table 3.4; accessed 22 January 2011

- *The reorganization of work.* The above structural changes have been
  accompanied by a broader reorganization of work whereby the entire
  Japanese employment system is perceived to have come under threat. On a
  symbolic level, perhaps the greatest challenge has been delivered by 'the
  freeter lifestyle' among young adults (Kosugi 2008), as described in more
  detail below. Dispatched workers (*haken shain*) have dealt another blow to
  Japanese employment as conventionally envisioned, reflecting the demise
  of company belongingness and the rise of 'a self-oriented process where
  occupational specialization assumes greater importance and the way
  people work is a matter of free choice' (Fu 2011:128). Yet job mobility has
  increased somewhat also among 'standard' *seishain* workers with permanent contracts.[3] In light of higher overall mobility, it seems increasingly more
  appropriate to speak in terms of 'long-term' rather than 'life-time' employment
  relations as characterizing the core of the Japanese labour market.

A host of other subtle changes have unfolded. In the 2000s, employers
used the term *sokusenryoku* to express a growing interest in recruiting

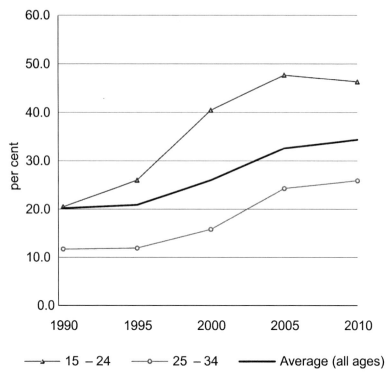

Figure 1.4 Trends in irregular employment among Japanese youth as a share of total employment (1990–2010), %

Source: Statistics Bureau (www.stat.go.jp/data/roudou/longtime/03roudou.htm#hyo_2); long-term time series data, table 10; accessed 22 January 2011

flexible workers who could make themselves 'instantly useful', usually outside the framework of the long-term employment system. This Japanese notion of employability is mirrored in the increasing popularity of various portable qualifications (*shikaku*) and vocational institutions that provide related training (see Borovoy 2010). Relatedly, the personal qualities of 'self-directedness' (*shutaisei*), 'individuality' (*kosei*) and 'creativity' (*sōzōryoku*) as well as strong communication skills have been framed as essential for success in the new economy (see Cave 2007 regarding the roots of these terms in 1980s' educational discourse). Lacking clear definitions, these terms have left many students confounded – including those whom I taught at Kyoto University, an elite institution, in the late 2000s – especially when actual job interviews have revealed a persisting corporate preference for obedience and 'cooperativeness' (*kyōchōsei*) over self-assertiveness. It has been felt that only those who can skillfully 'read the situation' (*kūki wo yomu*), balancing conventional and newly demanded attributes, are likely to succeed in the new economy. There is evidence from psychological experiments that much of the confusion that many young adults now feel springs partly from a growing discrepancy between explicitly held values and behavioural scripts, emphasizing independence, and values and scripts that are held at the implicit level, which still tend to emphasize interdependence (Toivonen, Norasakkunkit and Uchida 2011). The Westernized, though uniquely articulated, language around work may thus be as significant a factor in the labour market experience of young people as are the associated structural changes.

It is important to add that, for those who fail to enter the core workforce in today's Japan, employment conditions can be relatively harsh: long hours are expected even of nominal 'part-timers'; labour law violations are widely tolerated (especially when it comes to working hours); and there are limited institutional protections and oversight for the 80 per cent of workers who do not belong to a labour union (Weathers and North 2009). While too many and complex to sufficiently review here, the narratives of the youth support staff and supported youth whom I met during fieldwork reflect many of these issues (see Chapter 6 in particular).

- *The erosion of the school-to-work transition system.* Japan's sophisticated institutional school-to-work transition machinery (mentioned in the Preface) has likewise changed with post-industrialization, leading authoritative scholars to write it off as 'dysfunctional' (Honda 2004). Up to the 1980s, it could still be said that school-to-work transitions unfolded predominantly through extensive institutional mediation, with schools and companies playing a major role under the coordination of public employment offices (known in Japan as *Shokuan* or Hello Work). At this time, school-mediated transitions (*gakkō keiyu no ikō*) were underpinned by semi-formal employment contracts (*jisseki kankei*) whereby schools agreed to recommend suitable students to companies who in turn agreed to recruit a consistent number annually regardless of actual labour demand, based on long-term trust relations (Rosenbaum and Kariya 1989). Hiring decisions were made several months ahead of graduation and the practice of periodic mass recruitment (*ikkatsu saiyō*) meant that the vast majority of students could enter their new jobs according to a unified schedule at the beginning of April.

    Key factors that have eroded this once-functional system include the increase in non-standard employment as well as the growing popularity of higher education and post-secondary vocational schools. Non-standard employment, now the destination of a large share of high school graduates, is by definition outside the scope of the established system. Those moving into positions here tend to find them through earlier part-time jobs – an alternative recruitment channel (Brinton 2001) – or through publicly available job adds. Since just about half of all high school graduates in Japan now proceed to university (almost always at 18 years of age), while another fifth enter post-secondary vocational schools known as *senmon gakkō* (Goodman, Hatakenaka and Kim 2009), most youth entirely bypass institutionalized school-to-work transition channels at the high school level. They do come within the scope of various 'career services' at tertiary institutions, but these send students off into a recruitment race that is predominantly based on impersonal applications and increasingly sophisticated interview processes (Chiavacci 2005), without a commitment made by employers to recruit a certain number of students annually. Responsibility for outcomes is thus increasingly individualized. Yet institutions still matter in another sense, for graduating from an elite university seems to now be more important than ever for securing a stable job at a large firm (Kariya 2011).

The institutionalized school-to-work system nevertheless remains highly relevant to those interested in youth unemployment and joblessness in Japan. As Brinton (2011) has so insightfully shown, it is the uneven erosion of this system – whereby industrial high schools, in particular, remain well-connected to companies, but where low-ranking general schools are all but cut off from such all-important recruitment networks – that may best explain the 'production' of workless youth in today's Japan (Brinton 2011:138–43). We shall revisit Brinton's findings in the final chapter of this book.

- *Crucial continuities.* While a lot has thus changed in the youth labour markets, the organization of work and the school-to-work transition system, certain continuities remain important. By far the most important of these is the practice of 'periodic mass recruitment' (part and parcel of the legacy of school-mediated transitions) that persists as an essential component of youth transitions despite tremendous tensions. As one consequence, university students longing to secure stable jobs face enormous pressures to do so during their third and fourth years, lest they miss for good the opportunity to enter a company under a fresh graduate (*shin-sotsu*) scheme that comes with the best career advancement prospects, stability and full occupational training (see Kariya and Honda, 2010 for a state-of-the art analysis of job-hunting issues). For those who fail, it remains extremely difficult to enter the core workforce at a later stage, producing a strong sense that young people in Japan enjoy few 'second chances'. Because of such an institutional continuity – a key mechanism of labour market exclusion and marginalization – the post-industrial employment dilemma has taken on a particularly cruel edge in Japan (though labour market dualization, on the whole, seems to be deepening elsewhere also; see Emmenegger *et al.* 2012). As Esping-Andersen rightly points out, all other issues aside, it makes a world of difference for a person whether he/she is channeled into a 'dead-end' job that is literally just that – an end to good career prospects – or into one that is a stepping-stone to something more rewarding (Esping-Andersen 1996; also see Arnett 2004 on the role of transitional jobs during what he calls the emerging adulthood life-stage in the US).

How to interpret these changes?

This speedy review of the emergence of the post-industrial youth employment dilemma in Japan, marked by higher unemployment and less stable jobs, has been analytic in nature, reflecting academic knowledge on the matter as well as relevant statistical data. Yet the vital thing to note is that these changes were never so obvious or one-dimensional as to allow straightforward, unanimous definition among Japanese academics, government officials or the media. Indeed, multiple and even radically different interpretations of key causes were (and remain) possible, and the same applies to prescriptions regarding 'solutions'. While I have attempted to inform the reader, in the foregoing pages, of what I consider the most relevant underlying socio-economic factors, could it not be that youth themselves, instead of economic and labour market structures, are the main cause of the trend toward higher job mobility and unemployment? Rather than being pushed by ambiguous forces of social change, is it not possible that shifting values among Japanese youth could have caused them to make dramatically different, even 'counter-cultural', choices about their work involvement in the 2000s? Such queries and related arguments were in fact far from uncommon in the public debate, as we will soon find.

However, before turning our attention to the public appearance and interpretation of the post-industrial dilemma in 2000s' Japan, it is instructive to further examine the ideological and ideational landscape in which this dilemma appeared. To this end, we will take a brief look at how the youth employment dilemma has been tackled in Western Europe and North America – the model regions that Japanese decision-makers came to consult in the 2000s – to uncover the dominant policy ideas and paradigms based on which new measures were crafted in Japan.

The post-industrial dilemma elsewhere: The lure of activation

As Figure 1.1 shows, several affluent Western societies faced youth unemployment of significant – even disastrous – proportions from the 1970s and 1980s onwards (and indeed continue to do so as of the early 2010s). Countries such as Italy and Spain stand out as extreme cases, followed by Finland in the 1990s. With the impact of the oil shocks and deindustrialization, the labour market detachment of young people became a serious concern in the 'flexible' liberal market economies of the UK and the US also, well before the rise of this problem in Japan. The deepening of labour market insecurity coincided with a shift of dominant economic ideology from Keynesianism towards monetarism as well as with the further globalization of the world economy (Hall 1993). The speed and precise nature of post-industrialization and related labour market changes, it should not be missed, differed across national contexts so that, in addition to politics, existing institutional legacies strongly shaped these processes (Esping-Andersen 1999; Emmenegger *et al.* 2012). Curiously however, despite such variation and diversity in circumstances, by the 1990s almost all governments were agreed that there was one major policy response, in the increasingly challenging economic and labour market environment, that they could not do without – that which came under the paradigm of 'activation'. Due to its high relevance to youth policy and practice in post-industrializing Japan, it pays to briefly consider the meanings and practical applications of activation here.

First, as opposed to pre-existing labour market measures – such as unemployment insurance schemes and benefits that came to be recast as 'passive' measures – advocates of the idea of activation suggested that policies could go much further to mobilize inactive citizens so as to reinsert them into employment, thereby creating a new 'active society' (see especially OECD 1989; Kalisch 1991; Holmqvist 2009). Seen as the best cure to perceived benefit dependency within the 'underclass' (see MacDonald (ed.) 1997) – that some said were living a life of leisure at the expense of scrupulous tax-payers – active labour market policies were expected to reduce social expenditures while increasing state tax income. The lure of this promise proved hard to resist for the vast majority of OECD governments, financially pressed as they tended to be, at a time when they had already begun to pay keener attention to various groups that lay outside the formal labour markets.

For Gilbert (2002), this global ascendancy of activation has implied a fundamental shift from the welfare state to the enabling state, a state concerned more with the productive than the protective element of social programmes.[4] Variably referred to as the 'social investment state', the 'Schumpeterian workfare state' or simply the 'active state', such an entity no longer guarantees social citizenship – in short, the right to live according to standards prevailing in society by virtue of being a citizen (Marshall 1950) – but instead provides stronger incentives for people to reach self-sufficiency via paid labour. According to Gilbert, the most prominent changes to concrete social programmes for the unemployed and non-employed people include: restricting entrance and accelerating exit; the segmentation of participants; the introduction of contractual obligations; and the formulation of work-oriented incentives and services (Gilbert 2002:76). By the 1990s, most Western governments had recalibrated their employment initiatives along these lines to move those outside formal labour markets – including groups of young people, single parents and the disabled – to jobs with less regard to pay conditions, quality of employment or the personal preferences of the worker. These efforts focused much more on 'correcting' individual behaviour and enforcing responsibility than on boosting aggregate labour demand or creating new work opportunities.

While a wide spectrum of training schemes and job-seeking support services have now emerged internationally, it is arguably the stronger use of compulsion that defines the kind of active labour market policies (ALMPs) that we have seen develop since the 1990s. This compulsion essentially rests on the conversion of former entitlements into benefits that are conditional on participation in training and/or job-seeking activities. Hence the contention of critical scholars that ALMPs have marked the demise of unconditioned social citizenship (King and Wickham-Jones 1999) and the rise of more market-oriented, paternalistic – and possibly coercive – social policy that aggressively recommodifies individuals (Peck and Theodore 2000; Standing 2009).

This conversion of entitlements into conditional benefits (linked to partici-pation in activation schemes) did not, of course, take place overnight. British youth policy serves as an example of a gradual, politically mediated progression that culminated in a full-scale activation regime under the New Deal for Young People in 1998, whereby unemployment entitlements had transformed to 'Jobseekers' Allowances' that elicit participation in activation programmes. Peck and Theodore trace this process back to the 1978 Youth Opportunities Programme which, according to the authors, signalled a shift away from the old demand-side rationale towards a supply-side one that emphasized improving the work ethic and skills of young people (Peck and Theodore 2000:733). In parallel with the further destabilization of the youth labour markets and the demise of the UK's apprenticeship system – one reason why youth transitions were becoming protracted and possibly more 'risky' as well as fragmented than before (Jones and Wallace 1992; Furlong and Cartmel 1997) – eligibility conditions were thereafter progressively tightened under conservative rule. By the mid-1990s, an integrated system of benefits and programmes had materi-alized, which New Labour developed further under its New Deal package. While in many ways more 'user-friendly', well-resourced and successful in terms of short-term outcomes than its predecessors (see Kemp 2006 for an excellent review), the New Deal famously did not give unemployed youth the option of non-participation – lack of cooperation was to be met with pro-gressive benefit sanctions. Equally important, as Kemp (2006) notes, was the fact that this bundle of training, education, counselling and job experience measures remained focused on the supply of youth labour and on young people's personal attributes, conforming to a so-called deficit-model that highlights youth's personal failings to the exclusion of issues around labour demand.

As we will find in Chapter 4 in particular, British youth policy under New Labour captured the interest of central Japanese youth policy analysts, open-ing up an important pathway along which ideas of activation entered into this domain of policy activity in Japan. However, it is instructive to note at this point that, unlike their British counterparts, Japanese policy-makers did not have at their disposal the option of incentivizing 'inactive' youth by manipulating the benefits system, for the simple reason that there was no pre-existing youth unemployment benefit system to be manipulated. Hence their need to turn to alternative means and examples, which incidentally included the (English) Connexions counselling service created by New Labour for teenagers – including 16- and 17-year-olds whose right to cash benefits had been abolished in 1988 – who were possibly at risk of 'social exclusion'. Whereas the New Deal continued to exert a measure of government control and surveillance over older cohorts of young people (young adults), Connexions was an alternative attempt to reach out to, and exert control over, a group that was effectively outside the jurisdiction of employment services and workplaces, as well as edu-cational institutions (see Furlong 2006). Although sometimes better characterized as a 'social inclusion' measure insofar as it has provided much-needed assistance to children under severe distress, Connexions can be seen as an extension of the familiar activation paradigm into a different context. That is, it enables the state to access and activate a portion of the population that used to be inaccessible through previous policies, but for the same eventual purpose of enhancing participation in training and work.

To sum up, the experiences of affluent Western countries with post-industrialization and rising unemployment led, in the 1990s, to the ascendancy of the paradigm of activation that was framed as the main cure to labour market inactivity, including that among youth. While the only specific example given above was that of British youth employment measures, essentially similar schemes that mix supportive counselling and training elements with coercive incentives have emerged across Western welfare states from Scandinavia to the US and Canada. Such salience of activation-oriented, workfare-style responses made it nearly inevitable that Japanese policy-makers – who historically turn to other advanced societies for policy examples and precedents (see Kasza 2006) – would consider advocating them as the post-industrial dilemma emerged in Japan in the 2000s. In doing so, they would face important difficulties that ultimately contributed to the emergence of symbolic activation as the dominant mode of getting inactive youth back to paid work in Japan.

Having reviewed the essential socio-economic and ideational context for youth employment problems in Japan we can now turn to the specific ways in which these issues arose as an object of heated public debate in the 2000s. This is an essential step in building a broad understanding of how youth policies and support practices unfolded in this era, because of the deeply interwoven nature of such policies, practices and media youth debates.

Fear of the *freeter*: Young workers in the public spotlight

> Now, young people are emerging who are unimaginable in the past Japan; the word 'furiitaa' [a freewheeling, unskilled, irregular worker] is used to describe them … . This is a problem of the social structure of Japan; they can't be fit into existing organizations. People in the mainstream are frightened of these people.
>
>   A senior employee at a Japanese company (Mathews 2004: 130)

It is not an exaggeration to say that the predominant political approach, until the 2000s, to issues surrounding young people in Japan was to produce various morally driven 'youth problem debates' that highlighted the presumed deficiencies of specific groups of young people rather than socio-economic changes or pressures. There is accordingly a vast legacy of 'problem youth' labels that is testimony to the preponderance of this tendency (see Chapter 2) which goes hand in hand with a rather uncritical, even static view of society itself as being beyond scrutiny and without major structural problems (Toivonen and Imoto 2012). It is therefore less than surprising that the post-industrial youth employment dilemma would first enter the Japanese public consciousness in the form of particular youth categories that were cast negatively and sharply contrasted with 'ideal' normative statuses such as that of the regular (or standard) worker, *seishain*.

The first major issue that embodied youth employment worries in the late 1990s and early 2000s was, without doubt, that of the so-called *freeters*. Originally a term exploited by Recruit, a leading personnel service in Japan, to portray in consciously positive terms the lifestyle of 'free part-time workers' (*furī arubaitā*, from the English for 'free' and German for 'worker'), this neologism eventually became associated with a society-wide scare over young people's diminishing commitment to work (see Smith 2006). *Freeters* properly became an issue around the year 2002 when statistics seemed to indicate that their numbers had topped the 2 million mark (Figure 1.5), showing that this 'lifestyle' was no longer being adopted by a negligible minority.

In many respects, the discourse on *freeters* came to be influenced by that on *parasite singles*, the provocative youth debate, sparked by Yamada Masahiro's coining of the term (Yamada 1999), that raged in the Japanese media just before youth employment issues moved centre-stage. Yet the *freeter* issue stirred up much graver public concern than *parasite singles* ever did, in part because this term came to be linked to decreasing work morale and engagement among males. The *parasite singles* debate, by contrast, had focused more on women in their twenties who were supposedly happy to postpone marriage and enjoy a life of luxury and leisure at the expense of their hard-working parents (see Lunsing 2003). As Slater (2010) notes, the other reason why *freeters* aroused such concern had to do with the threat that part-time-working lifestyles and low pay posed to the middle classes. This threat had great force because it flew in the face of ideals connected to the long-cherished lifetime employment

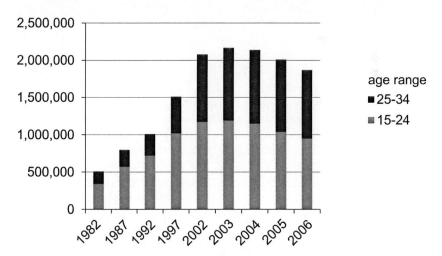

Figure 1.5 The increase in part-time working youth known as *freeters*, 1982–2006
Source: MHLW (2007a:26); the figures for 1982–97 and 2002–06 draw on different surveys and slightly different definitions of '*freeter*'

system as well as related notions of adulthood, masculinity and appropriate life-courses (see Chapter 3).

Partly as a consequence of these ascribed attributes and the public's appetite for controversy, *freeters* received harsh criticism from the conservative media and initially from many conservative academics such as Yamada around the turn of the Millennium. But there were also those who had more sympathy for young part-timers, whom they saw partly as the victims of economic recession and shifting employment structures. The now well-known labour market economist Genda Yūji was the one to deliver the most influential counter-argument in the *freeter* debate: with reference to statistical data, he posited that it was young people rather than the middle-aged who, despite the media's overwhelming concern over the latter, had lost most jobs following the 1990s' recession (Genda 2001). He moreover pointed out that not all *freeters* engaged in temporary part-time work voluntarily, helping to transform the image of this group from a 'self-actualizing' one that actively chose to espouse an alternative lifestyle to a disempowered one that no longer had the choice of becoming a protected permanent worker (*seishain*). The sub-text was that, in a conservative and change-resistant society ruled predominantly by the middle-aged, youth were increasingly underdogs rather than rebels. This theme was echoed in another influential book by the youth policy authority Miyamoto Michiko (2002), who portrayed young people as a new 'vulnerable' social group (*jakusha*).

Whatever one's position on its causes and implications, it is clear that it was through the *freeter* panic that the post-industrial youth employment dilemma properly made its presence felt in mainstream Japanese society. It would, of course, be naïve to assume that the 'problem' of part-time-working youth somehow naturally or automatically emerged from socio-economic change alone. In the background, key actors such as Kosugi Reiko and other researchers affiliated with the Japan Institute for Labour Policy and Training played a vital role in focusing the attention of the public as well as policy-makers by producing new definitions and statistics that could 'prove' that *freeters* were a major social problem. The dynamics of this strategic activity around *freeters* bear so many similarities to the campaign around non-employed youth that its main elements will become clear to the reader from the remainder of this account (see Chapter 3 especially). Suffice it to say, however, that these efforts were successful not only in convincing the public that there were over 2 million *freeters* as of 2002, but also in that they created a platform for a series of new policy responses under the umbrella of the Youth Independence and Challenge Plan (2003) – the first major response to youth employment problems in post-industrial Japan (Chapter 4).

Enter *NEETs*: At the heart of the dilemma?

Although the *freeter* discourse had done a great deal to raise the salience of youth employment issues in general, mainstream Japan was hardly ready for what was to emerge next – a fresh social scare over youth who were 'neither *freeters* nor even unemployed'. This puzzling problem around non-employed, formally inactive young people who came to be identified as *NEETs* in the mid-2000s was morally alarming partly because, as opposed to part-time-working youth who may have exhibited a new 'lifestyle' but who nevertheless kept working, it seemed to suggest that more youth were giving up on employment altogether.

The fact that, prior to 2004, there was no convenient word in the Japanese language to denote youth who were disengaged from work speaks of how rare, or at least how rarely spoken of, youth joblessness used to be in the Japanese context. The official term for the condition of worklessness among youth, *jakunen mugyōsha* (literally, a young jobless person/persons), was technical and cumbersome to pronounce, hardly lending itself to casual, everyday use. The more commonplace label of *shitsugyōsha*, on the other hand, referred to the unemployed who, in order to be counted as such, had to actively make themselves available for work; this term also implied the loss (*shitsu-*) of employment that had been previously held. Of course, those familiar with Japanese youth problem debates will know that there was indeed one pre-existing category that described a form of inactivity among youth – that of *hikikomori*, or social withdrawal (Horiguchi 2012). But the problem with the *hikikomori* concept, in the eyes of many Japanese youth and labour market experts, was that it was so bound up with debates about mental health issues, violent incidents and family relationships that it tended to deflect attention away from matters of employment.

This situation was to soon be rectified with the introduction of an entirely new label for youth inactivity that key actors framed first and foremost as an employment issue. In 2003, while the general public still by and large remained ignorant of the possibility of widespread non-employment among Japanese youth, a government-commissioned research project led by Kosugi Reiko of the Japan Institute for Labour Policy and Training 'discovered' 760,000 so-called *NEETs* in Japan (Kosugi and Hori 2003). Borrowing the British-born acronym that had been used to bring attention to 16- to 18-year-olds who were 'not in education, employment or training', Kosugi and others implied that Japanese *NEETs* – all those who in surveys had indicated that they were not looking for work for the time being – were quite different in their characteristics compared to their namesakes in the UK. Much older on average, it was proposed that the relevant age-range for Japanese *NEETs* should be set at 15 to 34 and that those with university degrees should also be included in the target group of future policies. Following this initial, rather dry and technocratic construction of the issue, Genda Yūji (see above) soon took active steps to familiarize a wider audience with non-employed youth whom he began to refer to, using Japanese *katakana* script, as *nīto*. While lodging a rather nuanced argument that strived to bring some attention also to the plight of those with very low educational credentials (see Chapter 3), Genda injected a number of key themes into the debate, including the notion that *NEETs* lacked confidence in themselves and in their communication abilities. These seemingly innocuous moves reflected the rise of a new agenda in Japan to activate the formally inactive young people who lay beyond the reach of conventional employment services and who seemed to be benefitting less and less from the fruits of Japan's postwar affluence.

Incidentally, the *NEET* issue quickly took on a dualistic nature as it became diffused through the Japanese media (Toivonen 2011a). On the one hand, it was framed as a serious policy issue with consequences for the economy and the welfare system. As such, it was appropriate for the state – that espoused Genda's characterization of non-employed youth as lacking in confidence and communication skills but wanting to work – to respond to it with various new countermeasures. On the other hand however, *NEET* was turned into a popular, universally recognized social category by the mainstream media that branded this group as predominantly lazy, unmotivated and essentially uninterested in finding employment. As Chapter 3 will explain in more detail, both sides of the argument prevailed to some extent: while a deeply unfavourable view of *NEETs* became entrenched across mainstream Japanese society, sections within the government succeeded in enacting new policy measures thanks to the high salience of the debate on non-employed youth. It was these measures – much less publicly visible than the *NEET* label itself – that would come to embody the more creative, inspiring side of the quest to get young people 'back to work' in post-industrial Japan.

Tangible measures to activate inactive youth took the form of a residential training programme and a rather versatile counselling service. The first went by the title of the Youth Independence Camp (*Wakamono Jiritsu Juku*) which, at least officially, was charged with providing jobless youth with a three-month dosage of 'work and life' training to boost their motivation and confidence. The second measure was called the Youth Support Station (*Chiiki Wakamono Sapōto Sutēshon*) and it was tasked with furnishing support that was more tailored to meet individual needs through dedicated counselling as well as through building local youth support networks. Needless to say, the overriding official objective of both interventions was to insert young support-receivers into paid jobs, preferably to permanent *seishain* positions. Yet those in charge of implementing the programmes on the ground level all but transformed their nature, enacting communities of recognition and nuanced practices of exploring the user, as suggested at the top of this chapter.

Setting aside the perplexities of these programmes for the moment, how could activation proceed at all, in the Japanese context, if there were no tools to build a conditional 'rights-and-responsibilities' framework (as in the UK) using cash benefits as incentives? Was 'independence support' for non-employed youth simply a token policy without any real force, or was activation catalyzed by some alternative mechanism, or a set of mechanisms, quite different to what we have seen in Western countries?

Symbolic activation – returning *NEETs* to work

It is one central argument of this book that the policies that emerged for non-working Japanese youth came to constitute, on the whole, a peculiar system of symbolic activation. Activation of this kind is rooted in the power of symbolic youth categories. Here, normative, universally diffused youth labels – rather than 'carrots and sticks' in the form of social benefits conditional on participation in state activation schemes – are deployed to prompt young adults to seek jobs as well as (in some cases) outside support.

However, it needs to be clarified that symbolic activation is not in all respects dissimilar to active labour market policies in Western Europe and the US, for it is based on interpretations of the same globally transmitted ideas of 'activation' and 'social inclusion'. The focus everywhere is on improving labour supply and the 'employability' of individual workers. But one major difference is owed to the fact that Western welfare states have had two to three decades longer than Japan to translate the concept of activation into firmly institutionalized policies. By contrast, Japan, for several reasons, currently lacks an institutionalized machinery for activating the formally inactive among its youth. Notably, the absence of pre-existing entitlements to social assistance and unemployment benefits among those with modest work histories has rendered it impossible to implement activation via the progressive conditionalization of such benefits there.[5] Policies and practices emphasizing the role of the family as a welfare provider and safety net (sometimes denoted with the term familialism in the social policy literature), driving youth to rely much more on their parents than the state to pay for education, training and welfare, have further complicated matters. These two points have meant that Japanese policy-makers interested in developing a Western-style activation regime have faced the dual challenge of activating youth without the aid of (coercive) financial incentives and without being able to access inactive individuals except through parental families. One may recall here that the institutional system that Japan did possess until recently and that was facilitated by strong linkages between schools and companies (see above) has not only unravelled, but simply lacks the practical tools to reach out to those not physically found in classrooms, workplaces or even the public employment offices. With the weakening of local communities and with schools' declining willingness to intervene in (what are perceived to be) private family matters, those not reporting to official institutions have increasingly fallen into an institutional grey zone.

These constraints did not entirely stop youth labour market activation from taking root in Japan, but they did affect its form. Crucially, the label *NEET* not only identified a new target for activation (Chapter 3), but, becoming rapidly diffused via the mainstream Japanese media, generated a powerful symbolic means for pressing young people – usually via their less secluded parents – to seek work rather than stay 'idle'. To be a *NEET*, it was made amply clear in the mid-2000s, was worse than being a part-time-working *freeter* or even an unemployed person who at least was looking for work; it was a normatively undesirable, shameful and increasingly unacceptable state for anyone within the reach of middle-class work norms. Hence, *NEET* was more than just a fashionable category with certain culturally defined meanings: it acted as a powerful trigger of social action (Turner 1975) by allowing actors to articulate a set of problems and solutions that had not yet been articulated and by prompting parents and inactive youth to seek employment opportunities as well as outside support. While distinctive in its logic compared to more institutionalized modes of activation, the kind of symbolic activation that has unfolded in Japan has had a real influence on behaviour by introducing a new category to daily vocabularies and by linking it to new services that are formally voluntary (for the user, or support-receiver) but are offered in a normatively pressurized context. The Internet has greatly facilitated this linking-up as it offers a discreet, anonymous means for contacting potential sources of support.

A significant part of this book deals in one way or another with the emergence and underpinnings of symbolic activation in Japan: Chapter 2 examines relevant earlier youth problems and labels, Chapter 3 how *NEET* came to be constructed as the prime target of activation, and Chapter 4 the making of policy interventions for this new group.

However, as was already suggested at the top of this chapter, the government-endorsed activation paradigm came to be challenged by the very same youth workers and managers who were tasked with delivering independence support measures in practice. Whereas the goal of youth independence support has officially been to guide young jobless people into stable jobs, youth workers recognized that such jobs are usually out of reach, in a deregulated labour market context, for those with long blanks in their CVs. So youth supporters opted to modify activation practices so as to avoid funnelling support-receivers into poorly protected low-paid service sector jobs – the most likely destination for non-employed youth who failed to find employment of the permanent sort in Japan in the 2000s. Instead, supporters placed youth in positions within their own internal job markets or within their network of trusted employers. This they did while exploring the user – relying on a diverse set of staff members to gain a deep understanding of individual youths' circumstances and abilities. These practices differ markedly with the orthodox paradigm of activation and were carried out within communities of recognition that often continued to provide a measure of belongingness and protection even after a young person had been formally 'activated'.

Figure 1.6 offers a simple illustration of how symbolic activation unfolded in mainstream Japan after the mid-2000s. This illustration shows how the family acts as a critical link between the category of *NEET* and support-seeking/job-seeking, suggesting that symbolic activation amounts, to a certain degree, to 'activation through the family'. It should be stressed here that it is not the main purpose of this book to either endorse or condemn symbolic activation, but rather to shed light on it as an empirical phenomenon. In

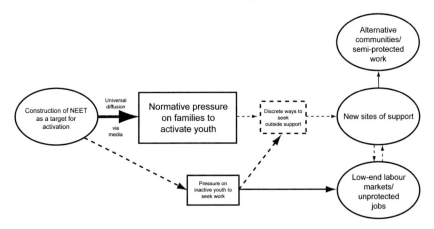

Figure 1.6 The process of symbolic activation in the case of *NEETs*

order to help the reader distinguish as clearly as possible between dispassionate empirical analysis and critical reflection, a critique of symbolic activation as well as the *NEET* category is reserved for Chapter 7.

I do not wish to suggest in this book that symbolic activation is particular to Japan or that activation policies in other countries do not have a symbolic dimension. The very status of 'unemployed' is one commonplace example of a powerful symbol with implications to activation; various labels that denounce 'welfare dependence' are another. Neither do I claim that symbolic activation is entirely new to Japan: important elements of it were in fact present in previous youth debates that similarly linked labels such as *futōkō* (children who are repeatedly or continuously absent from school) to certain support measures. Yet it was in the 2000s that these elements first converged and became connected to an explicit, congruent policy agenda founded on the Western-inspired idea of activation.

Research design matters

Having set out what may seem a rather bold argument about Japanese efforts to mobilize its formally inactive youth, it is important to discuss in some detail the methods and research design that have yielded the underlying empirical findings. The research design that powers this book differs somewhat from that adopted in most other prior works on youth, labour market activation and social policy in three main ways. First, it is ethnographic in orientation, with particular attention given to key actors, their practices and to the 'cultural translation' (Goodman 2002a:6) of key categories in each important sub-domain. As such, there is a strong exploratory element to the present inquiry that, in the absence of previous in-depth research on youth activation in Japan, seemed to me both necessary as well as capable of revealing previously unacknowledged phenomena, with symbolic activation a case in point. It may be pointed out here that, the existing body of literature on school-to-work transitions that was reviewed in the first half of this introductory chapter, though extremely important, has not yet dealt with the novel Japanese youth support programmes that surfaced in the mid-2000s.

Incidentally, overlapping with my own fieldwork period that ran from April 2007 to March 2008 (with additional research conducted in August and November 2008), the OECD also flew its researchers into Japan to take stock of the country's emerging activation policies for youth. This produced perhaps the best policy-oriented English-language overview of such initiatives to date (OECD 2008). However, due to its tight focus on the formal, conventional dimensions of employment measures as well as on policy recommendations, the otherwise insightful OECD report captured little of the wider, nuanced processes of negotiation around young people and work that are the subject matter of this book. It is hoped that the research results conveyed here will persuade readers (some of whom may be accustomed to more technical literature on active labour market policies, or 'ALMPs') of the value of adopting an inductive ethnographic approach whereby it becomes possible to interrogate not only what people say they will do – as this tends to indicate what they think they should do – but also what they actually do.

Focusing exclusively on micro-level practices in separate sub-domains without drawing links between them would do poor justice to the full potential of the ethnographic approach to social policy. Following Wedel, Shore and others, I therefore stress the fundamental interconnectedness of policy-making, public media discourses and policy practices on the one hand, and of the local, regional, national and international levels on the other (Wedel *et al.* 2005:39–40). This awareness helps break down the artificial separation of these realms and allows the analyst to begin discerning their points of interaction. In line with this holistic orientation, the second notable feature of this book's research design is a 'three-dimensional' structure that focuses on the following levels:

1) media debates on non-employed youth (*NEETs*) which played an essential part in building a case for new youth policies (Chapter 3);
2) strategic policy-making processes led by individual bureaucrats and key scholars with relevant institutional affiliations (Chapter 3 and Chapter 4);
3) youth work practices, carried out at various sites of support, partly reflecting, but ultimately contesting, official policy prescriptions (Chapter 5 and Chapter 6).

By expanding our notion of the 'field' in this way, it becomes possible to capture more fully the dynamism of the processes by which the activation of jobless youth proceeded in 2000s' Japan. This approach contrasts with many existing studies that focus predominantly on the dimension of the media or alternatively analyse youth issues mainly through quantitative surveys and labour market data. Observing reflexively the interactions of several actors, groups and networks offers many benefits, including the ability to detect acute tensions between various actors, bringing to life the classic observation that society is characterized not as much by consensus and harmony as by ubiquitous conflict between competing interest groups (Dahrendorf 1958).

The third notable methodological feature of this study is that it abstains from judging the effectiveness of the labour market measures that it examines. Or to be more specific, no effort is made to evaluate the 'performance' of such programmes according to any single set of criteria, for such criteria would require a normative and ideological commitment to certain forms of behaviour, social structure and economy. As was noted in a previous section, activation policies have come under fire from critical scholars for the reason that they tend to foreground the (presumed) moral and behavioural faults of the individual while ignoring serious social structural matters (see e.g. Honda *et al*. 2006). There is, moreover, an obvious sense in which activation measures strive to funnel individuals into low-paid, low-skilled sections of the labour markets that are characterized by precariousness, making it questionable whether they promote 'social inclusion' in a fundamental sense. Instead of basing my study on narrow assumptions about what activation measures should be achieving, I wish to lay bare competing sets of criteria advanced by distinctive social groups. Indeed, despite a certain degree of official consensus regarding the function and goals of activation across OECD governments (including the government of Japan), such consensus vanishes from sight once we scratch the surface and go beyond official statements and prescriptions. That said, my fieldwork indicates that there were three more-or-less coherent sets of positions regarding 'how to get youth back to work' in Japan in the 2000s – that of the mass media, that of 'sympathetic bureaucrats' and affiliated researchers, and that of youth supporters – though even each of these were, as we will see, characterized by a fair amount of heterogeneity.

So, in terms of methodological orientation, I adopt an ethnographically-driven approach to examining how the issue of youth (non-)employment has been renegotiated across multiple societal levels in contemporary Japan, not to judge efforts at youth activation with reference to a narrow set of criteria, but to reflexively expose competing sets of ideals that often lead to conflict but that sometimes also produce innovation and (temporary) settlements. An existing study that resembles mine in its research design – and that has closely informed my approach – is Goodman's inquiry into the changing status of the so-called returnee children, or *kikokushijo*, between the 1960s and the 1980s (Goodman 1990). The offspring of expatriate families who had received some part of their education abroad, returnees came to be problematized as culturally and/or educationally inadequate upon returning to Japan and therefore as needing special educational attention. Goodman's analysis not only deconstructed the cultural meanings assigned to the label *kikokushijo*, but illuminated how a cast of interested actors mobilized around this new 'problem', how the advantageous class position of the parents of *kikokushijo* resulted in a positive reframing of returnee children as the representatives of an internationalizing Japan, and how the latter were consequently made into targets of positive discrimination in educational policy. In this book, I make similar efforts to decode socially constructed meanings as well as the process by which non-employed youth were problematized through so-called claims-making activities where certain presumed conditions are framed and promoted as problematic in a public arena (Spector and Kitsuse 1977). I also pay considerable attention to behind-the-scenes policy-making strategies and to interactions between key domains during a relatively compressed time period (primarily, 2003–08). I also critically draw on the theoretical literature on the relationship between the 'deserving' versus 'undeserving' status of social policy target groups and the generosity of the policies that these groups 'receive' (Schneider and Ingram 1993, 2005, 2008; see Chapter 3).

Encountering the field

In concrete terms, conducting the fieldwork for this book meant long-term immersion in two distinctive, albeit overlapping, communities, these being what I call Japan's 'youth policy community' and its 'youth support community'. The former consists essentially of government bureaucrats, policy entrepreneurs and experts. Bureaucrats (*kanryō, yakunin*), I found, remain very much in control of hands-on policy-making processes and programme frameworks, although they engage with other parties to seek ideas and to improve their policy designs.[6] They are not a monolithic, universally conservative group, but have diverse views and goals, although all bureaucrats must negotiate similar constraints when promoting their ideas. Policy entrepreneurs are those who aggressively set the agenda and the basic definitions for policy. They comprise esteemed researchers at the University of Tokyo and the Japan Institute of Labour Policy and Training (JILPT) as well as at other academic institutions. Such actors tend to have tremendous influence over social problem discourse. On the other hand, youth support experts (*senmonka*) have rather less power, but they are also consulted in policy-making processes; they give statements to the government and the media based on authority that derives from long years of youth work practice and management, and that is thus 'self-made'. Some experts are what I call veterans: they are the 'pioneers' of youth support in Japan who tend to belong to the 1970s *anpo*-generation (that took part in anti-government activities then to protest against the US-Japan security treaty) and have great authority across the field of youth support due to their long-standing experience and wide networks. However, they also tend to be heavily opinionated and strong-headed, positioning themselves in different ideological camps, which has a divisive effect on the Japanese youth support field. Appendix A lists the most important members of Japan's youth policy community, all of whom I interviewed (see Appendix B for a list of interviews) – several times whenever possible – to ensure that I was able to adequately capture their viewpoints and strategies.

It should be pointed out that many of the members of Japan's youth policy community have public personae in the sense that they publish books and articles in their own name while also appearing in various other media such as television. I have therefore chosen to use the real names of those of my informants who routinely appear in the media (while respecting their privacy by not dealing with personal matters). This applies also to the central 'experts' who often also publish in their own name. At the same time, I have refrained from naming the government officials I interviewed since they mainly appear in their capacity as the representatives of particular organizations. Another point in need of clarification here is that I use key Japanese-language sources not only as general references to ascertain 'facts' or socio-economic trends, but primarily as the statements of strategic actors (policy entrepreneurs and experts). I argue that the majority of books and articles on youth problems such as *NEETs* and *freeters* that appeared in the mid-2000s need to be situated firmly within the relevant debates of the day and viewed as forming part of (political) claims-making activities aimed at shaping these debates. This is not to downplay the frequently high academic and literary skill that has gone into the writing of such works, but their nature as the vehicles for certain causes needs be explicitly recognized.

In addition to its policy community, Japan's youth support community was equally central to my fieldwork. This community is based on various physical sites of youth support such as the Youth Support Stations and Independence Camps across Japan. These sites are linked to one another closely through networks maintained by their leaders. Though the sector of youth support is in fact somewhat larger (see Chapter 2), I have chosen to focus on government-affiliated sites of support to keep my project viable and to stay in line with my research questions. Youth supporters (*wakamono shiensha*) play key roles at such sites, though they, in turn, are managed by the above-mentioned youth support experts (who are less directly involved in youth support practice though very much present at sites of support). Also referred to simply as 'staff' (*sutaffu*) or 'supporters' (*sapōtā*) – but never as 'teachers' (*sensei*) – these youth workers interact face to face with young people and their parents on a daily basis. At many centres, they are further divided into core staff, part-timers and volunteers, with the first group consisting of young workers in their twenties or thirties, the second group often of housewives, and the third of students and 'borrowed' members of other organizations. The supported youth (*shien sareru wakamono*) are themselves usually referred to as 'users' (*riyōsha*), 'camp students' (*jukusei*), or simply as 'youth' (*wakamono*) or 'children' (*kodomo*), but rarely as 'youngsters' (*seinen*), never as 'customers' (*kyakusan*), and hardly ever as 'clients' (*kuraiento*).[7] Parents are typically called 'guardians' (*hogosha*), although in the majority of cases it is mothers who most actively liaise with youth support groups. To ensure a thorough understanding of the youth support community, I chose to carry out participant observation at 15 separate sites of youth support out of which I continuously visited two as an official volunteer staff member (see Appendix C).

Japan's youth support community consists largely of non-profit organizations and is thus located in the civil society. Until the 1990s, civil society was regulated by the Japanese state to such an extent that the kinds of small groups that currently engage in youth support could not have acquired legal status, which in turn would have made cooperation with the state difficult. However, spurred partly by the Great Hanshin-Awaji Earthquake that hit Kobe in 1995 and that elicited an active relief effort from the public, as well as by concerted advocacy by various citizen groups, a new NPO (not-for-profit organization) Law was finally passed in 1998, reducing incorporation to little more than a formality (Schwartz 2003:14–15). It thus became possible for a vast range of groups to acquire legal status, having an invigorating effect on Japan's civil society, including the field of youth support. Although some groups had hitherto functioned as unincorporated voluntary groups (*nin-i dantai*), the NPO status made their operations greatly more viable, affording them not only legal but social recognition and therefore a higher measure of trust. On a related note, though Japanese civil society groups have been characterized as 'apolitical' until recently (Pekkanen 2003, 2006; Avenell 2010), there is currently something of a revival of activism taking place in this realm (Cassegard 2010).[8] Accordingly, all the youth support groups that feature in this study, while implementing state-commissioned programmes, find themselves able to simultaneously resist the government's objectives and priorities. Some are explicit in their resistance, while others strive to strike a fine balance between cooperation and criticality.

In this introductory chapter, I have chosen not to provide 'an arrival story' with which more orthodox ethnographic works tend to commence, but those interested will find a short description of my fieldwork experiences in Appendix D. Besides highlighting the sometimes messy but always fascinating human experience of conducting fieldwork in Japan, this description also gives some indication of the 'invisible labour' that, as with any immersive ethnographic inquiry, has been invested in the making of this study.

The structure of this book

Following the present introductory chapter, Chapter 2 provides an overview of the rather fragmented history of Japanese youth policy. This review highlights an important earlier programme – the Working Youth's Homes – but also places considerable emphasis on earlier youth problem debates that, in many ways, foreshadowed *NEETs* and symbolic activation in the 2000s. Also examined is the sector of private youth support groups which eventually came to provide the infrastructure for new government-coordinated youth activation measures. The second half of Chapter 2 investigates the Youth Independence and Challenge Plan that emerged in 2003 and that marked the beginning of a new era in Japanese youth policy.

Chapters 3 to 6 form the empirical core of this book. In Chapter 3, I trace the construction of *NEETs* as a social problem between 2003 and 2006 by investigating the actions of key policy entrepreneurs and their implicit strategies. Such actors, in striving to create an entirely new target for activation measures, faced the challenge of having to justify the expenditure of public funds on a group viewed by the public as largely 'undeserving'. In this chapter I distinguish the policy target category *NEET* from the social category *nīto* to untangle the dynamics of the social problem construction process and its mixed implications for policy-making efforts. That *NEET* became so universally known among the Japanese public leads me to argue that it has strongly contributed to the emergence of symbolic activation in Japan, something that is different in its logic to more institutionalized activation practices in many Western countries.

The mixed implications of *NEET* are explored in depth in Chapter 4 in which I turn to the hands-on policy-making processes, led by sympathetic bureaucrats, that eventually produced the Youth Independence Camp and the Youth Support Station. Although these measures could indeed not have materialized without the *NEET* debate that supplied the necessary momentum, many of the key ideas they embody in fact existed well before *NEETs* emerged as a social problem. This observation makes it clear that the *NEET* category was made to serve a largely hidden process whereby certain bureaucrats legitimized their pre-existing 'solutions' (i.e. policy ideas) with reference to a new 'problem' (youth non-employment). The key bureaucrats confronted resistance to *NEET* measures by emphasizing the costly consequences of inaction and by portraying their programmes as punitive and 'disciplinarian', reflecting the undeserving status of this group as well as the disciplinarian legacy associated with Totsuka Hiroshi. After numerous constraints were imposed, the Independence Camp and the Support Station were implemented with the cooperation of civil society actors.

Chapters 5 and 6 engage with youth policy practice through what are largely ethnographic accounts of the Youth Independence Camp and the Youth Support Station. These initiatives are examined from multiple angles through a limited number of cases, but the overriding concern is to elucidate their strategies of activation and the ways in which they negotiate, and indeed transform, government-designed blueprints. The Youth Independence Camp, essentially based on collective living and training activities, appears, at first blush, to stand in considerable contrast to the more 'professionalized' and individualistic Youth Support Station. However, these two initiatives differ mainly in terms of accent, with the former illustrating most lucidly how youth support unfolds within communities of recognition, while the latter demonstrates how staff explore the user to gain a deep understanding of his/her preferences, needs and abilities, which then further facilitates training and work placement.

Chapter 7, instead of simply summarizing the main findings of the book, begins with a head-on critique of symbolic activation and the particular category of *NEET*. Both are found to possess fundamental flaws at several levels. The focus is then shifted to the alternative methodologies of activation (or: alternatives to dominant ideas of activation) embedded in the practices of Japanese youth workers who deliver the Youth Independence Camp and the Youth Support Station. The attractive elements of these models are underlined and discussed. Finally, it is argued that, rather than through formal politics, 'scaling up the alternatives under the radar' offers the best hope, in Japan as in most other advanced countries, for a more diversified society that affords recognition to young people and resolves the post-industrial employment dilemma.

One final caveat is in order before concluding this introductory chapter. Some readers may by now be wondering about the relative absence of young people's own voices from this account. Issues of ethnic diversity and gender may also seem underemphasized. Such suspicions are reasonable, and I agree that one cannot fully comprehend the state of Japanese youth without actually talking to individuals from varied backgrounds. However, in this book I have made a conscious intellectual choice to primarily analyse how various powerful groups treat young people and how they define particular groups of youth in modern-day Japan. Indeed, I maintain that, without a critical understanding of how 'problematic' youth groups are defined and by whom, any interview-focused study that takes its cue from well-known categories such as *NEETs* and *hikikomori* risks being heavily biased from the outset (Toivonen and Imoto forthcoming). My empirical findings confirm the suspicion that the primary targets of youth support policies – in this case those referred to as *NEETs* – tend to exercise little voice and have little chance to define public discussions about themselves, being all but sidelined by strategically situated (older) experts, bureaucrats and media establishments. Time will tell whether the events triggered by the triple disaster of 11 March 2011 and the further diffusion of information technologies will empower troubled youth to exert a greater influence on policies and institutions that centrally affect their lives.

Equally striking is the fact that the Japanese government's youth support policies thus far make no reference to the possible ethnic or cultural dimensions of employment integration, partly because of the extreme sectionalism and ethnic biases that characterize policy-making in Japan. *NEET*, as I will explain in more detail in other chapters, was almost from the beginning framed as a problem of 'Japanese' youth belonging to the middle classes and not as an issue of diverse groups of youngsters who might happen to be out of work as well as outside education. Fortunately, I had the chance to talk to around 100 supported youth as well as dozens of youth workers (of whom some were ex-support-receivers) over the course of my fieldwork, which allows me to show that considerable heterogeneity in fact exists within – and indeed is central to the very logic of – the world of youth support. Due to the vulnerable state of many of the young people I encountered, I refrained from trying to conduct interviews with more than a handful of individuals (recruiting a balanced sample would have been extremely difficult and possibly invasive), but actual young people's voices nevertheless inform my account. Their stressful circumstances – which I related to throughout my fieldwork – allow me to consider the policy-focused issues examined in this book from the perspective of their actual users.

2 The emergence of youth independence support policy

The previous chapter charted the appearance of what may be called the post-industrial employment dilemma – the choice that policy-makers seemingly have to make between higher unemployment or a mass of insecure, low-mobility jobs – in Japan. It was argued that the response to youth non-employment put forth by the state and affiliated groups took the shape of 'symbolic activation', whereby prominent youth categories, and in particular that of *NEET*, were employed to mobilize formally inactive young people to consult new youth support services (the option taken by a significant minority) or to join the low-end, low-security labour markets (the default choice for the majority).

Despite the air of newness, in the mid-2000s, around youth non-employment and concepts such as *NEET*, the youth policies that emerged and that are a key subject matter of this book have far-reaching roots. In broad terms, these roots can be divided into four sub-plots that then converge in the 2000s to create a novel type of 'activation' dynamic. This chapter offers a review of each of these sub-plots, beginning with the so-called Working Youth's Homes of the 1970s. A look at this programme, astonishingly similar in terms of its blueprint to current youth support measures, demonstrates that Japan has in fact had a type of youth support policy all along.[1] The second relevant domain that receives attention here is Japan's long legacy of colourful, highly controversial youth problem debates and labels. The centrality of well-known youth types – such as 'school-refusers', the 'single nobility' and *parasite singles* – to policy-making is highlighted, and the extent to which such labels encapsulate changing meanings of youth is also considered. The third sub-plot concerns the presence, since at least the 1970s, in Japan of a peculiar sector of small youth support institutions. This sector is critical to understanding current policies because it is the more 'accommodating' groups within it that came to serve as the main infrastructure for youth support programmes in the 2000s.

The fourth and latest part in the long plot leading to the eventual materialization of symbolic activation comprises the rise, in the Koizumi-era which many associate with the proper arrival of neoliberal economic ideology on Japanese shores, of youth independence support policy (*wakamono jiritsu shien seisaku*). This policy effectively consisted of a broad administrative framework stressing individual self-responsibility (*jiko sekinin*) and the utilization of the private sector in youth employment support provision. It also contributed to the flourishing of many new small educational and employment-related programmes, two of which provided direct models for the Youth Independence Camp and the Youth Support Station discussed in Chapters 4 to 6.

The present chapter therefore takes us from the 1960s all the way to the 2000s, focusing on everything but (the erosion of) the school-to-work transition system that was outlined in Chapter 1. The objective is to identify the direct antecedents of recent programmes and the larger scheme of symbolic activation. This will create a basis for understanding not just the emergence of support policies for inactive youth in the mid-2000s, but also for grasping important – oftentimes surprising – continuities in the realm of Japanese youth policy.

Providing respite to working youth in the 1960s and the 1970s

Immediately following the Second World War, Japan found itself in the position of a poor developing country struggling to rebuild itself and to overcome the social confusion that followed its defeat. Owing to the dire socio-economic conditions of the day, poverty and child labour were widespread, and war orphans in particular remained vulnerable to human trafficking.[2] Many youth survived by selling flowers or polishing shoes on the street; amphetamine addiction was, according to some, a big social problem; and a large share of children were forced to skip school for extended periods because their families could not get by without their economic contributions (Yamaguchi 1972:1–3). At this time, the major preoccupation of the welfare and labour administration was the protection of children and youth from exploitation and unduly long working hours via new regulations and improved enforcement.

As Japan recovered and as its economy began to expand from the late 1950s onwards, the situation of young people – and of teenagers especially – was transformed drastically: in place of unemployment there was, by the 1960s, a growing labour shortage that led to a phenomenon of 'collective hiring' or 'mass hiring' (*shūdan shūshoku*; Kariya *et al.* 2000:2) whereby thousands of lower secondary school graduates migrated from rural areas to industrial growth centres where they worked mainly in manufacturing (see Chapter 1 on the recent erosion of mass hiring). This bred new urban youth problems that were said to comprise, among other ills, delinquency, prostitution and drug abuse as well as poverty. Increasingly, even those who worked in essentially legitimate jobs at small and middle-sized companies were also found to face significant social issues. The government, though not necessarily as soon as some had hoped, eventually decided to commission surveys into undesirable behaviours and conditions with an eye to developing novel disciplinary and welfare-oriented measures.

Yet it was not the central government but local civil society organizations (including churches) that were the pioneers of welfare support for youth in the late 1950s and the 1960s. Such actors appeared to be more sensitive and responsive than the government to the plight of many of the thousands of youth who had migrated to industrial towns at an early age and who reportedly suffered from loneliness and severe exhaustion (Sakaguchi 2007). Although omitted in official national-level and local governments' reports, that a number of surveys showed suicides to be a regular occurrence among working youth in the 1960s speaks of the grimness of such young people's living conditions (interview with Sakaguchi Junji, 17 March 2008). Ikoi no Ie of Toyota City (Aichi) and Fukagawa Kinrō Seishōnen Sentā of Tokyo were the two notable centres that acted as prototypes for subsequent government youth programmes, furnishing care and relaxed social spaces to hard-working migrant teenagers.

In a pattern that would recur in the 2000s, the government grew more interested in developing tangible national-level welfare measures for working youth in the late 1960s after having learned about the kinds of local initiatives just mentioned. The efforts of an enterprising and, according to his successors, exceptionally broad-minded bureaucrat by the name of Yamaguchi Masaji were instrumental to this turn. Dubbed the 'father of Japanese youth policy' by his juniors, Yamaguchi worked as the chief of the Youth Labour Section of the Women's and Youth's Bureau at the Ministry of Labour and actively engaged with the field of youth welfare both domestically as well as internationally (he took a special interest in German postwar youth policies in particular). If Yamaguchi was, in terms employed in Chapter 4, the key 'innovator' who drafted the main proposals and designed the central programmes in this era, it was Hara Kensaburō (1907–2004), the then minister of labour (1968–70, 1971–72), who played the crucial role of a 'sponsor', ensuring the political survival of such programmes.

Minister Hara was said to have had a passionate interest in improving the welfare of 15- to 24-year-old working youth who then comprised one-third of Japan's total working population, reflecting a demographic reality starkly different to that of the present day. Hara viewed such hard-working young people as a highly deserving group and, when promoting new policy, lamented the fact that, whereas roughly 1 million yen was spent annually by the state on each upper secondary school student, employed youth of the same age received only 1,000 yen per person in terms of government expenditure (Yamaguchi 1972:151). The following argument that he made at large national youth workers' conferences summarizes well the spirit of emerging youth welfare policy at this time:

> Work is the basis of everything; it is precisely work motivation that lies at the root of prosperous living. Yet, at the same time, a human being cannot lead a rich life if he neglects relaxation, sports, recreation and other leisure activities. I want it to be a principle that [youth] work well and play well; live strongly and robustly; and thereby become proud professionals (*shokugyōnin*).
>
> (Yamaguchi 1972:152)

In minister Hara's mind, commitment to work was clearly to remain as essential a prerequisite to 'prosperous living' as before, but it was to be supplemented by meaningful recreational activities that would promote the development of robust and independent young adults with a high work ethic. The assertions of both Hara and the bureaucrat Yamaguchi were in line with a broader trend in Japan of the 1970s where economic growth-centrism came under criticism, leisure gained a much higher status than before and calls for environmental protection and more generous welfare proliferated (Goodman and Peng 1996). The way the two worked together to realize a new youth policy, it may be added, foreshadowed, to a truly remarkable degree, the making of activation policies for young adults in the 2000s (see especially Chapter 4).

However, new youth policies – most centrally the Working Youth's Welfare Law of 1970 that contained an article regarding the establishment of Working Youth's Homes – were usually justified with direct reference to a mix of alarming social problems. This provides us with an early example of how, virtually without exception, youth policies are always intimately linked to youth problems, and vice versa. First, it was found in the late 1960s that the majority of serious criminal acts by those aged 14 to 19 were committed by working youth (*kinrō seishōnen* being the relevant label); second, employers and the wider economy were said to be suffering from the high turnover rates of young people (curiously resembling the concerns of Japanese society about part-time working *freeters* in the 1990s and 2000s); and third, working youth were found to waste away their leisure time 'passively' by listening to radio or watching TV (or consuming other forms of entertainment), the majority not participating in club activities that could foster solidarity and personal development (Yamaguchi 1970).

Because frequent job-switching was associated with both economic losses and delinquency, better occupational counselling was offered as one solution, and 'active leisure' was to be promoted through the Working Youth's Homes.[3] The underlying point was not simply to provide welfare but to furnish 'labour welfare' (*rōdō fukushi*), a type of welfare that would support economic activity without questioning its primacy and that would have wider positive societal effects. There is thus an intriguing parallel between the Working Youth's Homes and youth employment measures in the 2000s, as both were tasked with 'activating' youth to engage in desirable activities, albeit in a drastically different labour market context, the ultimate goal of which, at least on the level of rhetoric, was to contribute to economic progress. Another remarkable feature of the Working Youth's Welfare Law was that it designated the third Saturday of July as the 'Working Youth's Day' to honour the contributions of such young people, reflecting the labourism of the era that valorized commitment to work and company.

We will see in Chapters 4 to 6 that Japan's new inclusion policies have many further features in common with these classic policies for working youth, although the former are, in the words of the youth work pioneer Sakaguchi

Junji, 'from-welfare-to-work' policies while the latter are more aptly characterized as 'to-welfare-from-work' measures (as they supported the leisure
activities of employed youth who were often overworked; interview with
Sakaguchi Junji, 17 March 2008). This partly springs from the fact that they
were the creations – though creations influenced by pre-existing models – of
the very same section of the government, namely those of the Youth Labour
Section of the Women's and Youth's Bureau (at the Ministry of Labour) that
later became the Career Development Support Office (CDSO) of the Human
Resources Development Bureau (now under the Ministry of Health, Labour
and Welfare). The idea of *tamariba* (a hangout) was embodied in the design
of the Working Youth's Homes, predating the more recently popularized
concept of *ibasho* ('a place for being oneself') that is now often applied to
sites of youth support. Moreover, the old policies stressed the recruitment, as
staff, of committed and enthusiastic youth workers, for which a new training
programme was designed by Sakaguchi Junji – himself a social worker and
psychologist who imported British youth work ideas to Japan in the 1970s
(Sakaguchi interview, 17 March 2008).[4]

It should be noted that the total number of the Working Youth's Homes
across Japan grew to around 500 in the 1970s, which was the heyday of this
programme. However, in the 1980s and 1990s this scheme rapidly lost relevance due to social changes that produced more university and vocational
college students, fewer 'working youth' and plentiful alternative sources of
entertainment, but also due to paralysis within the scheme itself. There was
arguably little incentive for this programme to change since state funding for
it was guaranteed by law. Moreover, Working Youth's Homes lacked innovative leaders and thus failed to adapt to the times by reaching out to new
target groups such as school non-attendants or socially withdrawn youth
(although there may have been individual exceptions, with Kyoto City standing
out as a particularly energetic administrative actor). By contrast, private
groups such as those to be discussed below moved far more swiftly to seize
new opportunities, though they initially lacked the reach and coverage of an
integrated national programme. Chapter 4 will recount how, despite this
situation, the engineers of new youth inclusion policies failed to gain the
cooperation of the Working Youth's Homes – around 400 of which still
remained – in the early 2000s.

Youth problems and changing meanings of 'youth' in affluent Japan

The production of mainstream youth problems

While Japan enacted few extensive youth services beyond the Working
Youth's Homes in the postwar period, it produced an all the more colourful
repertoire of youth problems that have inspired successive high-profile media
debates.[5] These include, but are not limited to, the 'moratorium humans', *student
apathy*, the 'single nobility' (*dokushin kizoku*), *parasite singles*, the socially

withdrawn *hikikomori* and the part-time-working *freeters*.[6] Well-known children's and teenagers' problems which emerged in the same era – including school non-attendance (*tōkōkyohi* or *futōkō*, said to relate to apathy and anthropophobia), *kikokushijo* (returnee children), *enjo kōsai* (compensated dating), *ijime* (bullying), *taibatsu* (corporal punishment) and *jidō gyakutai* (child abuse) – have followed a similar general pattern (or 'career') as social problems that focus on young adults.[7] Table 2.1 charts the most notable socially

Table 2.1 Notable Japanese youth problems, 1970–90

Time period	Socialcategory (label)	Initial meaning
1970s	Tōkōkyohi	Children who refuse to attend school and are therefore deviant (surfaced in the 1950s, but became prominent in the 1970s); also, the phenomenon of school refusal
	Kikoku shijo	Returnee children said to suffer from various cultural and educational deficiencies upon returning to Japan
	Moratorium ningen	'Moratorium humans' who postpone important transitions, especially into university and jobs
1980s	Dokushin kizoku	'Single nobility': wealthy single young adults who live alone in a manshon while postponing marriage
	Otaku	Obsessive sub-culture consumers and creators; originally perceived as mentally sick
1990s	Adult children	Immature young adults who continue to live with their dysfunctional parental families
	Freeters	First, freelancing youth who avoid company drudgery to pursue their dreams; in the 2000s, involuntary young part-time workers (the term was invented in the 1980s)
	Parasite singles	Affluent (mainly female) youth to whom work is a 'hobby' and who consume luxury items while living at home with their parents
2000s	Hikikomori	Socially withdrawn and isolated youth who are not only immature but also mentally ill (the term first appeared in the 1990s)
	NEETs (nīto)	Lazy and immature jobless youth who intentionally avoid work and live off their parents
	Sōshokukei-danshi	'Herbivorous' men who are more interested in style and their hobbies than in meeting women and achieving career success

Source: Toivonen and Imoto (2012)

constructed youth problems in the preceding four decades. These debates deserve attention because they constitute direct precursors of the *NEET* discourse and remind us that youth problems and policies have always been interconnected. Even more importantly, in relation to this book's key argument on symbolic activation (see Chapter 1), understanding that Japan had a significant legacy of popular categories, operating according to a consistent logic, makes it easier to see why youth labels could eventually become so central there to practices of labour market activation.

How, then, were youth problems produced in postwar Japan? What are the key sociological mechanisms that turned them into such high-profile affairs in the Japanese media? Toivonen and Imoto (2012) propose, in an in-depth treatment of this topic that builds on a growing constructionist literature on Japanese youth problems, that the following features are shared by all mainstream youth problems in Japan, and quite possibly in other advanced societies as well:

1) Mainstream youth problems, rather than simply being 'caused' by young people themselves, are always the outcome of broader social activities that define certain issues as 'problems'.
2) Individual youth problems proceed as 'waves' of collective attention, characterized by relatively short episodes of moral panic, followed by longer two-to-three-year policy cycles, after which some issues wane and others re-emerge.
3) Lending a tangible form to youth debates and giving expression to interests, recognizable 'industries' emerge around high-profile youth problems.
4) Youth problem discourses tend to fall within predictable boundaries, with 'translators' (claims-makers) synthesizing specific areas of knowledge into general media discourses. However, discursive spheres that are initially discrete can also converge around shared symbols.
5) Different youth categories are linked in their underlying moral vocabulary and form a distinctive 'youth problem pedigree'. All these categories, however, should be seen as symbolic and open to manipulation and change.
6) Youth problems have, in the Japanese context, been strongly defined by middle-class values and interests.

(Toivonen and Imoto 2012:16–23)

Chapter 3 of this book will amply demonstrate that it is this same logic, embodied in a long pedigree of youth problems, that manifested in and governed the construction of *NEET* as a social category in the 2000s.

Three further reasons why Japan's youth problem legacy is relevant to the purposes of this book need to be emphasized here. First, related research shows that perceived youth problems do not correspond in any straightforward way with socio-economic conditions, even if they partly reflect the economic, educational and demographic concerns of the day. They are rather driven by 'industries' of interested actors, commercial enterprises, private or semi-private youth support groups, the media and the government. This interactive process is led by claims-makers (Spector and Kitsuse 1977), individuals who 'translate' their concerns to the wider public and promote the popularization of certain issues and interpretations. Second, although older mainstream youth problems do not predetermine the meanings of emerging problems, the former shape the latter in critical ways so that there is a high degree of continuity in the 'moral vocabulary' and popular responses across issues that may be temporally distant. For example, where the so-called 'school-refusers' (*tōkōkyohi*) were criticized, in the 1970s, for making the unthinkable choice of forgoing school, *NEETs*, the 'work-refusers' of the 2000s, received much the same treatment (as well as the same defence) for resisting entrenched work norms (see Chapter 3). The more recent category of the presumably fashion-conscious but sexually lacklustre *sōshoku-kei danshi* ('herbivorous men'), further demonstrates how new categories are, to some extent, mere reincarnations of earlier youth types, for this recent debate clearly contains elements from the *parasite single, freeter* and *otaku* discourses, which have revolved around the violation of middle-class gender norms (e.g. women lacking in feminine qualities and readiness to play the 'proper' female role and males lacking in the ability or willingness to step into the masculine role of the male breadwinner). Third, in comparison to such underlying themes that have tremendous resilience, 'booms' around particular categories and problems are often short-lived, lasting no longer than a few years, but nevertheless create opportunities for relevant policies to be changed or introduced.

Salient types of youth discourse

As already argued, behind a dazzling range of categories, images and interpretations, one finds significant continuity on several levels, and this includes recurring positions pertaining to the causes of and solutions to a given youth problem. In her discussion on the debate around children who forgo school for an extended period, the *tōkōkyohi* (later reframed as *futōkō*), Yoneyama (1999) identifies the following four types of adult discourse:

1) psychiatric discourse: *tōkōkyohi* as a mental illness
2) behavioural discourse: *tōkōkyohi* as laziness
3) citizens' discourse: *tōkōkyohi* as resistance to school
4) socio-medical discourse: *tōkōkyohi* as school burnout.

(Yoneyama 1999:191)

The major point of contention that characterizes these discourses is whether *tōkōkyohi* is a personal or structural problem and whether it is an illness or not. Table 2.2 illustrates economically, building on Yoneyama's schema, how a given youth problem is usually interpreted and the types of solutions that are proposed.

The psychiatric and behavioural discourses are highly similar in that they attribute the problem to individual youth themselves, or to their parents, The

Table 2.2 Four dominant types of youth problem discourse

Youth problem X is:	An illness	Not an illness
Personal adjustment or moral problem	Psychiatric discourse Solution: medical treatment, confinement	Behavioural discourse Solution: discipline and punishment
Structural problem caused by society / particular institutions	Socio-medical discourse Solution: good rest, medication if required	(3) Citizens' discourse Solution: total acceptance by others, support network, social reform

Source: Adapted with some modifications from Yoneyama (1999:191–92)

key difference here is that the former speaks in terms of 'maladjustment', syndromes (as in *gakkō kyōfushō*, school phobia syndrome) and parental excesses or deficiencies (as in 'over-interference' and 'over-protection', or lack of a father figure), while the latter finds fault with individual youth who are said to be lazy, lacking in discipline, spoilt or plain selfish (Yoneyama 1999:194, 201). The solutions that these two discourses directly imply are also highly similar and centre around coercive and punitive strategies, delivered, for instance, at correctional boarding schools or at hospitals for the mentally ill. I refer to these kinds of measures broadly as comprising 'disciplinarian rehabilitation'. This is the formerly dominant, but now discredited, model of youth support that was charted in the Preface. It may be further noted briefly that, though rather curiously, despite the fact that disciplinarian methods have recently become less acceptable in Japanese society, the psychiatric and behavioural discourses are alive and well. This discrepancy helps to explain the need felt by youth policy bureaucrats in the 2000s, as will be charted in Chapter 4, to moderate the disciplinarian elements of their policy blueprints – closely derived from the popular, harsh discourse on non-employed *NEETs* and sometimes endorsed by senior bureaucrats – so as to ensure that actual practices are far 'softer' and safer than what punitive discourses seem to demand.

The citizens' discourse and the socio-medical discourse are agreed that the main problem lies with social structure and institutions, not with individual youth or with parents per se. The former discourse rejects any claims that the youth at the centre of a given problem are 'sick' and posits that they are simply resisting structures that threaten them. On the other hand, the socio-medical discourse focuses on physical disorders such as chronic fatigue, nausea or depression but attributes them primarily to social or work environments. In terms of solutions, both of these discourses essentially suggest non-coercive support strategies that I generally refer to as 'accommodating rehabilitation' and which may be delivered by alternative schools or residential youth support organizations (see Miller and Toivonen 2010, where a typology of disciplinarian and accommodating rehabilitation philosophies is developed in more detail). This is generally the approach taken by the Youth Independence Camps and Youth Support Stations that will be examined in depth Chapters 5 and 6.

It is clear that discourses one and two above are fundamentally opposed to discourses three and four, as the former allocate blame to the individual while the latter focus on social structure and institutions. One additional observation to make is that the former two are decidedly in favour of the status quo while the latter tend to demand change (although the extent of this can vary from the establishment of small alternative and accommodating institutions to the promotion of wider attitudinal or political change). Each of these four discourses may manifest in a single youth problem debate, so that we see a plurality of interpretations regarding causes and solutions. More often than not, however, a particular youth problem tends to be discussed predominantly within the parameters of one dominant position in a given period. For example, work-related youth problems such as *parasite singles* and *freeters* were (at least first) talked about as issues of behaviour and morals or 'lifestyles'. On the other hand, the socially withdrawn *hikikomori* have been discussed mainly as a psychiatric matter though, in all of these cases, the relevant discourses shift over time. It is all too often overlooked that how a particular problem is framed depends to a great extent on the professional background and social position of the central claim-maker(s): psychiatrists, psychoanalysts and psychologists are liable to speak in terms of the psychiatric paradigm, whereas civil society groups and social scientists more readily embrace the citizens' discourse and structural explanations.

Changing meanings of 'youth'

Rather than an objective, static category, the meanings assigned to the term 'youth' – as a life-stage and a demographic group – vary significantly across time and context. Hence it is important for social scientists to refrain from defining youth simply as a particular, neatly delineated age-group – such as 15 to 24, or 20 to 29 – but to first query the key cultural definitions of youth as well as possible shifts in such definitions. In most societal settings, 'youth' are defined in opposition to 'adults' and are seem as not having undergone signal transition events, such as entry into stable paid work and marriage, for example. This means that, even in today's advanced societies, someone in his or her thirties who is 'still living like a student' and who remains jobless and/or unmarried, may be considered less of an 'adult' than a 22-year-old with a full-time job and children. As we will see, the policy-relevant age bracket for 'youth' in Japan in the 2000s was 15 to 34, but this should not be taken to imply that policy-makers and Japanese citizens generally think that 35 is the threshold for adulthood in their country. Rather, this age-group, as will be set out in detail in Chapter 3, was singled out as a potential target for employment support interventions, with the employment situation as the de facto arbiter between 'youth' and 'adult' statuses. Cultural definitions of youth and adulthood are in actuality a highly nuanced matter, as will be suggested by a review of the multiple dimensions of 'independence' (*jiritsu*) below. First, however, let us examine a few particular ways in which the meanings of 'youth' have shifted in the postwar era.

As was already set out, Japan grew from a poor developing country in the 1940s and 1950s into a rapidly developing, manufacturing-driven economy in the 1960s and 1970s, and subsequently into a post-industrial society where most jobs were to be found in the service sector. Over this period, average educational levels and the number of years spent in education rose dramatically, strongly contributing, along with later marriages, to the prolongation of the period that can potentially be thought of as 'youth' (Miyamoto 2005). Remarkably, roughly 90 per cent of teenagers complete upper secondary school in Japan, with 50 per cent of the total population of youth also now graduating four-year university courses. This has clearly created a framework for a prolonged youth life-stage. The 1990s' recession and the subsequent wave of labour market deregulation have further complicated the 'school-to-work transition' (itself now a rather outdated term), making it less predictable, protracted and possibly more risky (Kosugi 2008).

Mainstream youth debates reflect these socio-economic changes, but only to an extent. Rather, they encapsulate the dominant socially constructed meanings – produced against the backdrop of broader debates and trends perceived by interested actors and the media – of 'youth' and associated 'problems' at certain points in time. For example, the 1960s' term 'working youths', as examined above, mainly referred to 15- to 19-year-olds (who were employed immediately upon leaving lower secondary school), who were said to suffer from excessive work and high rates of offending as well as job-switching.

Interestingly, *parasite singles* may be seen as a refashioning of the 1980s' 'single nobility' discourse under the conditions of the economically stagnant, depressing 1990s (retrospectively, the Lost Decade). Although 'parasites' still led luxurious and brand-embellished lives, unlike the *dokushin kizoku*, they could not bring themselves to leave their parental homes.

Observing the ever-expanding time that youth required to gain full adult status in Japan, Miyamoto Michiko penned the concept 'post-youth' (*posuto seinenki*) in the 1990s to propose a new life-stage between youth (*seinenki*) and adulthood (*seijinki*) (Miyamoto 2002:46). However, Miyamoto's take on this life-stage was less optimistic than that of her American counterparts (see especially Arnett, 2004, on 'emerging adulthood') as she pointed out an increase in young people who could not, even after years of trying, become independent either economically, mentally nor socially. While Yamada, who collaborated with Miyamoto at this time, took this as evidence of the proliferation of parasitic youth (Yamada 1999), Miyamoto maintained that the appearance of post-youth was due to the breakdown of 'post-war-type adolescence' (Inui 1999). This hitherto standard pattern of adolescence had rested, it was suggested, on a stable, functional triangle of families, schools and companies, between which human and economic resources flowed smoothly (see also Honda ed. 2007:20). Though clearly an idealized image of a past model that was not always as 'functional' as assumed, a highly efficient school-to-work transition system (see Chapter 1) meant that there was a measure of truth to this interpretation.

Although Miyamoto, drawing on empirical social surveys, was more concerned with part-time working *freeters* and the social status of young people in general, it was the socially withdrawn *hikikomori* that became the epitome of immaturity and of the failure to reach adulthood around the turn of the millennium. The key claims-maker to construct withdrawn youth as a serious social problem, Saitō Tamaki, claimed that there were up to 1 million such youth in Japan and defined *shakaiteki hikikomori* as:

> A condition where a youth withdraws into the home and does not participate in society for a period of over six months, of which mental disability is not likely to be the primary cause.
>
> (Saitō 1998:25)

Saitō thus portrayed *hikikomori* youth as suffering from a long period of social isolation (whether voluntary or not) and initially associated it strongly with the trappings of adolescence (*shishunki*). Despite being a psychiatrist, he insisted carefully that *hikikomori* was not an illness as such, even if it coincided with certain mental health problems. However, many nevertheless came to see social withdrawal as a kind of illness during the *hikikomori* 'boom' of the early 2000s (Horiguchi 2012).

The reason the *hikikomori* emerged as the epitome of immaturity was because socially withdrawn youth were seen to be deficient in not just one, but in up to four, dimensions of 'independence' (*jiritsu*) – not just an important cultural concept, but also a key youth policy term in the 2000s (see below). Insofar as withdrawn youth were dependent mentally on their parents, they were psychologically dependent; as long as they were unable to form proper relationships with others, they were socially inept; since they were not earning their own living, they lacked economic independence; and since they were unmarried, they were also sexually immature (Kaneko 2006:345). So, in order for the hikikomori to become accepted as mature adults (*ichinin-mae no otona*), they had to achieve independence on all of these counts, usually beginning with independence from parents, leading to economic and sexual independence, but only through first gaining the ability to enter social relationships. Considerable disagreement remained, however, regarding the substance of independence on each of these dimensions. For instance, Saitō Tamaki, the main authority on *hikikomori*, favoured the 'Japanese independence model' – which positions living together with one's parents and taking care of them as an integral part of maturity – over the markedly different 'Western model of independence' under which a mature person is, presumably, expected to maintain physical distance from his or her parents.

There are two further ideas that have critically shaped postwar perceptions of youth and debates surrounding young people. The first of these is the notion that parents are ultimately responsible not only for the education of their children but for looking after them until they reach adulthood, however long this may take (Miyamoto 2005:76–78). This means that their offsprings' attainment of 'independence' becomes a matter of enormous importance to most families. While no doubt setting the family up as the main safety net for those who struggle to become self-reliant, as Miyamoto and Yamada argue, the norm of family responsibility may have simultaneously led to the concealment of various pressures, including youth poverty, within parental households (Miyamoto 2005:78; Yamada 2006:35). It seems plausible that this may have led to less momentum towards generating new youth policy measures in Japan, and that youth as well as parents have been discouraged from seeking outside support even when some local support measures may already have existed. This helps to explain why Japan's activation programmes in the 2000s came to serve a relatively 'old' youth demographic, including those in their late twenties and early-to-mid-thirties. Another implication of prescribing the family as the main safety net is that reaching out to youth tends to be harder in the Japanese context compared to more individualized settings where parents are not held responsible for the livelihoods of their offspring after a certain age.

The second idea is that of work as the ultimate arbiter of social worth and deservingness, especially for males. While not a feature peculiar to middle-class Japan alone, the high work ethic enforced by Japanese society tends to contribute to relatively brutal public reactions towards those who do not work but who are nevertheless seen as being physically and otherwise capable of working. In the late 2000s, there were several well-documented cases where unemployed men starved to death following the denial of livelihood security payments by local welfare offices (Yuasa 2008), though this is but one manifestation of dominant work norms interacting with austere institutional practices in the context of growing labour market insecurity.

Underlying dominant Japanese work norms – which are not necessarily shared by all people in Japan but remain strongly enforced by mainstream institutions – is the peculiarly egalitarian idea of 'potential', articulated well by White (1987) as follows:

> [I]n Japan eventual success is not assumed to depend on one's innate capacities but on virtuous characteristics one can develop. Hence potential is regarded in Japan as egalitarian – everyone has it but some work harder to develop it than others.
>
> (White 1987:19, cited in Hertog 2008:199)

This belief suggests that everyone can indeed do well at school and in their careers as long as they try hard and persevere. The reverse implication is that those who are not doing well must simply be lacking in effort. This strong belief lingered on in the 2000s despite social disparities becoming a salient concern with the prominent *kakusa shakai* debate (see Goodman 2012b on how the efforts of middle-class children have been aided by considerable investment, by affluent parents, in expensive cram school courses). As we will see in Chapter 3, it is exactly this common Japanese notion – crystallized in the old but still popular proverb that 'those who do not work shall not eat' (*hatarakazaru mono kuu bekarazu*) – which made non-working *NEETs* so provocative a phenomenon in the mid-2000s.

Adaptive youth support organizations

In addition to past policies, youth problems and shifting meanings of 'youth', we also need to take a glance at Japan's peculiar sector of private youth support institutions in order to understand the dynamics of youth activation in the 2000s.[8] Unrelated to the above-mentioned Working Youth's Homes, a small number of private groups emerged in the 1970s to cater to the needs of various young people seen to be struggling with education and employment. Many such private initiatives looked after young people – predominantly 'school-refusers' at first, but later also socially withdrawn, jobless youth – on a full-time basis in residential settings that tried to build a family-like atmosphere. As was the case with the pioneering Wada-juku (Odawara City, Kanagawa Prefecture) of Wada Shigehiro, and Tame-juku (Fussa City, Tokyo) of Kudō Sadatsugu, founded in 1974 and 1977, respectively, they had often evolved from academic cram schools and had gone on to develop highly original pedagogic philosophies (see Chapter 5).[9] These elusive organizations which, according to a private research project carried out in the early 2000s, numbered around 80 (Purattofōmu Purojekuto 2003), suddenly became relevant to Japanese youth inclusion policy by the mid-2000s as they were then seen as 'youth support professionals' or 'pioneers'. Key policy-makers decided that they would harness the facilities and practical know-how of such organizations in implementing new youth support programmes.

It is vital to make four observations about these groups. First, it is clear that two broad genres of private residential youth support institutions have taken shape over the past four decades. The more famous – or rather, infamous – of the two consists of disciplinarian, boot camp-style training schools, already described in Chapter 1, which have provided correctional training to youth in line with the behavioural discourses discussed above. The three best-known examples of disciplinarian institutions include the Fudōjuku, the Kazenoko-Gakuen and the Totsuka Yacht School, each having experienced student deaths between 1979 and 1991 apparently due to the application of physical punishment (Yoneyama 1999:93–95). Of these, the Totsuka Yacht School is by far the most famous institution, not only due to its highest death count (five student deaths altogether, of which one seems not to have been related to disciplinary practices) but also owing to its leader's active participation in educational debates in which he has continued to advocate the use of corporal punishment for the improvement of students (Miller 2012). Totsuka's activities have, it is fair to say, defined the very image of residential youth training in the public consciousness since the late 1970s. This inevitably complicated the operation of government programmes such as the Youth Independence Camp that many saw as belonging to the Totsuka tradition of youth support (see Chapters 1, 4 and 5).

Yet also an 'accommodating' genre of residential youth support institutions took shape in the same era, with the above-mentioned Tame-juku and Wada-juku offering two examples. While not necessarily renouncing all kinds of discipline, they have come to view violence by and large as an inappropriate and ineffective method for rehabilitating the kinds of youth – often characterized as insecure, lethargic and withdrawn – that they receive.[10] Some such institutions can be categorized as 'free schools' that serve as alternative places of learning and communication for non-attending school children, most of which appeared in the late 1980s and which typically are not residential.[11] However, it is the residential facilities that are of higher relevance here due to the fact that residential training came to be seen by many decision-makers as an effective method for rehabilitating jobless *hikikomori* and *NEETs* in the 2000s.

The second point to make is that residential youth support has been tremendously adaptive: it has survived through ever-changing public youth debates, always reframing its activities in terms of the most recent problem youth discourse. This is why many groups in this sector have switched from targeting delinquent youth (*hikō*), 'emotionally disturbed' children (*jōcho shōgai-ji*) and 'school refusers' (*tōkōkyohi*) in the 1970s and 1980s to serving 'school non-attendants' (*futōkō*) and socially withdrawn youth (*hikikomori*) in the 1990s, only to re-emerge as *NEET* supporters in the 2000s. This does not necessarily mean that the types of children and youth actually accommodated at residential institutions have substantially changed, only that it has been necessary to justify and advertise the activities of such institutions in terms of the pressing social problems of the day. Doing so has probably made them more appealing to parents in addition to sometimes leading to additional funding from local governments and to bank loans (which is certainly among the goals of those groups that contribute to the construction of youth problem debates). One thing that such adaptability speaks of is the relatively ambiguous, weakly institutionalized position of private youth support services, at least until the 2000s, in the context of the Japanese welfare state. While not a theme pursued further in this book, it may be precisely this lack of institutionalization, together with the private ownership of most youth support institutions, that makes recurrent youth problem campaigns 'necessary' from the point of view of this sector and its sponsors.[12]

The third point that merits attention here is that residential support institutions have exhibited considerable diversity in both their practices and philosophies: some are Buddhist, others Christian or non-religious; some, as we have seen, endorse corporal punishment while others employ markedly 'softer' approaches; a few appear reclusive while others integrate thoroughly into local society and broad networks. Such diversity has arguably been facilitated by the creativity and originality of the groups' (sometimes strong-headed) leaders, alongside an almost complete lack of regulation pertaining to residential institutions – that are neither schools nor official welfare facilities.

Fourth, although it is difficult to make generalizations about this fragmented field, some have reported that the emphasis of *hikikomori* groups was shifting towards a greater stress on training for economic independence in the early 2000s (Ishikawa 2007:20–22). At the same time, there seemed to be a shift towards 'accommodating' approaches (over disciplinarian training) where violent methods of discipline have become marginalized, as suggested in the Preface. The growing interest among support institutions towards more systematic work training may have been prompted, in part, by the relative aging of withdrawn youth and their parents, or it may have reflected users' frustrations with a communication skills-oriented approach. In any case, if there indeed was an increasing grass-roots-level preference for employment-focused youth support at this time, the government-supported *NEET* campaign of 2004 and 2005 seems to have been more or less in line with ongoing trends in the youth support field. It is instructive to add here that there was, in the early 2000s, a closer relationship between private youth supporters and the government, with Kudō Sadatsugu, the single most influential person in the youth sector in this period, reportedly having established a 'channel' between himself and the Ministry of Labour (Adachi 2006:9). There is no doubt that such relations between employment-oriented youth supporters and the government contributed to making employment-focused training the dominant mode of support in the second half of the 2000s (though, as further chapters will show, 'employment-focused' does not entirely capture the essence and diversity of actual support practices).

'Independence support' as a new framework for youth policy

The foregoing sections argued that Japanese youth policy, social problem debates and private support measures evolved in parallel with vast socio-economic changes and growing material prosperity. However, after decades of high and moderate economic growth, Japan experienced a deep recession after the bursting of the economic bubble at the start of the 1990s. This marked yet another drastic change in conditions faced by young people: the youth labour market deteriorated, the school-to-work transition system came under pressure, and part-time work proliferated (see Chapter 1). These changes inspired key actors to bring in a whole new era in youth policy in the 2000s. This was the era of government-led 'independence support'. This shift in the policy realm was symbolized by the Youth Independence and Challenge Plan of 2003 and the Youth Independence and Challenge Action Plan of 2004. The appearance of these Plans immediately preceded the *NEET* debate and activation policies that appeared in 2005 and 2006, as will be discussed in subsequent chapters. The developments described in this section are important because they set out the administrative principles and programmatic features of symbolic activation while also highlighting some of the dilemmas that emerging policies faced when trying to mobilize formally inactive Japanese youth.

The 'independence support' policy discourse

While debates on the closely related topic of individuality (*kosei*) have a long history in Japan,[13] the cross-sector policy discourse on individual self-reliance or independence (*jiritsu*) is relatively new.[14] Though the role of the family in supplying care and in keeping down social spending was certainly stressed in the 'Japanese-style social welfare system' discourse of the late 1970s and early 1980s (Goodman and Peng 1996:193), under conditions of near-automatic school-to-work transitions and low unemployment which lasted until the early 1990s, public discussions on the independence of particular target groups such as youth were rare (even as discipline and youth socialization remained hot topics; see Foreword).

The breakthrough of the notion of independence in the realm of policy and politics coincided with the era of Prime Minister Junichiro Koizumi (2001–06) who forcefully leveraged the idea of self-reliance in advancing his 'structural reforms' (*kōzō kaikaku*) (Hook and Takeda 2007). Koizumi's ideas were 'neoliberal' in the sense that they encouraged maximum reliance on the market and minimum state interference. 'Self responsibility' (*jiko sekinin*) was another of Koizumi's central rhetoric devices which drove home the message that individuals and families, rather than the government, were ultimately in charge of outcomes in the labour markets and in terms of welfare.[15] The state's appropriate role, by implication, was merely to support the independence and self-reliance of individuals.

The emergence of the 'independence support' discourse in social policy in this era can be traced to a particular report issued by the welfare-side of the MHLW in January 2002. Outlining the conclusions of a project team tasked with designing a 'new livelihood support system for low-income earners', this report stressed that the aging of the population would lead to an inevitable increase in Japan's overall social security burden and thus it would be necessary for all those who were able to do so to shoulder part of the costs (MHLW 2002). Interestingly, to bolster its case, the brief report cited 'broad trends' in a number of foreign countries towards new kinds of welfare, highlighting specific examples in the UK and the US as well as Germany where new 'welfare-to-work', 'work-first' and 'active labour market programmes' had recently been implemented. What the report called for were independence support measures (*jiritsu shien saku*) that consisted essentially of employment support (*shūrō shien*) and welfare loans to those 'who had the motivation and the ability to work'.[16] Clearly then, something very similar to the European and OECD-endorsed activation paradigm, discussed in more detail in Chapter 1, was being adopted for use, in the guise of independence support, in Japanese policy-making circles at this time.[17]

While the above report discussed support measures for low-income earners, the disabled, single mothers and the homeless, it did not mention youth as a distinctive target group. This was less than surprising however, for the particular project team behind the report worked within the welfare (rather than labour) side of MHLW: unemployed youth were not much of an issue for it since young adults do not, when lacking extended work histories, qualify for social security benefits in Japan. New activation measures for young adults would hence not have immediate impacts on welfare budgets. Moreover, it is worth emphasizing that, as of 2002, employment-related youth problems had not yet become a major government policy concern, though this would come to change very soon.

The 'Youth Independence and Challenge' plans

Indeed, in the year 2003 the independence support discourse finally crossed over to the realm of employment-related youth policy with the enactment of a novel inter-ministry youth policy package, the Youth Independence and Challenge Plan (*Wakamono Jiritsu Chōsen Puran*). Marking the start of a new era in youth policy, this plan brought together the three ministers of Health, Labour and Welfare (MHLW), Economy, Trade and Industry (METI), and Education, Culture, Science and Technology (MEXT), with Takenaka Heizo, the specially appointed minister for economic and fiscal policy, in a coordinating role. Although situated far lower on the government's list of priorities at the time than, for example, the handling of bad loans and administrative reforms (led by the Keizai Zaisei Shimon Kaigi), the initiative had tremendous significance since nothing as comprehensive or cross-ministerial had hitherto been attempted in the realm of Japanese social policy for youth.[18] It moreover brought a nearly ten-fold increase in the MHLW's youth employment support budget alone.[19]

The Youth Independence and Challenge Plan signified a growing awareness within the government that youth employment problems were becoming serious to the point of threatening Japan's economic competitiveness and skill base (Cabinet Office 2003:1). In a more direct sense, however, through my interviews a few years later I learned that the plan was the result of the activism of the then-director of the Industrial Policy Bureau (Sangyō Seisaku Kyoku) of METI. In 2003, he had paid a visit to the director of the Occupational Security Bureau (Shokugyō Anteikyoku) of MHLW, boasting that his own ministry was designing youth measures and inviting the welfare ministry to jump on board (interview, 'sponsor', 26 November 2008). The two executives were good friends who had graduated from the same university in the same year (i.e., were so-called *dōki*); this clearly predisposed them to collaborate on policy despite operating in a bureaucratic environment where sectionalism tends to limit cooperation (see Chapter 4). Sharing a certain awareness regarding what needed to be done, the two sought cooperation from other governmental players and eventually persuaded the Ministry of Finance to give a go-ahead to their scheme.

The original Youth Independence and Challenge Plan of 2003 asked relevant ministries and the private sector to cooperate so as to formulate an 'integrated human resources policy'. The proclaimed purpose of this was to prevent economic malaise, halt the expansion in unstable labour and stop inequalities from widening. Additional concerns that were to be addressed included the weakening of the general social security system and the low birth rate. Prompting some analysts to view the declaration – at this point it was little more than that – as a 'hopeful moment' in the development of Japan's youth policy, the Independence and Challenge Plan recognized at the outset that youth employment issues arose not simply from a lack of effort on the part of the youth, but largely from a deterioration in the demand for young workers (Cabinet Office 2003:2). The inability of pre-existing training and employment systems to keep up with far-reaching structural changes was acknowledged. Youth themselves were also attributed part of the blame and were said to lack sufficient planning skills and initiative.

Under the new plan, the three ministries would be responsible for concrete programmes according to their respective areas of expertise, with the Ministry of Economy, Trade and Industry assuming leadership and designing one of the flagship programmes, the Job Café. Appendix E summarizes the key features of both the Youth Independence and Challenge Plan as well as the Youth Independence and Challenge Action Plan that was meant to turn the original vision into tangible measures for real young people.

The Youth Independence and Challenge Plan contained an impressive range of individual programmes, showcasing bureaucratic innovation and giving new prominence to many pet projects of high- and middle-ranking officials. In addition to an emphasis on inter-ministry cooperation, the max-imum utilization of the private sector (*minkan*) was a key tenet. This referred to a variety of corporations, NPOs and educational institutions that were to be relied on for the delivery of specific services, the training of workers and the cultivation of work motivation and awareness among youth. The role of localities (*chiiki*) and local governments (*chihō jichitai*) was strongly emphasized, the 'self-directedness and diversity' of which were to be respected by the initiatives enacted under the Youth Independence and Challenge Plan.

However, the Youth Independence and Challenge Action Plan of 2004 did not, in the end, deliver what could have been expected based on the liberal interpretations of the labour market situation put forth in the preceding 2003 Plan. It was devoid of tangible measures for addressing two of the key con-cerns highlighted in the original blueprint, namely the dearth of employment opportunities for youth and the inability of Japan's employment system to adequately respond to recent structural changes. On the contrary, the 2004 Action Plan appeared to place greater importance on young people's 'work motivation' and 'confidence' through introducing the Youth Independence Camp and the Youth Job Spot that seemed to shift the focus squarely onto individual behaviour rather than institutional reforms.

This change in tone was interpreted by scholars such as Honda Yuki as a sign that the government had, after a moment of sound analysis, relapsed into a moralistic approach that, once again, cunningly obscured structural problems and corporate behaviour and foregrounded the presumably deficient character-istics of individual youth (interview, Honda Yuki, 18 January 2008). Yokoi (2006) observes a similar turn based on the stronger emphasis that the government put on '*NEET* countermeasures' (*nīto taisaku*) from 2005 onwards (Yokoi

2006:112). It is indeed difficult not to come to such a conclusion from a close reading of official government documents.

Some of the omissions of the Youth Independence and Support Action Plan are summarized well by Higuchi (2007). While recognizing the government's move to address areas that had hitherto lain outside official concerns, he points out that none of the attached programmes was linked to any income security measures (Higuchi 2007:236). According to Higuchi, this is particularly odd in light of growing rates of poverty among households headed by youth aged under 30 (although he does not mention that the majority of those in their twenties live in their parents' households).[20] Another important issue highlighted by the same author is the tendency of Japanese youth to not use public services to begin with, suggesting that there is a persisting reliance on family welfare. This implies that increasing the accessibility and visibility of youth services is one precondition to their success. Finally, Higuchi argues that the Independence and Support Action Plan was overly concerned with getting youth into work and not concerned enough with improving the working conditions of those who were in employment (Higuchi 2007:237). If it is assumed that youth employment problems relate to a wider set of issues, the Plan can sensibly be criticized for a narrowness of vision and compartmentalization that lingered despite cross-sector aspirations.

The Job Café and the Young Job Spot

Two new services that were introduced under the Youth Independence and Challenge Action Plan deserve to be highlighted here because they are intimately related to subsequent policies crafted for harder-to-reach inactive youth (*NEETs*). These two programmes are the Job Café (formally, One-Stop Service Centre for Youth, or *Wakamono no tame no Wan-Sutoppu Sābisu Sentā*) and the Young Job Spot, overseen, respectively, by METI and MHLW. The first was charged with furnishing a range of essential employment services at a single location, while the second was tasked with fostering young people's work motivation. Out of the two programmes, Job Café was given far higher priority in the government's plans. Its main target groups comprised *freeters*, students and unemployed youth. Described in a ministry press release as the core measure within the Independence and Challenge Plan, the Job Café was to offer an 'integrated service' that embodied the principles of the government's new youth policy (METI 2004). The most important of these principles were:

1) actively utilizing the private sector (*minkan*) in delivering services
2) 'listening to young people' and providing carefully tailored support
3) producing (measurable) results subject to performance evaluations
4) requiring active initiative from local governments
5) strengthening cooperation between local governments, companies and educational institutions (*renkei*)

6) putting more stress on career consulting and experiential activities (e.g. internships) than before.

(Cabinet Office 2003:9)

These central principles capture crisply the direction of government youth policy from the early 2000s onwards, although they also reflect wider discursive trends in social services and education. Based on my fieldwork observations, 'utilizing the private sector' refers to anything from the wholesale contracting-out of services to private companies and NPOs, to the more limited outsourcing of particular programme components and to the hiring of staff with private sector experience. The second principle can be taken to indicate a turn towards a more individualized and 'client-based' approach, while the third promotes an 'audit culture' and the introduction of presumably objective performance criteria within youth policy.[21] Career consulting by qualified counsellors and the expansion of 'work experiences' (*shokuba taiken*) are equally relevant developments here.

Although a few opened their doors as early as 2003, most Job Cafés began operating in April 2004. By 2005, there was one in 46 of Japan's 47 main administrative regions (i.e. its 43 prefectures, Hokkaido, the Tokyo metropolitan area and Osaka-fu and Kyoto-fu, the *todōfuken*; METI 2008). Over three-fourths of these were attached to a Hello Work public employment office. It was reported that, collectively, all Job Cafes received 1.6 million users in 2007, out of which just under 90,000 found paid employment with assistance from the service (METI 2008). It is, however, necessary to observe such figures sceptically since practices relating to the collection of statistics vary so that sometimes 'visits' rather than the actual number of individual users may be included (see Chapter 6).

Analyzing the findings of her research team, which interviewed staff at every Job Café in Japan between late 2004 and early 2005, Takahashi (2005) discerns several interesting aspects of this service. First, most Job Cafés operate near train stations or in other highly accessible locations. Also, they have relatively long opening hours and boast bright, even cheerful interiors that contrast strikingly with typical public employment services (Takahashi 2005:57–58). So as to respect users' privacy and to not deter them from dropping in, initial sign-up is made very easy. Most Job Cafés strive to create an 'open' atmosphere by eschewing the use of partitions, although there is usually a counselling booth for sensitive discussions. Chapter 6 will show that design of the Youth Support Station closely resembles the innovative features of this service.

In looking at the actual operation of the Job Café, Takahashi makes the following key points:

1) Even though the service is charged with supporting young adults' employment, most centres in fact lack the right to engage directly in job-brokering (*shokugyō shōkai-ken*).

2) A large share of users lack work experience, 'work consciousness' and a clear idea of what kind of work they want to do.
3) Many users would require intensive support in order to get employed, but staff cannot furnish such support without compromising the quantitative targets of their centre: i.e., there is a conflict between the support needs of some and official performance evaluation criteria.
4) Some centres are developing 'advanced' job-brokering practices that bypass Hello Work and make use of detailed information of potential openings and of job-seekers' qualities, striving to improve job matching.
5) It is recognized everywhere that the Job Café cannot provide sufficient services to *NEETs*; cooperation is thus sometimes sought from NPOs that specialize in *hikikomori* and *futōkō* support.

In addition to these points, Takahashi highlights the fact that Job Cafés build on long-term relationships with users – whom it is recruiting fairly successfully – but that significant problems follow from points 1), 2) and 3) above. Moreover, direct job-brokering (4) remains very limited in terms of scope, although the METI emphasizes that recent deregulation had made it possible for localities to apply for job-brokering rights (METI 2004).[22] Takahashi emphasizes that most Job Cafés feel enormous pressure to meet quantitative performance criteria with their limited resources and suggests that policy-makers should pay more attention to qualitative aspects of support, especially when programmes must deal with hard-to-employ youth (*shūshoku konnansha*).[23]

The limited participant observation I conducted in 2005 confirms many aspects of this account. Visiting and using the Job Café in Tenjin, Fukuoka revealed also how certain kinds of employment guidance can be more important in Japan than in countries that may have more streamlined job-seeking customs. An important example is the résumé (*rirekisho* or *keirekisho*). This is a document that must be written by hand on a standardized form according to standardized rules. It matters a great deal that one's handwriting is both legible and aesthetically pleasing, conveying a positive impression of the writer to the reader. The tricky aspect regarding the content of the résumé is making it stand out while keeping it firmly within accepted conventions. It is also mandatory to include one's facial photograph on the *rirekisho*, the quality of which may be crucial. For many new job applicants with little prior job-seeking experience, authoring proper personal statements and mastering correct business manners ahead of interviews (including bowing to an appropriate angle and using honorific language when answering questions) pose further challenges. Hence, quite understandably, the bulk of the Job Cafés' counselling and seminar activities focus on teaching such basic yet demanding skills that seem not to be taught thoroughly at all schools or universities (despite the recent efforts of universities, in particular, to strengthen career services).

Alongside the more visible Job Café, the smaller Young Job Spot was incorporated in the same Youth Independence and Challenge Plan. Interestingly, the Young Job Spot appears, on paper, almost identical to its larger cousin: it was tasked with actively attracting youth through conveniently located service centres that would furnish job information, counselling services and Internet access. The scheme was to support the 'occupational independence' (*shokugyōteki jiritsu*) – a long-held concern of the MHLW – of young adults on the local level while making use of private organizations (Cabinet Office 2003:9). The semi-autonomous Koyō Nōryoku Kaihatsu Kikō (the Employment and Skill Development Institute) was recruited to oversee the practical operation of the programme which, at its peak, comprised only 16 centres across Japan (however, most of these were phased out by 2007).

Unlike the Job Café, which focused on youth who were relatively employable, the key policy-maker behind the Young Job Spot had wished to target those young *freeters* who required time to think more deeply about work and its meaning before even beginning to look for employment. When searching for methods to stir work motivation, the bureaucrat drew inspiration from the practices of the American Job Clubs which made use of mutual support between job-seekers. It was clear though that he also wanted to introduce a new kind of *tamariba*, or a hangout, reminiscent of the Working Youth's Homes that had by the early 2000s become all but dysfunctional (see above). In retrospective interviews, the same bureaucrat conceded further that two particular domestic private support groups had influenced his thinking regarding youth support (contributing, by extension, to the Youth Support Station that emerged three years after the Job Spot under the leadership of the bureaucrat). It is possible to view the Young Job Spot either as an initiative that failed to distinguish itself from the Job Café and thus quickly perished, or as a 'pilot programme' for the Youth Support Station – a more advanced scheme which benefited not only from a stronger concept but from the fortuitous timing of the *NEET* debate (see Chapter 4).

Emerging 'preventative' approaches: career education

As the following chapters will show, Japan's new activation policies for youth have, to a surprising extent, targeted 'older' youth so far, i.e. those in their late twenties and early thirties. Yet the limitations of such a focus have become widely acknowledged and the importance of earlier, possibly preventative approaches is increasingly realized within Japan's youth policy community.[24] The most salient of such approaches so far is so-called career education (*kyaria kyōiku*).

Although new thinking on career education had begun to emerge in Japan a few years earlier, the Youth Independence and Challenge Plan and the subsequent Action Plan gave it higher visibility in policy and practice. Reflecting the expectations of policy-makers, measures for the enhancement of career education at schools were enumerated in the very first section of the Action Plan (Cabinet Office 2004:1–2).

According to the first official definition by a leading MEXT policy council, career education refers to:

> education that, along with imparting desirable occupational and work attitudes as well as occupational knowledge and skills, fosters the capacity and attitude for understanding *the 'individuality of one's self'* so as to support the choosing of one's future path in a self-directed way.
>
> (MEXT 1999; my emphasis)

The more recent definition used by the MEXT in its guidebook for schools designates that, based on a holistic view of 'career' as the sum of a person's work-related positions and related meanings, career education is something that 'supports the career development of each individual student and fosters the kinds of motivation, attitudes and skills that are necessary in developing a career that is appropriate for him or her' (MEXT 2006:3).

In such broad and ambiguous conceptualizations of career education, students' individuality (*kosei*) is positively stressed alongside the fostering of 'desirable' or 'appropriate' attitudes and skills. While the exact content of 'desirable' attitudes and skills is not specified, the underlying assumption clearly is that, because society is undergoing rapid change, flexibility and individual adaptability are the crucial attributes of all workers. In order to improve their adaptability, students are required to become more 'self-directed' (*shutaiteki*) and 'active' (*sekkyokuteki*), thereby ensuring that they will reach 'independence' (*jiritsu*) and avoid becoming passive 'drifters'. This change in rhetoric presents a marked paradigm shift compared to earlier thought on 'career guidance' (*shinro shidō*), under which students were expected to rely heavily on their teachers in making decisions about their future paths (Chapter 1 outlines the school-to-work transition framework of which teacher-led 'career guidance' was an integral part).[25] Now they are required to become proactive, reflexive crafters of their own destinies, a rather fundamental shift in philosophy. Clearly, educational bureaucrats and council members put great emphasis on raising youth with stronger agency, but only in a limited apolitical sense within the framework of flexible neoliberal labour markets that de-emphasize individual rights and social protection.

Such formulations of career education are consonant with new youth services such as the Job Café in terms of other key principles as well: they stress networking and cooperation between various sectors – schools, PTAs, boards of education, employment services, local governments and business associations – in the delivery of what primarily comprise experiential activities. Short-term 'work experiences' (*shokuba taiken*) and internships form the core of such activities, their purpose being to raise the 'work consciousness' and motivation of students through allowing them to observe actual places of work for five days or more (an initiative known as the Career Start Week). Conversely, current workers and professionals are invited to visit schools to discuss their experiences for much the same purposes.

However, the real educational practices behind such shifts in discourse have hardly been analyzed yet.[26] The effectiveness of new schemes remains, hence, assumed rather than proven. It is obvious that formidable obstacles exist to career education on the level of individual schools, where teachers may be simply too burdened with other duties to dedicate themselves to such pursuits.[27] Also, teachers and many educational decision-makers are likely to contest state-advocated ideas regarding how education and work should be bridged – they may view career education as a Trojan horse that allows self-interested companies to encroach on 'their' turfs by stealth. It is furthermore puzzling what the relationship will be between career education and citizenship education, the former attempting to raise 'active workers' who can reflexively build their careers and adapt to social change, but who are not necessarily encouraged to think of themselves as 'citizens' with rights to social protection and political influence. It is thus possible to predict that the model of self-directed yet apolitical 'individual' of new career education plans will come under fire from those who see such individuals as highly vulnerable and disempowered at a time when unstable and low-paying jobs continue to proliferate.

'The State-Society Movement to Raise the Human Competence of Youth'

Finally, some attention needs to be paid to a peculiar campaign called 'the State-Society Movement to Raise the Human Competence of Youth' (*Wakamono no Ningenryoku wo Takameru tame no Koku-Min Undō*).[28] Launched in 2005, this campaign was the public face of the Youth Independence and Challenge Plan, formulated for the purpose of 'selling' fresh youth measures to important sectors in society.[29]

'The State-Society Movement to Raise the Human Competence of Youth' of 2005–08 called for active collaboration from schools, families, communities, public agencies and companies, as well as from the media and labour unions. Its executive council (the *Koku-Min Kaigi*) was presided over by Mr Mitarai, the chairman of Keidanren, the federation that represents large employers in Japan. The 22 other members comprised representatives of the mass media, local governments, middle-sized and small companies, and academics such as Yamada Masahiro and Genda Yūji. In this sense, the council was rather comprehensive and covered sectors that had strategic importance from the point of view of youth employment measures. It managed to hold a total of five meetings between May 2005 and February 2008 (there were no meetings in 2007), producing first a declaration that promised to 'make efforts' to ensure that:

1) Youth will be able to develop 'confidence and power for living' (*ikiru jishin to chikara*) before entering society through fostering their ability to think about life as well as communication skills from an early age, along with deepening their understanding regarding work;
2) youth who are about to enter society will enjoy many opportunities, and that they will be able to take on work-related challenges and be active at work;

3) youth will be able to continue improving themselves independently through preparing various systems to make it possible for them to study while working;
4) youth who feel insecure and confounded about work will be able to try again without hesitation and take on new challenges.

(MHLW 2006:236)

This loose set of commitments reflected the dominant youth policy rhetoric of the time, implying that some youth needed more confidence, better communication skills and higher work motivation, while hinting only very cautiously that there was also a need to rethink elements of the labour markets (this closely reflected key themes in the *NEET* debate that was unfolding at the time; see Chapter 3). It was stated clearly that the main purpose of this 'movement' was to raise awareness on youth issues and stimulate (*unagasu*) the creation of autonomous support measures on the local level, as well as to send a 'message to the Japanese people' (MHLW 2005a:274). In terms of concrete activities, companies were asked to extend work trials and internship opportunities to more youth; educational institutions were exhorted to actively support such activities and provide 'diverse second chances for study' to those youth who wished to become independent; and local communities were asked to support and counsel families and their offspring.[30] The government would coordinate the collaboration (*renkei*) between different areas of policy and support the initiatives of other institutions.

Youth themselves were conspicuously absent from the executive State Society Council, illustrating poignantly the limits of the 'youth-friendliness' of new measures for young people. Some youth and parents were, however, engaged in discussion through public symposia held in Osaka, Tokyo and regional cities,[31] but this did not stop many youth supporters from dismissing the whole campaign as a 'failure that was not welcomed by the people', not least because of Mitarai – the head of Keidanren and Canon, who was quite generally despised by youth supporters and labour activists (Iwanaga, Young Job Square Yokohama, 26 March 2008).

It is difficult to gauge whether this campaign contributed significantly to the popularization of new youth policies, but it was certainly important for what it symbolized. A massive effort was made to 'brand' youth measures by hiring Dentsū, Japan's top advertizing agency to create a youthful image for the campaign and to design a *Waka-chare* ('youth challenge' in abbreviated form) symbol for use on websites, pamphlets and bright posters. Yet, behind such a gleaming image was an operation planned largely by senior bureaucrats and mainly conservative leaders from business and local administrations. To be sure, as is the case with most youth programmes, many of the actual activities – such as school visits by representatives of various occupations – were delivered by youth support staff in their twenties and thirties, but such younger actors did not shape the basic parameters of the campaign. Finally, in the spring of 2008, this endeavour ended quietly – and rather disappointingly – with a nebulous two-page 'public appeal' that reaffirmed family responsibility over youth problems, exhorting parents to spend more time 'talking about work' with their children.

Summary

This chapter sought to uncover the institutional and political roots of what eventually emerged, in post-industrial Japan, as symbolic activation as defined in Chapter 1. Four distinctive sub-plots were identified here, comprising an important earlier youth support programme (the Working Youth's Homes); a rich legacy of youth problem debates and labels; an adaptive sector of private youth support institutions; and the Youth Independence and Challenge Plan, which was enacted during the prime ministership of Junichiro Koizumi. Each of these sub-plots will serve as vital reference points for the reader when studying Chapters 3 to 6. Next, this book will turn to the topic of how *NEETs* – a policy term imported to Japan from the United Kingdom – came to be constructed as a new target group for activation towards the mid-2000s.

3   *NEET*: Creating a target for activation

As a rule, all social policies require what may be called target groups. In other words, policy actors must delineate a particular group of people (or sometimes, institutions) that they can argue deserves, or otherwise is in need of, policy attention before any programmes or laws may be implemented. Japanese youth policy in the 2000s was no exception: very little could be done by policy-makers about the destabilized school-to-work transitions, growing youth unemployment and temporary jobs described in Chapter 1 before a clear definition was given of the types of people who required special attention.

We have seen in the preceding chapter that growing concerns around young adults' employment, and about part-time-working *freeters* in particular, were essential to the creation of the Youth Independence and Challenge plans in 2003 and 2004. Without the problematization of youth employment issues with recourse to a new salient target group – *freeters* – it would have been scarcely possible to justify new programmes to support young adults. However, a strong sense lingered among certain parties that the initial targets of the new policies – essentially, part-time workers in Japan's expanding peripheral labour markets – were still relatively well off and 'active'. They were, after all, working, or at least looking for work, rather than idle. A handful of policy analysts, government bureaucrats and youth workers began, around the launch of the Youth Independence and Challenge plans, to voice suspicions that there was another sub-set of young people that was not served sufficiently by measures such as the Job Café and that was in sore need of further support.

This chapter tells the story of how these concerns eventually, though not inevitably, found public articulation through what was, in the Japanese context, an entirely new youth category – that of *NEET* (Not in Education, Employment or Training). Conceptually distinct from *hikikomori*, a salient earlier category that denotes inactive young people withdrawn into their rooms for months or years at a time (see Horiguchi 2012), *NEET* was to become Japan's first official target group for youth activation measures. As such, over and beyond enabling the making of policy, it evolved into the very engine of what I call a system of 'symbolic activation' whereby symbolic youth labels play a more important role than cash incentives (the hallmark of activation in most Western countries) in mobilizing formally inactive youth to seek for work.

The first task of this chapter is to trace the steps through which *NEET* came to be defined and constructed, in this brief period, as a relevant social policy target group. Next, I also observe how it emerged as a prominent and universally recognized social category. The product of a strategic 'campaign' with certain unintended consequences, that this category 'went viral' and quickly entered the everyday vocabularies of people living in Japan proved critical to its activation power: literally, to its power to trigger actions (job-seeking, support-seeking) among many non-employed youth as well as their parents. After untangling this dual process of definition, this chapter notes a curious hierarchy among interrelated youth categories such as *hikikomori* and *freeter* and explores what may be called 'the language of youth support' disseminated by central youth support experts. Because the origins of the term *NEET* lie in the British and European discourse on 'social exclusion', the ways in which being 'Not in Education, Employment or Training' has been associated with exclusionary processes in Japan are set out briefly.

This chapter builds on the classic research strategy associated with the constructionist study of social problems in sociology (Spector and Kitsuse 1977; see also Hilgartner and Bosk 1988; Best 1989). This strategy posits that social problems can be best defined not as objective conditions caused by particular target groups, but as the 'claims-making activities' of various individuals and groups. Such activities sometimes succeed in producing broadly shared, though contested, understandings of what counts as a legitimate 'social problem' in society. Based on this, we have previously defined a 'youth problem' as a putative condition or a situation surrounding 'youth' – however defined – that is labelled a problem in mainstream arenas of public discourse and action (Toivonen and Imoto 2012). With this definition in mind, the objective of the present chapter is to shed light on how the particular issue of *NEETs* came to be 'labelled a problem in mainstream arenas of public discourse and action', namely the Japanese mainstream media, the bureaucracy and political apparatus, as well as the field of youth support. As key data, I rely upon the writings of, and extensive interviews with, key actors belonging to powerful institutions such as the Ministry of Health, Labour and Welfare (MHLW), Tokyo University and the Japan Institute for Labour Policy and Training (Nihon Rōdō Kenshū Kenkyūjo –JILPT). I also critically review statistics that have been strategically employed by these actors and analyze relevant newspaper articles. The account that follows contributes to a growing critical literature on Japanese youth problems (Goodman, Imoto and Toivonen 2012; Kinsella 1998; Kaneko 2006; Leheny 2006; Allison 2009) that has significant implications to the study of youth issues across various national, sub-national or transnational settings.

Once again, the concept of *NEET* and the specific ways in which it came to be understood in Japan is absolutely central to processes of symbolic activation. While the present chapter examines the definition and popularization of *NEET*, Chapter 4 tackles in greater detail micro-level policy-making techniques and strategies of legitimization. Chapters 5 and 6 then show how youth workers, as well as jobless youth themselves, have responded to, and indeed contested, the *NEET* category. It is important to note that the initial definitional activities traced here are crucial because they set the conceptual basis for how relevant actors could subsequently address the issue of non-employed Japanese youth, with implications for how youth policy would unfold in the subsequent years and perhaps decades.[1]

The definitional process[2]

NEET *as a new target group category*

How did *NEET* become a salient and legitimate target group for policy measures in the mid-2000s? Chapter 1 has already revealed the broad outlines of the 'career' of the *NEET* concept in Japan, including the fact that it was initially highlighted by Japanese labour market scholars in the first half of the 2000s. It is important to note that, as they sought to ground their arguments regarding this puzzling new phenomenon, all salient Japanese-language publications in the 2003–05 period cited one key report: *Bridging the Gap: New Opportunities for 16–18 Year Olds Not in Education, Employment or Training* (Social Exclusion Unit 1999). The interesting thing is, of course, that this document was issued by the Cabinet Office of the United Kingdom – with absolutely no reference to Japan – in the early years of the Blair era, amid growing fears over the 'social exclusion' of 16- to 18-year-olds and the UK's relatively low educational participation rates in the context of the EU. Roughly a tenth of British youth in this age-group were found to be inactive at any one time due to factors such as 'educational underachievement and educational disaffection' as well as 'family disadvantage and poverty'. Not surprisingly, inactivity was found to be disproportionately concentrated among those from working-class and ethnic minority backgrounds.

Japanese writers in the early 2000s usually omitted the fact that the roots of *NEET* in fact stretch back much further. In the mid-1990s, some British researchers employed the term 'Status Zer0' – based on the technical, residual statistical category 'status 0' – to denote essentially the same demographic, but since this was deemed too derogatory by some, 'Status A' came to be used in its stead (see for instance the report on *Young People Not in Education, Training or Employment in South Glamorgan* by Instance, Rees and Williamson, 1994). The concept then continued to transform amid the interaction of researchers and politicians, mutating from 'EET' to 'NETE' and then finally, to NEET. Although criticized as excessively 'sanitized' or otherwise misleading by prominent youth scholars, NEET became popular in high levels of the government due to its catchiness and marketability (Williamson 1997:82).[3]

It was hence this evolved, but contested, version of the British 'status 0' category that came to be picked up by leading Japanese labour scholars in 2003. Despite appearances to the contrary, this was not an entirely random incident: NEET found its way to Japan through two pivotal policy reports officially commissioned by the Occupational Skill Development Bureau of the MHLW with the purpose of generating ideas and knowledge to bolster fresh policy initiatives. This took place in a context where, jolted by the 'discovery' of 2 million *freeters* in 2002, labour bureaucrats within the MHLW began to turn their attention from retraining measures for 'restructured' middle-aged workers to youth employment problems (interview, the former chief of the Career Development Office, 4 July 2007).

Both compiled by the government-affiliated think tank, JILPT, the first of the above reports investigated active labour market policies for young people in Western countries; the second focused on existing institutions in Japan that supported youth in their 'school-to-work' transitions (Kosugi (*et al.*) 2003; Kosugi and Hori 2003). It was the latter of the two that first applied the NEET concept explicitly to Japan. In hindsight, it was this seemingly innocuous move that produced the first sparks in what would later flare up into a full-blown *NEET* scare.

Not unpredictably, authors Kosugi and Hori found that the '*NEET*-layer' within the Japanese youth population had indeed grown drastically in size in the preceding years. Drawing on the National Census (*Kokusei Chōsa*), they calculated that in the year 2000 there had been as many as 760,000 15- to 34-year-olds who 'expressed no will to work', leading the authors to argue that appropriate countermeasures were badly needed. By excluding those non-employed youth who were reportedly engaged in housework (*kaji*), Kosugi and Hori had effectively produced a formulation of 'Japanese-style *NEETs*' that would become entrenched as more or less the standard definition over the subsequent years.

Curiously enough, however, no full explanation was given by the authors as to why the *NEET* category should include youth up to the age of 34 as opposed to 24 or 25 as in most other OECD countries (it was only remarked that there had recently been an increase in inactive 30- to 34-year-old young people in Japan). I thus resolved to inquire further into this issue through interviews with several key actors.

First, the research director in charge of the above reports, Kosugi Reiko of the JILPT, conceded that the 15- to-34 age-range was chosen partly because, as of 2003, it was already being applied to part-time-working *freeters*: using the same range for *NEETs* would facilitate comparisons and more integrated analyses of these two issues. Another contributing factor was that since Japan had no pre-existing policy measures for inactive youth, there was no need for more finely-distinguished gradations just yet and a catch-all approach seemed most appropriate (interview, Kosugi Reiko, 17 May 2007). This meant, among other things, that university-educated middle-class youth who failed to enter employment upon graduation could also be included among the potential targets of any new measures (Kosugi interview in *Asahi Shimbun*, 2 October 2004a). This choice reflects not only Japan's high educational participation rates but also the fact that the *NEET* debate was, at least in its initial years, preoccupied with middle-class youth rather than with the offspring of relatively deprived families.[4]

Offering a more historical perspective, a key labour bureaucrat at the MHLW posited that the 15-to-34 age bracket followed from the gradual expansion of the state's general definition of 'youth' in the postwar era: whereas the so-called working youths (*kinrō seishōnen*) of the 1960s and 1970s fell between ages 15 and 19 (see Chapter 2), the upper age ceiling had thence crept up in small leaps, first to 24, then to 29, and finally to 34. Paralleling this quiet shift, the words used by the labour administration to denote 'youth' had also changed, morphing from *seishōnen* ('youngsters and juveniles') to *seinen* ('youngsters'), to *wakamono* and *jakunen* ('youth'; *jakunen* is used mainly in formal contexts). This shift serves as a good reminder of how the parameters of even basic, taken-for-granted categories such as 'child', 'youth' and 'adult' sometimes undergo substantial redefinition in a short span of time (see Chapter 2 for more detail on the shifting meanings of 'youth').

When I put the same question regarding the expansive *NEET* age-range to Kudō Sadatsugu, the most influential independent youth work 'veteran' in Japan, he started by highlighting cultural factors that led Japanese parents to feel intense responsibility over their offspring's education and careers while simultaneously allowing the latter to indulgence themselves (interview, 22 April 2007). Kudō also recalled, however, that he and a small group of scholars (including Kosugi Reiko and Miyamoto Michiko) had in fact made explicit demands to the MHLW in the early 2000s to extend the Ministry's upper limit for 'youth' to 34 (from 29), following the realization that there were a substantial number of over-30-year-olds requiring support on their way towards 'adulthood'. Another justification given by key bureaucrats (including the former head of the MHLW, the Administrative Vice Minister, referred to as 'the sponsor' in Chapter 4) as I interviewed them was that using the 15- to-34 range was necessary in order for statistics – and hence for policy – to grasp those young people who had failed to enter the labour markets during the 1990s' 'employment ice age' (*koyō hyōgaki*; see Rebick 2005), i.e. the youth who subsequently came to be called the 'Lost Generation'.

What is especially interesting about these explanations is that, despite covering issues of tremendous importance in their own right, they all but omit one obvious factor: by employing an extraordinarily wide, although culturally plausible, age-range, claims-makers could produce a higher total number of *NEETs* than would have been possible had they focused on a narrower demography such as 15- to 19-year-olds or even 15- to 24-year-olds. Being able to 'prove' with ostensibly objective data that there were hundreds of thousands of apparently idle jobless youths gave key advocates a powerful symbolic means to stir alarm and a sense of 'moral panic' through the media.

It is, of course, nothing new to note that actors manipulate statistics to support their own agendas, but it is worth briefly tracing how this 'numbers game' was played in the particular case of *NEETs*. Table 3.1 lists different numbers put forth by central researchers and think tanks between 2003 and 2006.

What this table tells us, first of all, is that a striking range of figures – from 400,000 to 2.5 million – were cited in the first years of the *NEET* debate. That

Table 3.1 The reported numbers of *NEETs* in 2003–06 and respective sources of statistical data

Number	Explanations and data sources
760,000	15–34-year-olds who were NEET (*excluding* those who did housework) in 2000 (Kosugi and Hori 2003). Data source: National Census (Ministry of General Affairs).
2.5 million	15–34-year-olds who were NEET (*including* women who did housework or cared for children) in 2002 (Genda 2004). Data source: Special Labour Force Survey and Basic School Survey.
400,000	15–24-year-olds who were NEET and expressed no desire to work or study in 2003 (Genda and Maganuma 2004). Data source: Labour Force Survey Detailed Results.
640,000	15–34-year-olds who were non-employed and not in education (*excluding* those who did housework) in 2003 (Kosugi Reiko; interviewed in Asahi Shimbun 2004a). Data source: White Paper on the Labour Markets 2004 (MHLW 2004).
1 million	A projection of the number of NEETs in 2010 (Dai-ichi Seimei Research Centre; quoted in Asahi Shinbun 2004b).
520,000	15–34-year-old NEETs in 2003 (*excluding* those who did housework; MHLW; quoted in Asahi Shinbun (2005b). Data source: White Paper on the Labour Markets 2004 (MHLW 2004).
847,000	15–34-year-olds who were NEET (*including* those who did housework) in 2002 (Cabinet Office; cited in Asahi Shinbun 2005a). Source: Employment Structure Basic Survey.
640,000	15–34-year-olds who were NEET (*excluding* those who did housework) in 2002–06 (MHLW, numerous articles and publications in 2004–06). *The most widely accepted and cited figure since 2005.* Source: Labour Force Survey.

these numbers drew on at least seven different surveys partly accounts for this diversity, but equally consequential were the intricate definitional battles fought in the background.

One pivotal conflict revolved around the issue of gender roles: were unmarried, formally non-employed women who reportedly engaged in housework (*kaji*) to be counted as *NEETs* or not?[5] The answer of Genda Yūji, a central claims-maker (see below), was yes, based on the contention that many female survey respondents preferred to say they were 'engaged in housework' when they really were 'out of work' (Genda 2007). The Ministry of Health, Labour and Welfare, however, disagreed, preferring to take the 'housework' category at face value and thus keeping to Kosugi's original definition.[6] Since the Cabinet Office nevertheless adopted Genda's definition, this meant that an intra-government conflict ensued over who should be considered a *NEET*. Eventually though, it was the MHLW that appeared to have won the feud as its figures – producing an annual number of 640,000 *NEETs* between 2002 and

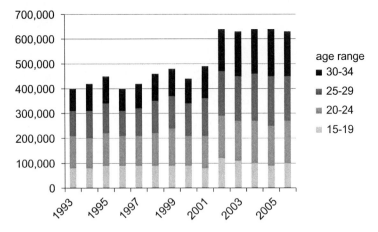

Figure 3.1 The number of *NEETs* in each age group between 1993 and 2006
Source: (MHLW 2007a)

2006 – became the most widely cited ones since the mid-2000s (see Figure 3.1). This was significant as the MHLW was the government organ directly in charge of developing new social programmes for non-employed youth (Chapter 4).

These battles over definitions and aggregate *NEET* statistics were coupled with a yet more subtle strategy of omission: in contrast to the debate in the UK, the percentage shares of non-employed youth were consistently de-emphasized in Japanese policy discussions and were almost never mentioned in the public debate. This was understandable as no more than a mere 1.9 per cent of 15- to 34-year-olds (2.5 per cent of 18- to 19-year-olds) were found to be outside education, employment and training as of 2003 (Kosugi (ed.) 2005:7–9). Although referring to the same phenomenon, it is clear that foregrounding the figure '640,000' in academic and general publications was far more effective a way to raise alarm over *NEETs*. Also conspicuously absent from the debate was any information regarding the length of time youth generally spent in the *NEET* category, which would have made it easier to grasp the nature of the issue.[7]

What we learn from the above is, first of all, that it was a select group of policy actors who initially introduced *NEET* to Japan and then went on to call for new measures to tackle this new issue. However, we also saw that the process of defining and counting *NEETs* was not only messy but characterized by substantial contestation and conflict between actors who were in the position – in other words, who had the power – to participate in the definitional process.

The social category *nīto*

> *NEETs* do not have confidence in themselves. One out of two *NEETs* feel that they are inferior in terms of sociability, initiative and communication skills compared to other people of their age.
>
> (Genda 2004:165)

Nīto are ravaging the wealth and pensions of the state and parents.
(Asai and Morimoto 2005:15)

How did *NEET* transform from a dry, mundane policy term into an almost universally known, even fashionable social category? While the definitional process of the policy category was all but monopolized by labour researchers, its colloquial mirror image was crafted through a less centralized process in the mass media between 2004 and 2006. As a result, *NEET* took on provocative symbolic meanings with significant social and policy consequences.

The beginnings of this process can be traced back to the efforts of Genda Yūji of Tokyo University, the author of the widely acclaimed *A Nagging Sense of Insecurity About Work* (*Shigoto no naka no Aimai na Fuan*, 2001/2005) and one of Japan's most prominent labour economists. He first engaged with the issue of non-employed youth in the February 2004 issue of *Chūō Kōron*, drawing attention to a layer of young people who were 'not fortunate enough to even become *freeters* or *shitsugyōsha*' (i.e formally unemployed) and who hence fell into the curious category of *NEET* (Genda 2004). They were hitherto all but ignored by society and policy, and the trend-setting scholar argued that it was high time to consider support measures for this group.

Citing the results of a small Internet survey, Genda first constructed *NEETs* as lacking in communication skills and confidence, which soon became a dominant theme in the youth discourse of sympathetic academics and practitioners (see below). These assumptions regarding the characteristics of *NEETs* were adopted in numerous articles as well as in official government publications (see e.g. the Health, Labour and Welfare White Papers for 2006 and 2007 – MHLW 2006, 2007a). By spelling the name of this category not in roman alphabets but in Japanese katakana script as *nīto*, Genda facilitated the 'indigenization' of this category as he lifted it from the narrow realm of labour market policy to that of public debate.[8]

Although JILPT's Kosugi Reiko also helped popularize *NEET* through interpreting the issue for the mass media,[9] the defining publication of the debate was without doubt *Nīto: Neither Furītā nor Unemployed* (*Nīto: Furītā demo naku, Shitsugyōsha demo naku*) by Genda and the freelance writer Maganuma, published in July 2004. Intended as a general-interest book rather than an academic volume, it explored the vexing puzzle of *NEETs* by drawing on a mix of statistical data and journalistic interviews. Although it did employ statistics to argue that there had been a dramatic increase in youth who were essentially inactive (Genda and Maganuma 2004:20–22), the main contributions of this best-selling book were conceptual and moral. First, by drawing a strict line between the new category of *NEETs* and the existing category of the officially unemployed,[10] and by portraying the youth whom Maganuma had interviewed as 'adult children', it aroused outrage over (intrinsically) lazy youth who were violating established work norms. This had clear elements of a 'moral underclass' discourse. Second, in an apparent contradiction of the first point, Genda emphasized that it was not that *NEETs* did not want to work; they simply could not, for one reason or another. The book therefore sent a highly mixed message striving to stir controversy while attempting to temper criticisms regarding the personal failings of 'unmotivated' youth. In a media environment where the disparagement of 'problem youth' had a long tradition (see Chapter 2), this would soon prove an impossible balancing act.

This volume by Genda and Maganuma was followed by a flurry of publications and public forums on the topic of youth (non-)employment.[11] Interestingly, alongside professional researchers, also youth support practitioners – mostly former *futōkō* and *hikikomori* supporters who now framed themselves as *NEET* experts – began to put out their own books. Futagami Nōki's *The Nīto of Hope* (*Kibō no Nīto*, 2005) was an early exemplar of this genre.[12] Based on experiences with hundreds of youth and parents whom Futagami had met during his career as a private youth worker and manager, his book bitterly criticized not just the Japanese family but also social structural factors that he said were producing youth marginalization. Others, including the young social entrepreneur Kudō Kei, soon followed suit by releasing books that explained their personal perspectives on young people and support practices (see e.g. Kudō 2005 and 2006). The tone of such expert-authored books was generally more down-to-earth than that of scholars, but in other respects they supplemented rather than challenged the assertions of Genda and Kosugi. They did, however, take serious issue with dominant mass media representations and public perceptions of non-employed youth that had, at this point, already coagulated. Table 3.2 summarizes the basic positions of key scholars and experts vis-à-vis nīto.

How, then, did the Japanese mass media construct *nīto*? Most major media were indeed more than happy to sensationalize *NEETs* and play up the

Table 3.2 How key scholars and experts constructed *nīto* in 2004 and 2005

Genda Yūji	*Nīto* are youth who do *want* work but are simply unable to do so; they typically lack confidence and communication skills; many have low educational qualifications and/or are drop-outs.
Kosugi Reiko	*Nīto* are not only a private issue but also a *social* problem that largely results from labour market change; four distinctive categories of *nīto* exist, one of which is universal and three of which are Japan-specific.
Futagami Nōki	It is a misunderstanding that *nīto* have simply no interest in work: they are victims of rigid social values, conservative parents, abusive workplaces and dire job markets.
Kudō Kei	*Nīto* are not lazy but in fact *desperate* to work and become financially independent; in Japan, it is vastly more stressful to remain jobless than it is to work.

Sources: Genda (2004); Genda & Maganuma (2004); Kosugi (ed.) (2005); Futagami (2005); Kudō (2005, 2006)

controversy of 'rapidly proliferating' workless youth, all the way from respectable broadsheets such as *Sankei Shimbun* to perhaps less respectable weekly magazines. For a large part, this served the interests of those wishing to popularize the problem of youth non-employment. What was less useful to the original claims-makers, however, was the aggressively asserted view that non-working youth were not only lazy and unmotivated, but essentially worthless and by implication undeserving of any public support. It was this strongly negative reaction to *nīto* – most unabashedly expressed in 'variety shows' on TV – as glaringly deviant that the youth workers I met while conducting fieldwork invariably resented and challenged.[13]

Yet, taking the most disparaging reporting as fully representative of all public opinion would be misleading: in reality there was – and still is – at least a modest spectrum of positions on *NEETs*. As a bureaucrat in charge of the MHLW's youth support policies so diplomatically put it, 'it is not that all Japanese people lean towards the same direction, calling for more [youth support] measures, or calling for existing measures to be abolished; there is indeed a variety of opinion on this issue' (interview, 30 May 2007, three bureaucrats in charge of youth measures, Career Development Support Office, MHLW).

There are several ways to make sense of this diversity of opinion. One is to study and compare different sources, including ethnographic evidence as well as newspaper reporting. What I did in a previous study was to analyse the views of practitioners as well as of dozens of supported youth (at altogether 15 Youth Support Stations and Youth Independence Camps) after which I conducted a content analysis of relevant *Asahi Shimbun* articles.[14] A striking finding that emerged was that, contrasting with the negative, damning social images of *NEETs* that youth workers thought were predominant in Japan, reporting in the *Asahi* in fact took a relatively 'constructive', even positive attitude to non-employed youth. Although a third of the articles I surveyed did associate *NEETs* with a lack of motivation for work or study, the broadsheet also called on society to provide more support to youth on their way to independence (*Asahi Shimbun* editorial, 2005c). Moreover, the voices of central claims-makers such as Genda, Kosugi and Kudō featured very frequently, positioning the *Asahi* essentially as an 'ally' of these actors (Campbell 1996), helping to build support for the latter's policy agenda. Table 3.3 summarizes dominant constructions of *nīto* based on newspaper reporting, ethnographic evidence and everyday discussions.

Notwithstanding such variation across parts of the media and distinctive interest groups, it is safe to say however that, from 2004, the category of *nīto* came to be constructed in predominantly negative terms in the public consciousness as referring to youth who were lazy, uninterested in work and generally low in motivation. At its most basic, this is consistent with what is known in British youth studies parlance as a 'deficit model' of youth that places blame on the moral shortcomings of individual young people and de-emphasizes social structural issues. This is in many ways highly unfortunate,

Table 3.3 Tracing the dominant constructions of *nīto* in Japan

Source	Content
Newspaper articles (the Asahi Shimbun, September 2004–September 2005)	'Those who do not commute to school, engage in work or receive occupational training' (*gakkō ni mo kayowazu, shigoto mo shiteorazu, shokugyō kunren mo uketeinai wakamono*); associated with a 'lack of motivation'; in need of support.
Youth support staff and supported youth (April 2007–March 2008)	*Nīto* are seen by mainstream society as lazy sluggards (*namakemono*), as disgraceful (*mittomonai*), worthless (*kudaranai*), spoilt and dependent (*amaeteiru*) and as having no work motivation (*hataraku iyoku ga nai*); yet *nīto* is less negative in its connotations than *hikikomori*.
General everyday contexts (April 2007–March 2008)	*Nīto* are often seen as lazy and irresponsible, but any young person who is even temporarily out of work can casually and sometimes jokingly be called a *nito*.

for recent empirical research makes evident the central role of institutional changes in the production and patterning of youth inactivity in Japan (Brinton 2011). In any case, since earlier youth problems such as the *parasite singles*, part-time working *freeters* and the socially withdrawn *hikikomori* had been debated in broadly similar terms in the late 1990s and the early 2000s, one notes considerable thematic continuity between *NEET* and such predecessors.

There is one crucial discontinuity in the way that *NEET* was constructed that needs to be foregrounded here. This concerns the reframing of youth inactivity as primarily a matter of employment rather than of mental welfare. As confirmed in Horiguchi's (2011) authoritative account, the *hikikomori* debate that directly preceded *NEETs* produced a medicalized, stigmatizing public discourse that suggested formally inactive youth were often violent and by implication mentally ill (or at least unstable). The consequence was that, despite its successful construction as a social problem by key actors such as Saitō Tamaki, as well as the mainstream media, the *hikikomori* came to be understood largely as a psychological concern and a family issue. While the Ministry of Health and Welfare did designate public health centres as the main institutions responsible for responding to *hikikomori* and supplied them with a set of guidelines, it was very difficult to justify substantial new national-level policy measures for this group. *NEET* was different in this respect: with the intervention of labour economists, youth inactivity was swiftly repositioned as an employment problem and therefore it could be claimed to have direct, measurable consequences to the economy as well as to the stability of the social security system. As shown by the quotes on the first page of this article, key claims-makers indeed drew a direct link between the increase in *NEETs* and the (presumably unsustainable) social security system which might suffer additional burdens were non-employed youth to be allowed to become welfare claimants.[15] This argument was, importantly, also adopted by the MHLW. We may thus contend that, in a conservative public policy context where 'welfare' (*fukushi*) – and mental welfare especially – was associated with the private sphere of the family, but where 'the economy' (*keizai*) was placed at the very centre of the public realm, shifting the issue of youth inactivity (whatever its empirically detected causes or solutions) towards the latter, more legitimate, frame made plenty of strategic sense.[16]

Interests

While the central claims-makers of the *NEET* campaign – scholars such as Genda and Kosugi, practitioners such as the two Kudōs (father Sadatsugu and son Kei), as well as several MHLW officials – have already been identified, the issue of interests is yet to be addressed. What were the driving motivations of these actors, and which other groups might have hoped to benefit from the *NEET* debate in one way or another?[17]

At the risk of over-simplification, one can identify three particular organizations and one distinctive 'industry' that clearly had a vital interest in the problem of jobless young people. First, the Career Development Support Office of the MHLW's Occupational Skill Development Bureau (that had commissioned the critical JILPT reports on youth labour market measures) had an institutional 'mission' that it was struggling to continue. The old Working Youth's Homes – the CDSO's classic youth programme that had at one time comprised over 500 activity centres across Japan – had by the early 2000s descended to virtual irrelevance, so there was strong interest within the Office to enact newer, up-to-date programmes (see Chapter 2). Beyond such an institutional state of affairs, the CDSO had a particularly enterprising chief in the first half of the 2000s who was keen to apply his personal youth policy vision to novel programmes.

The Japan Institute of Labour Policy and Training faced, if anything, much greater pressures as it was pressed to produce new research that could capture the public's interest and be seen as 'socially useful'. This was partly because, as of the early 2000s, the JILPT became widely seen as one of Japan's many corrupt and wasteful semi-governmental organizations where high-ranking bureaucrats found cushy post-retirement jobs as *amakudari* (this criticism resurfaced in 2009 following the historic election victory of the Democratic Party). While not necessarily a fair appraisal of the organization's contributions – the institute continues to be highly regarded by many domestic and international researchers – the JILPT has had to fight for its survival in the past decade and therefore it has had much potential benefit from the creation of new topics and 'social problems' over which it can claim expertise. The predicament of the Institute of Social Science of the University of Tokyo (where Genda is a faculty member) was somewhat less acute than that of the JILPT, but not altogether dissimilar: it, too, was under growing pressure to produce research that was not only of high quality, but also socially appealing and marketable and that could thus attract funding as well as continued government approval.

At the same time, though less visible and influential, Japan's youth support industry also had a critical interest in the debate on *NEETs*. While not necessarily a sector-wide campaign, some of the most well-situated youth work 'veterans' had been in regular contact with officials within the MHLW since the early 2000s, with Adachi (2006) documenting that a 'channel' (*paipu*) had opened between Kudō Sadatsugu and the MHLW around this time (Adachi 2006). Kudō consistently demanded that youth support institutions be recognized as providing a public service that benefitted not just individual support-seekers but the wider society and economy as well. Though there is little evidence that actors such as Kudō had played a direct role in devising the *NEET* category itself, they certainly helped raise awareness regarding youth issues within the MHLW, encouraging the latter to take official action. Once a new category did materialize, the former immediately began to discuss it in publications and reframed their own activities as '*NEET* support measures' (as opposed to *hikikomori* and/or *futōkō* measures), partly in order to qualify for government subsidies. These observations confirm the notion that private institutions indeed actively shape and are shaped by dynamic youth problem discourses (Goodman 1990).

It is puzzling that two other potential beneficiaries of youth policies – parents and young people themselves – appear to have played no marked role in lobbying for new youth measures through the *NEET* debate. The youth workers whom I met during fieldwork in 2007 and 2008 argued that parents with offspring who were formally inactive and/or socially withdrawn typically felt ashamed and thus grew rather isolated in their respective communities, making it difficult for them to collectively make demands for new social support measures (see related observations in Chapter 5 and Chapter 6). This, of course, is not the whole story as Japan is replete with various small parent-led self-help groups, some of which have become influential within youth support debates (see Horiguchi, 2011, for examples). Nevertheless, parents did arguably not contribute to the *NEET* campaign as a coherent, well-organized group.

With the exception of the aforementioned Kudō Kei, who took part in the planning of new support programmes, the voices of youth also remained largely absent. Once again, we witnessed a youth problem debate where the central objects of intervention were relegated to the status of a muted group.[18] It is of course possible to view influential youth support institutions and scholars such as Genda as acting as the *de facto* representatives of parents and youth: they rallied for new policies on behalf of these two groups, which were assumed to be in need of new support measures.

It is clear from this brief account, it may be added, that institutional and personal self-interest provided a strong catalyst to the *NEET* campaign. Yet, at the same time, it is possible to view 'self-interest' from an expanded perspective: for each main advocate of the *NEET* debate and associated policies, advocacy has also been a matter of personal commitment and passion. Influenced by their personalities as well as by direct contact with distressed young people, these enterprising actors have demonstrated a degree of empathy for youth who suffer from certain kinds of social exclusion. They can therefore be said to have engaged in the policy process with a strong sense of 'mission' and a desire to 'make a difference' (also see Chapter 6 regarding the motivations of youth support workers). The fact that activation policy for youth has not so far attracted the interest of heavyweight interest groups – nor has it been an obvious cash cow for commercial enterprises – has arguably given more space for individual initiatives based on empathy.[19] In this sense, some *NEET* support advocates resemble what are currently known globally as 'social entrepreneurs' (Nicholls 2006; in Japanese, *shakai kigyōka*) in that they seem to be motivated by a mix of considerations in addressing particular social problems. Now, as Chapter 7 will reiterate, this does not make the construction of *NEET* any less problematic a process or *NEET* a less problematic category, but accounting for diverse motivations as the drivers of youth support advocacy offers a more balanced understanding of such action compared to a view that assumes, *a priori*, narrow 'self-interest' as the sole motivator of policy-making efforts.

British vs Japanese 'NEET'

Having elucidated the processes and strategies through which *NEET* was constructed as a new target group and youth category in Japan, let us next contrast the category that emerged with the British definition of NEET. Table 3.4 summarizes the key features of both, first as a policy target group and then as a social category.

For one, this table underlines the very different gender implications of *NEET* in Japan: women who are married or engaged in housework (in the parental family) do not generally fall within its ambit. As will be discussed later, this stems partly from entrenched gender role expectations and partly from the assumption that married women are 'socially included'. These assumptions were espoused by the MHLW, which has been the most influential government department in defining the debate and thus was able to overturn a contesting Cabinet Office definition (see above). Also, single parents and the disabled have their separate categories in Japan and are thus not (at least explicitly) included in the *NEET* category. Importantly, the Japanese concept lumps together a vast range of age groups, which seems internationally peculiar. Needless to say, those in different age categories could sensibly be expected to face very different challenges. For instance, achieving basic qualifications is likely to be a more pressing concern for 15- to 19-year-olds than 30-year-olds, who might be more interested in quickly locating paid work. However, as we have seen, this expansive age-range must be seen in context and considered a strategic choice by policy actors.

In line with the younger age group and the overall definition given to *NEET*, promoting swift (re-)entry into education or training was clearly the priority for policy-makers in the UK context. In Japan, as the subsequent chapters of this book will document, economic independence through

Table 3.4 Contrasting the British and Japanese definitions of 'NEET'

	UK	Japan
	As a policy target group category	
Year of introduction	*1999*	*2003*
Age-group	*16–18*	*15–34*
Inclusion of:		
the formally unemployed	Yes	No
married individuals	Yes (in principle)	No
those engaged in housework	Yes	No (contested)
single parents	Yes	No
the disabled	To an extent	No
Population	181,000 (2002)*	640,000 (2004)** (the dominant figure)
Percentage of age-group	10% (the dominant figure)	Around 2%
Male/female ratio	n/a	Roughly 1:1
Main policy concerns	Educational underachievement, lack of opportunities	At first, low education and social isolation, but risks to social security system stressed later
Key solution	Education and training	Employment
	As a social category	
In common use	No	Yes (since 2004)
Dominant gender	n/a	Male
Character	n/a	Lazy, self-indulgent, low-work ethic
Class background	n/a	Middle or middle-upper class
Locus of blame	n/a	The individual and parents: not deserving of generous public support
Main concern	n/a	Employment: not a 'welfare' issue like the *hikikomori*
	Key 'NEET' policy achievement targets	
	A total reduction of 10 per cent (2002–04)	Employment of 35 or 70 per cent of those who show up

Source: * Office for National Statistics/Department for Education and Skills, *Statistical Release* SFR 31/2003; ** *White Paper on the Labour Markets 2005* (MHLW 2005b)

employment was the dominant remedy that was advanced both by the government and the media. Entry to long-term professional or vocational education was almost never raised as a desirable response there in the 2000s. This is somewhat ironic for, as we will see in Chapter 6, the real young people who came to consult new sites of support in fact faced a plethora of educational challenges and would almost certainly have benefited from a stronger stress on 'education' (e.g. supplementary, subsidized educational programmes) as a key 'solution' to the *NEET* problem.

Subtle hierarchies of labels, *NEET* taxonomies, and the language of youth support

The above analysis of how *NEET* was socially constructed by key actors and the media may leave the impression that the label emerged in relative isolation from other categories. This, however, was not the case. All youth categories are constructed and made sense of with reference to pre-existing categories. While dominant assumptions regarding 'youth' and 'adulthood' set certain frames for fresh classifications, in general discourse new classifications are routinely related to other popular, more specific cultural categories. In the case of *NEET*, the most immediately relevant other categories were *hikikomori* and *freeters* (socially withdrawn youth and part-time working young adults) and, to a lesser extent, *futōkō* (children who miss school for significant periods of time) and *parasite singles* (mainly female youth who live with their parents and presumably engage in luxury consumption).[20] We will see below how such earlier categories were evoked in new taxonomies of *NEETs*. Interestingly, as newly introduced and pre-existing categories are contrasted in popular discourse, they tend to also be situated into a hierarchical order vis-à-vis one another.

First, if analyzed as a social category, it is quite straightforward to distinguish *NEET* from *freeters*: the impression that they either could not work (Genda) or did not want to work (dominant construct) clearly set them apart from young part-timers who 'at least were employed'. A rather stark line was thus drawn between the two groups in mainstream discourse, even as some scholars such as Miyamoto protested that this was misleading and that the boundary between 'non-employment' and 'part-time employment' was in actuality quite fluid. Since employment remains the key determinant of a young person's social status in Japan, *NEETs* came to be ranked decidedly lower in the (mainstream society's) hierarchy of social categories compared to *freeters*. This hierarchy was implicit already in Genda's initial characterization of *NEETs* as 'youth who could not even become *freeters* or attain the status of formally unemployed'.

By contrast, the relationship between *NEET* and the socially withdrawn *hikikomori* has emerged as something more complex. In his best-selling book, Genda intentionally posited the *hikikomori* as a minor sub-category of *NEET* and conceptualized it as occupying the bottom range of the latter group

(Genda and Maganuma 2004). He thus acknowledged the links between the two youth issues, but framed *NEET* as the master category that subsumed all other inactive groups. As might have been expected, this led to some protests from *hikikomori* advocates who claimed that *NEET* had a confusing effect because there was a general tendency to equate, or at least mix up, the two issues. From a constructionist perspective, however, that there was significant overlap between *NEET* and earlier youth categories was hardly surprising and rather something to be anticipated. In any case, the outcome was that non-working *NEETs* came to be situated, as Kudō Kei promptly put it, as being 'above the *hikikomori* but below *freeters*' (*Asahi Shimbun*, 2004a). That such a hierarchy came to be created had, as will be seen in Chapter 4, some practical implications for youth support measures: policies came to target youth who might have previously been, but were no longer, in a state of social withdrawal, and who thus 'qualified' as *NEETs*. In such a progression from *hikikomori* to *NEET*, the 'natural' next stage for supported youth would accordingly be that of a *freeter* and indeed not that of a *seishain* (permanent worker). As suggested in Chapter 1, the *de facto* goal of symbolic activation as advanced by government discourse – which was to turn inactive young people into low-paid irregular workers – was consistent with these assumptions. Chapter 6 will highlight yet another particularly intriguing dimension in the hierarchy of labels and social statuses that *NEET* became part of, highlighting the fact that *NEET* was in fact a preferable category compared to a number of more low-status social classificiations. This, as I will argue, had significant consequences for support-seeking behaviour on the part of individual young people and their parents, leading certain kinds of inactive young people to flock to sites of support.

Somewhat more distance was perceived between *NEET* and the category of *futōkō* (non-school-going children). However, many experts and commentators were quick to posit that school non-attendance would inevitably lead to non-employment, implying an intimate connection between lack of educational qualifications and non-employment. Several *futōkō* support groups swiftly reframed their activities as constituting '*NEET* prevention', providing an example of the adaptability of private youth support practitioners to shifts in discourse. The most striking similarities between the two categories can, however, be found in the way that they were debated: just as it had been argued in the past that *futōkō* in fact 'wanted to go to school but simply could not' (Honda 2005), the same argument was now reworked by Genda who stressed that it was not that *NEETs* did not want to work – they were merely unable to do so. Just as school was portrayed as absolutely compulsory in the mainstream *futōkō* debate (Yoneyama 1999), the dominant *NEET* debate never questioned the assumption that all (able-bodied) young adults should work and be employed; those who did not conform to such expectations were singled out as deviants. And just as public discussion on *futōkō* was defined by essentially negative behavioural and psychiatric discourses, so *NEETs* were faulted for having moral deficiencies and sometimes analysed using psychological concepts. The key difference was, of course, that the former debate dealt with 'children' (*kodomo*) while the latter was concerned with 'youth' (*wakamono*). *NEETs* were thus treated with a higher degree of harshness, at least in the public debate, than the *futōkō*, although they were also more feared, since 'youth' could not be as easily controlled if they turned violent towards their parents or committed other criminal acts.

Kosugi Reiko of JILPT may have been the first to put forth a taxonomy of non-working youth. In an early phase of the *NEET* debate, she explained in a *Sankei Shimbun* (2004) article that there were indeed 1) yankee-type, 2) *hikikomori*-type, 3) 'paralyzed-type', and 4) 'stumbling-type' *NEETs*. In an interview that was published four months later, these categories had morphed into 1) the 'living for the moment'-type, 2) the 'self-actualization'-type, 3) the 'low confidence'-type, and 4) the *hikikomori*-type (Asahi Shimbun 2004a). Based on an exploratory interview survey of 51 youth – the selection criteria of which were not clear – these typologies arguably did more to construct sub-categories of *NEET* than to explain the phenomenon in any rigorous empirical sense. This is, of course, very interesting as it demonstrates how even labour market scholars feel obliged to explain *NEETs* not through rigorous empirical studies (that would, say, establish individual life courses instead of supplying miscellaneous assortments of disconnected 'data'), but through pre-existing, yet highly putative, social categories. On the other hand, the use of such categories seems to have been part of a wider strategy of advancing the *NEET* discourse in the popular media to bring about policy change. Chapter 6 will return to the question of whether it is possible to understand the highly ambiguous circumstances of many non-working youth through standard social science survey methods at all.

What is notable about the particular taxonomies offered by Kosugi is how they identify type one (the yankee, or 'living for the moment', type) – which is essentially code for delinquent youth (*hikō*) – as the type of *NEET* which is universal across the developed world, while all other types are said to be specific to Japan. In a later research report Kosugi specified that type one *NEETs*, raised in metropolitan families with poor economic situations and low expectations, closely match the image of 'socially excluded' youth that is found in many Western countries (Kosugi 2004:13). Conversely, she likened all the other types of *NEETs* to moratorium-type *freeters* – i.e. part-time workers who postpone important life choices – where the moratorium concept itself originates in Japanese youth debates of the 1970s (Kosugi (ed.) 2005; also see Chapter 2).

In sum, then, it can be said that *NEET* was constructed in Japan with close reference to earlier social categories such as *hikikomori* and *freeters* which inevitably shaped how *NEET* came to be understood. Such pre-existing categories were also employed in taxonomies of *NEET* that, it can be safely said, had little coherence as 'empirical' schema, but created perfectly logical links and hierarchies between an array of socially constructed youth categories.

The new language of youth support

In conjunction with the emergence of *NEET* as a policy term (target group) and social category, a related dialogical discourse was produced by a handful of policy entrepreneurs and youth support experts. I call this discourse the 'new language of youth support' since it was distinctive from the mainstream debate (that portrayed youth as 'lazy' or as lacking 'motivation') and since it offered a common set of paradigms for youth workers across Japan. This new language was actively disseminated by Genda Yūji who drew on both statistics and the ideas of youth support experts (including 'veterans') in creatively constructing his accounts, the first goal of which was to publicize the *NEET* issue and the second to explain it to a broad audience.[21] The conceptual landscape that he and a few other writers defined should hence not be viewed as a fully coherent set of thought-out empirical findings, but rather as an exploratory dialogue that began in 2004 and that by 2005 had produced clusters of issues around which explanations came to be structured. The most important of such clusters concerned the predominant attributes of *NEETs*, the role of the family and the impact of labour market change.

The foundational elements of the new youth support language were laid down by Genda Yūji in his first article on *NEETs* in 2004 where, based on a survey of 700 jobless youth, he made the following observation:

> *NEETs* do not have confidence in themselves. One out of two *NEETs* feel that they are inferior in terms of sociability [*kyōchōsei*], initiative [*sekkyokusei*] and communication skills [*komyunikēshonryoku*] compared to other people of their age.
>
> (Genda 2004:165)

Regardless of limited empirical evidence, among these observations especially the notion that *NEETs* suffer from a chronic lack of confidence and that they have poor communication skills became entrenched as key themes in the new language of youth support. *NEETs* were said to suffer from an acute sense of inferiority (*rettōkan*) and lack of ability (*nigate ishiki*), and they were even said to have lost all 'hope' (*kibō*) in work. Early accounts did not specify why this was the case, although sometimes a link was drawn between the 1990s' labour market 'ultra-ice age' (*chō-hyōgaki*) which had caused many young job-seekers to give up on working after repeatedly failing job interviews. That a large proportion of *NEETs* had no friends and no-one to consult in times of hardship (*sōdan aite ga inai*) was also pointed out from the start, with Genda arguing that youth in this group had no 'connections' (*tsunagari*) with society and enjoyed few 'chances' (*kikkake*) to associate with others. This was partly because they had 'nowhere to go' (*ikiba ga nai*) and no place where they could interact freely and 'be themselves' (*ibasho ga nai*). Although Genda did repeatedly highlight the higher risk of lower-secondary school graduates and school dropouts becoming *NEETs* (Genda 2004; Genda and Maganuma

2004), he consistently avoided reducing this issue to that of *hikikomori* or *futōkō* (school non-attendance), nor did he make direct reference to social disparities (*kakusa*) or poverty (*hinkon*).

There were several other – mainly psychological – disadvantages that non-employed youth were said to suffer from. They were found to be extremely 'serious' (*majime*) and 'docile' (*sunao*) to a harmful degree. More often than not, *NEETs* were so-called *ii ko*, good boys and girls who obediently followed their parents' wishes to the best of their abilities. This led to severe stress and pressure whenever they failed to fulfil their parents' expectations. Another problem was that *NEETs* in fact thought too much about work and were concerned that they had not found what they really 'wanted to do' (*yaritai koto*), which made them paralyzed and unable to take concrete steps forward. That *NEETs* had accumulated no prior 'failure experiences' (*zasetsu keiken, shippai keiken*) in their childhood and youth made them particularly vulnerable to such paralysis as, having led overprotected and overplanned lives, they had not learned how to rebound from difficulty.

It was universally agreed among all key writers that parents also played a key role in the 'production' of *NEETs*, even if there were was no unanimity about the details. In most cases though, parents were generally blamed for excesses of one kind or another: they were not communicating sufficiently with their offspring nor spending enough time with them, or, conversely, they were guilty of excessive interference (*kakanshō*). Some argued that mothers had allowed too strong an attachment to develop between them and their children (echoing the concept of *amae* developed by Takeo Doi), while dads – who anyhow were absent most of the time – talked too little about their careers, being unable to say anything positive regarding their experience of a 'salaryman life' (Futagami 2005). Moreover, parents were seen as highly reluctant to part with their children (*kobanare dekinai oya*) whose independence they were obstructing by fostering too much dependence. At worst, youth were pressured, even oppressed, by their guardians who acted as poor role models but obsessively urged their children to follow a 'standard life course' of studying at a 'good school', proceeding to a 'good university' and being hired by a 'good company' (Futagami 2005:7–8). Similarly criticizing parental over-interference, Genda (2005a:242) was not the only one to suggest that parents should not 'monopolize' their children as the latter would surely benefit from more contacts with other 'good adults' (*ii otona*) in society.

Although labour market themes had been conspicuously absent from scholarly and popular writings on *NEETs* in 2004, some came to be highlighted in the following year.[22] The keyword that emerged at this time was that of *sokusenryoku*, or 'instant work competence' (closely resembling the Western concept of 'employability'), that companies had come to demand of new hires as they wished to cut down on training costs and reduce the share of permanent workers (see Chapter 1 also). This concept was introduced into the language of youth support by Genda (2005a) who criticized it as a form of 'mistaken Americanism' (*ayamatta Amerika-ryū*) and perceived a trend – prompted by changes not only in company behaviour but also in government policy – towards self-responsibility (*jiko sekinin*) over skills training. Others emphasized that the requirement that new employees should possess *sokusenryoku* had the severest consequences not for fresh graduates (*shinki gakusotsusha*) but for those who were attempting to (re-) enter the labour markets as 'mid-career hires' (*chūto saiyō*), in particular for those whose CVs contained long blank periods (*kūhaku kikan*). In addition to this unwelcome development, by 2005, Genda began to put more stress on the role of excessive work (*kajō rōdō*) and poor work environments (*retsuaku na rōdō kankyō*) that sometimes led young workers to not only quit but to develop mental health (*mentaru herusu*) problems (Genda 2005b:176).

Whatever the balance of the above factors and whatever the circumstances of individual youth, the new language of youth support stressed, once again, that it was not that *NEETs* did not want to work; they simply could not, for one reason or another. This contention became popular among youth supporters who wished to confront the dominant image of *NEETs* as 'lazy' and as lacking motivation, perhaps partly because of its lack of specificity. The phrase could be used by those who mainly saw fault with families as well as by those critical of the government and the labour markets, and it left room, too, for altogether new explanations. Emphasizing in this way the various potential obstacles to employment instead of individual morality was, furthermore, compatible with the notion that this was an era when 'anyone could become a *NEET*' (see above). The framing of *NEET* as a universal risk functioned both as a normalizing, destigmatizing technique (*NEETs* were in fact 'normal youth') as well as a strategy to stir wider concern over the issue (*NEETs* were a general 'social problem').

As always, the problem conceptions that were embedded in the new language of youth support inevitably implied certain solutions, if only very vague ones. The perception that *NEETs* lacked confidence clearly suggested that there was a need to facilitate confidence-building. Insofar as poor communication skills were the problem, measures that could cultivate such aptitudes were required. If some youth were becoming isolated (*koritsu*) from society, they needed opportunities (*kikkake*) to re-enter it through acquiring more 'connections' (*tsunagari*). A master of counterintuitive interpretation, Genda came up with a broad list of further prescriptions in 2004 and 2005 that ranged from career education and five-day work trials for lower-secondary school students and the provision of 'failure experiences' (*zasetsu keiken*) to advise that overly 'serious' youth should refrain from excessive thinking and first establish a regular daily 'rhythm' (*kisoku tadashī rizumu*; Genda 2004, 2005a; Genda and Maganuma 2004). Borrowing the favourite phrase of the head of the NPO Children's Life and Culture Association (CLCA) in Odawara, Kanagawa-prefecture, Genda paradoxically exhorted *NEETs* to learn how to be 'properly roundabout' (*chanto iikagen ni suru*) so as to 'loosen up' and overcome their fear of failure. *NEETs* were also to train themselves to go to bed and wake up early (*haya-ne, haya-oki wo suru*) before troubling themselves over the difficult question of why they should work.

NEET and social exclusion

A final issue that requires clarification here is the relation of *NEET* to 'social exclusion' in the Japanese context.[23] As we have seen, the two concepts were very closely linked in the British youth policy debate under New Labour, and it is predominantly through the British case that social exclusion entered the Japanese youth policy discourse. Contributing to one of the landmark youth reports by JILPT (then called JIL, Japan Institute of Labour), Okita played a large role here by being among the first to cite the report *Bridging the Gap* authored by the Blair government's Social Exclusion Unit (Okita 2003:62). In addition to noting that, in the UK, 9 per cent of 16–18-year-olds had been found to be *NEETs*, Okita underlined that many of such youth – who often had few qualifications, low incomes and poor mental and physical health – fell into non-participation for prolonged periods of time. This, Okita recounted, was bound to lead to various social ills, from homelessness and drug abuse to criminal offending, incurring tremendous costs on government finances through lost tax income and increases in social benefit outlays (Okita 2003:63).

These points were echoed soon afterwards by Kosugi and Genda, the latter of whom stressed that *NEETs* were a 'significant minority' that could, indeed, due to being excluded from social participation, become a great 'cause of instability' (Genda and Maganuma 2004:27; see also Kosugi (ed.) 2005:3–6). Their message was that there were youth in Japan also who had been all but forsaken by society and policy, and that this was untenable due to the significant social costs and dangers that would result. On an implicit level, by omitting structural considerations and by invoking images of threatening problems such as homelessness, early parenthood and drug use, Okita, Kosugi and Genda strongly implied, whether intentionally or not, that social exclusion stemmed primarily from individual behavioral and moral reasons.

Even though the public media debate that ensued in 2004 and 2005 put overwhelming emphasis on the fact that *NEETs* lacked employment and work motivation, there are strong grounds for positing that the Japanese policy debate on *NEETs* was indeed concerned with social exclusion more broadly rather than with paid work only. Key policy actors scarcely believed that all youth who were (temporarily) outside education, employment or training were socially excluded, but they did think that there was a sub-set of formally inactive youth who indeed suffered seriously as a result of exclusion. Although one will look in vain for a clear definition of what exactly was meant by 'social exclusion' in the context of the *NEET* debate, by way of a summary, at least the following dimensions were invoked within it:

1. Labour market exclusion. *NEETs* have given up hope about finding work; they are 'not even' *freeters* who work part-time nor are they formally unemployed as they do not take active steps to seek for jobs.

2. Educational exclusion. Those with low education credentials, especially lower-secondary school graduates and drop-outs, fare poorly in the job markets and are over-represented among *NEETs*.
3. Exclusion from social relations. Those who do not work tend to have only a fragile relationship with society, and those who are also socially withdrawn have no regular contact with anyone but their parents.
4. Exclusion from public support. *NEETs* have so far been ignored by policy measures and they were not even originally incorporated in the Youth Independence and Challenge Plan that focused on *freeters* and students.
5. Future exclusion and deprivation. Exclusion at the present time could lead to more poverty, livelihood assistance claimants, homeless people and social disturbance, and less economic growth and lower tax revenues in the future.

Out of these, points one to three were standard observations in accounts on the characteristics of *NEETs*, while points four and five were repeatedly made by policy entrepreneurs in their books and articles, arguably to justify the enactment of new youth measures. There were also some voices that suggested that the labelling of youth as *NEET* or non-employed could itself produce stigma and thus lead to exclusion (Chapter 6 will return to this issue).[24] In any case, although the terminology of 'social exclusion' was not always directly employed, *NEET* was clearly conceptualized (at least by leading policy entrepreneurs) as a multi-dimensional, dynamic issue marked by the exclusion of some youth from several important social spheres, setting it apart from a mere labour market problem.

Yet, in spite of such a concern with multiple types of exclusion, discussions of poverty and economic deprivation in general were muted in the debate on *NEETs*. As was noted a few sections ago, Kosugi posited that only one of her (speculative) *NEET* categories was characterized by poor economic conditions and low expectations. Genda, on the other hand, carefully avoided explicitly mentioning poverty and inequality in his writings on *NEET* in 2004 and 2005. This may have been simply because he wished to consistently frame *NEET* as an employment issue so as to attract public employment-related responses in a deeply conservative political climate. Stressing poverty as a key factor behind youth non-employment would not have suggested any new policies (beyond those related to livelihood assistance, or *seikatsu hogo*). At the same time, in the public eye, *NEETs* came to be viewed as the offspring of relatively affluent families who could afford not to work since their basic needs were being taken care of by parents. At worst, poverty was raised as a looming future risk that would inevitably materialize when the parents of *NEETs* grew frail and could no longer provide for them.

Conclusion

The construction of *NEET* as a new target category was a vital step in the campaign for creating policy measures for non-employed youth in 2000s'

Japan. It was an 'agenda-setting' process in the broadest sense of the term, for *NEET* was made known, in the brief period from 2004 to 2006, not only in the policy world but across the general population. Symbolic activation, as defined in Chapter 1, would not have come into being without it: the popularization of *NEET* enabled the making of policy and this very category turned also into a powerful symbolic trigger for support-seeking and job-seeking activities on the part of young adults and their parents.

It is important to stress here that the framing of youth joblessness into a public issue was indeed more than just a strategic feat for central policy proponents within and without the government: defining the problem of non-employment was, from the start, a matter of articulation and interpretation. There was, as I have suggested before, not one correct way to diagnose the post-industrial youth employment dilemma in the Japanese context (or anywhere else), but multiple possible diagnoses. Interestingly, key claims-makers – Genda in particular – had a keen sense for exploring this issue as something that was, as of the early 2000s, fundamentally unknown and ambiguous (very much in the spirit of innovation and 'search' as discussed in Stark, 2009).

But Genda and others, while appreciating the complexity of the situation (and being in favour of an ongoing creative dialogue with various actors), also knew that, in order to get their thoughts on youth non-employment across to a wider audience, their novel ideas had to be articulated with firm reference to pre-existing, familiar themes. It is precisely when they did this that the process of constructing *NEET* became heavily influenced by an existing legacy of youth problems (Chapter 2) that was predominantly conservative and conducive to 'youth bashing'. In a sense, then, deep-rooted themes in Japan's youth problem pedigree and the media forces that reproduce them 'hijacked' the *NEET* discourse, imbuing it with explanations highly reminiscent of the preceding debates on *freeters*, the *hikikomori* and *parasite singles*. It is somewhat strange that leading claims-makers (who did not wish to blame young people for their lack of employment) were not able to foresee that this would happen and to take precautionary actions.

Either way, the upshot is that key actors did succeed in setting a new youth policy agenda through *NEET*, but this agenda ultimately became constrained because of the 'undeserving' image of the *NEET* category in the domestic debate in the mid-2000s. All actors involved in the field of youth support in Japan have thereafter had to address this image in one way or another. Widespread negative understandings of non-employed youth – as lazy and as personally responsible for their lack of work – therefore also made the task of hands-on policy-makers much harder than it might otherwise have been (had a more favourable interpretation become entrenched). It is the manoeuvrings of such 'sympathetic bureaucrats' and their allies, keen to craft novel support programmes but confronted with a hostile climate, that I turn to in the following chapter.

4 Crafting policy: Sympathetic bureaucrats in a hostile climate

In the previous chapter I examined the particular ways in which the post-industrial youth employment dilemma came to be constructed, and vigorously debated, in Japanese public discourse in the early 2000s. The acronym *NEET*, referring to those 15- to 34-year-olds who were neither in education, employment or training (but with a predominant accent on employment in the Japanese context), was at the very centre of the agenda-setting efforts of actors such as Genda and Kosugi. But once it had become broadly accepted that *NEETs* were indeed a problem worthy of public debate and policy attention, it was time for hands-on bureaucrats, with support from politically influential superiors, to craft actual youth employment programmes with real budgets, outcome targets and evaluation criteria.[1] Not nearly as visible a process as the *NEET* debate that unfolded in the national media where everyone could follow it, the two programmes of interest here, the Youth Independence Camp (*Wakamono Jiritsu Juku*) and the Youth Support Station (*Wakamono Sapōto Sutēshon*), were moulded largely behind the scenes by a small number of bureaucrats. This chapter provides the first in-depth, independent account on how these policies were developed, resisted, modified and ultimately rolled out by influential actors within Japan's central government.

I argue that the two above-mentioned youth support programmes (that appeared in 2005 and 2006, respectively) were a product of the efforts of 'sympathetic bureaucrats' working in a 'hostile climate'. Sympathetic towards jobless youth whose circumstances they viewed as complex and nuanced rather than as purely self-inflicted, these bureaucrats were faced with considerable resistance to their policy plans on three specific counts. First and perhaps most interestingly, the key official in charge of concrete programme planning had to negotiate the wishes of more senior decision-makers who wanted to to implement a disciplinarian training regime à la Totsuka Hiroshi (see Chapter 1). Second, the same official and his colleagues found it very difficult to argue that programmes for *NEETs*, widely perceived as 'lazy' and therefore 'undeserving' in Japan, should receive more than a token amount of taxpayer money. Paradoxically, even though the *NEET* category was indispensable to raising youth non-employment onto the public agenda, it thereby also severely constrained the making of substantial employment programmes.

A number of harsh conditions imposed by the Ministry of Finance within a social insurance-oriented welfare system constituted the third predominant set of obstacles.

By closely tracking how 'pro-youth' bureaucrats drew on their agency and creativity to counter each of these challenges, this chapter moves forward our story on the emergence of a new kind of youth policy – essentially, two policy frameworks within the larger Youth Independence and Challenge framework that was set out in Chapter 2 – in post-industrial Japan. While the substance of these initiatives becomes more apparent in Chapters 5 and 6, it is possible to draw three important policy lessons from the following sections. The first lesson aligns with the theories of Schneider and Ingram (1993, 2005, 2008) and has implications for the making of youth policy beyond the particular case of *NEETs*: not only is it difficult to generally promote youth employment support policies within the Japanese social security system, but whenever a target group is constructed in mainly negative terms as 'undeserving', it is virtually guaranteed that the resulting programmes will turn out weak, poorly funded and possibly punitive. While not a topic explored here, a demographic situation where young adults – those from their late teens to their early thirties – are a shrinking group within a rapidly ageing population, may further aggravate this dynamic. The second, more unexpected, policy lesson is that youth policy solutions often predate youth problems: both of the programmes reviewed here had in fact been partly designed before the emergence of *NEET* on the public radar. Finally, we also learn about the counter-intuitive relationship between foreign and domestic 'models' in the making of youth policy.

In terms of structure, this account will first unpack the origins of the residential Youth Independence Camp, Japan's first support programme for *NEETs*, which evoked powerful images of Totsuka Hiroshi-style disciplinarian training. The origins of the Youth Support Station, a counselling initiative, are probed next. The underlying concept of this scheme, as set out by policy-makers, can be summarized as 'supporting youth through more tightly integrated local networks of social services and employers'. The third main section delves further into the strategic dimensions of policy-making in a hostile climate, with a focus on legitimization strategies. Before concluding, I take a glance at how the Ministry of Health, Labour and Welfare moved its new schemes towards the implementation stage with support from various intermediaries.

The data for this chapter come predominantly from in-depth, repeated interviews. The main informant was the former head of the Career Support Development Office (Kyaria Keisei Shien Shitsu) within the MHLW who oversaw, and indeed actively led, the development of the two programmes that I examine in this chapter. I refer to this official as 'the innovator' to acknowledge his role in the youth policy process. Thanks to an introduction from my academic host in Japan (see Appendix D), I was able to interview the innovator first in July 2007 at the MHWL in Kasumigaseki, Tokyo, after which we met about a dozen times in the subsequent 18 months. Through interviews with 'the sponsor', the former head of the MHLW and the most

Table 4.1 The development of Japanese youth activation policy (overview)

Year	Policy event
2003	The Youth Independence and Challenge Plan is announced; the Job Cafe launches
2004	The Youth Independence and Challenge Action Plan is enacted
2005	The Youth Independence Camp is launched; the State-Society Movement to Raise the Human Competence of Youth begins
2006	The Youth Support Station opens
2008	The Youth Support Station is converted from a 'pilot' into a 'regular' government programme

influential supporter of the new youth policies, as well as with a number of other officials at the CSDO and related institutions, I have been able to contextualize and relativize the information provided by the innovator. This was indeed a crucial strategy; one of the most interesting findings I will share below has to do with open disagreements and contrasting positions between the actors interviewed. I therefore make no claims that the narratives offered here present the only 'true' account of the making of youth support policy in Japan, but they do reveal key dynamics in the policy process and demonstrate the very human, socially interactive and contested nature of policy-making – something that does not always receive much attention in mainstream social policy scholarship.

The origins of the Youth Independence Camp: A disciplinarian policy-maker's dream?

The Youth Independence Camp (YIC), Japan's first and by far the most symbolic support measure for non-employed *NEETs*, was launched in 2005. Compared to the counselling-based Youth Support Station that appeared a year later, the YIC was tasked with furnishing residential 'work and life training' to small groups of young adults who consistently suffered from joblessness. Where did the core concept for the Independence Camp scheme come from, and who designed the programme? What kind of obstacles stood in its way? In the brief account that follows, we will find that the Youth Independence Camp, like the Support Station, was the pet policy of a particular bureaucrat – in this case, one with a disciplinarian orientation – who vigorously promoted his ideas within the MHLW. We also find that the core concept for the programme had been conjured up well before the emergence of the debate on *NEETs*, which nevertheless proved critical to the enactment of the scheme.

The genesis of the Youth Independence Camp concept

The making of the Youth Independence Camp is essentially a story of bureaucratic initiative as well as of changing government priorities. The scheme's direct origins stretch back to the early 2000s when an increase in part-time working *freeters* was rousing social concern and when the *NEET* category did not yet exist in Japan (see Chapters 1 and 2). While youth policy was hardly on the government's agenda at this point, a handful of officials were beginning to develop modest policy measures as they felt something needed to be done about young adults' increasingly difficult employment situation. The Young Work Plaza, a job brokering and counselling service attached in 2001 to five Hello Work centres across Japan (and that predated the Youth Independence and Challenge plans reviewed in Chapter 2), was the first of such initiatives to take concrete shape. The interested bureaucrats, however, fought an uphill battle: the prominent view within both the ruling Liberal Democratic Party as well as the mainstream media was that *freeters* (the foremost target group for potential policies) were indeed a problem, but that they had voluntarily chosen insecure part-time jobs over regular work commitments due to low work motivation and carefree attitudes (see Chapter 1). Hence, it was hard to argue that such youth deserved public support and resources. Moreover, the fact that leading politicians were preoccupied with sorting out bad debts (*furyō saiken*) in the banking sector – resulting in the need to quickly develop retraining and re-employment programmes for middle-aged bread-winners who were being made redundant – did not make matters easier from the point of view of crafting employment measures for young people ('sponsor', 26 November 2008).

This was why the proposal of a high-ranking bureaucrat – whom I refer to as the 'sponsor' in this chapter – to design a new type of programme for involuntary young part-timers was squarely rejected by the leading Liberal Democratic Party in 2002. Serving as the director of the Shokugyō Antei Kyoku (Occupational Security Bureau) at the time, the official in question had, as of the early 2000s, become deeply concerned over unprecedented levels of youth unemployment and insecurity. He was moreover alarmed by the fact that up to three-quarters of *freeters* – who had a reputation for staying up in the night and sleeping through the day – lived with their parents, from whom many received economic support. The director's idea was to break precisely such dependence on parents and to teach youth to live according to a regular day rhythm (*oyagakari no seikatsu kara kirihanashite, kisoku tadashī seikatsu wo saseru*). This could be done best in a camp format that would encourage participants to wake up early in the morning, work during the day and rest during the night ('sponsor', 26 November 2008).

The bureaucrat believed that camp-style residential training could return young people to what he viewed as the very 'essence of work' (*rōdō no genten*), i.e. to experiencing physical labour ('working while moving one's body') through engaging in agricultural and construction work. Such work could instil in youth desirable work habits, enabling them to escape from a vicious cycle of insecure part-time employment. In addition to these concerns, the key official was galvanized into action by the dire trends in final-year upper-secondary school students' recruitment rates (*naiteiritsu*), which showed that fewer and fewer students had a job lined up for them prior to graduation (see Chapter 1). European countries such as France and the UK that had experienced consistently high levels of youth unemployment and labour market precariousness served as negative examples for the director as he was thinking of new responses. The official feared that youth unemployment would become entrenched in Japan also, if not actively tackled at the earliest possible stage.

Luckily from the director's perspective, the mood within the leading Liberal Democratic Party suddenly became more favourable to new youth programmes in 2003. In this year, JILPT and its director, Kosugi Reiko, surveyed Japanese labour market changes from a comparative perspective and introduced the *NEET* concept to labour bureaucrats and politicians in Japan (Chapter 3). Reports published by JILPT, alongside a pre-existing societal concern over *freeters*, made youth issues relevant for politicians, eventually prompting Mr Tanihata, the vice minister for Health, Labour and Welfare at the time, to order his ministry to prepare appropriate policy responses. The official who received the vice minister's request was the very same official discussed above, i.e. the 'sponsor'. Incidentally, he was now attached to the far more powerful post of administrative vice minister (*jimujikan*) – the top administrative post within the MHLW – and jumped at the chance. The official quickly replied to Tanihata that he in fact had an idea that had already been 'warmed up', and he was soon given the go-ahead to launch a project team to develop further a scheme that would eventually emerge as the Youth Independence Camp.

By this time, the 'sponsor' had come to view *NEETs* as a valid target group for his programme (alongside *freeters*, the target group he had originally had in mind) since he thought they were in a particularly serious state, having fallen outside the labour force and often suffering from social withdrawal (*hikiko-mori*). The fact that European countries such as the UK also had '*NEET* countermeasures' made targeting this group seem even more sensible to him.

Designing the programme: Moderating the disciplinarian leanings

In designing the Youth Independence Camp, numerous challenges had to be negotiated before reaching the state of programme implementation. The onus for dealing with these challenges fell on the chief of the Career Support Development Section of the MHLW who had previously displayed great commitment in youth measures in enacting the Young Job Spot (see Chapter 2). The chief – whom I refer to as the 'innovator' due to his pivotal, creative role in designing Japan's two main youth inclusion programmes – had to tackle two key issues from the outset: locating pre-existing models that could be presented as 'precedents' (which are something that bureaucrats in Japan are typically required to study when preparing policy proposals) and moderating the desire, on the part of more senior bureaucrats, to give the Independence Camp a strong disciplinarian slant.

The innovator proceeded by conducting deliberations with an internal project team. This team was launched in late 2003 and it consisted of six members, all of whom were MHLW labour bureaucrats. It puzzled over the basic features of the Youth Independence Camp and, despite the distinctiveness of this scheme, managed to locate what they argued were relevant policy precedents and models. One of these was the Job Corps in the US; another one was the training programme of the Okinawa Sangyō Kaihatsu Seinen Kyōkai (The Okinawa Industrial Development Youth Association).[2]

The project team bureaucrats contended that the Job Corps had mainly served ethnic youth from poor backgrounds – many of whom had reading difficulties – and hence any 'Japanese version' of the scheme would have to be quite different.[3] Therefore, while this American programme gave the Youth Independence Camp some legitimacy, it never was used as a model in the literal sense of the term. Instead, the project team was more interested in the domestic private sector schemes they discovered. It was these schemes that seemed to embody ideas highly similar to those of the administrative vice minister (the 'sponsor'). No particular Japanese programmes were singled out as explicit policy models either (unlike in the case of the Youth Support Station), but the existence of camp-style training programmes on Japanese soil convinced the key bureaucrats that Japan indeed had a pre-existing 'climate' (*fūdo*) that was hospitable to *juku*-based training in communal settings. This made the policy-makers more assured of the viability of the Youth Independence Camp.

The project team disagreed over whether to build new facilities to house the new scheme or to utilize existing infrastructure. The innovator persuaded the others that investing funds in the construction of new buildings would be unwise as a new programme could very well fail, and as its delivery could be delegated to various pre-existing private institutions. This was as far as the initial project team took the scheme; further design aspects were largely left up to the chief of the CDSO.

The chief had to next deal with the wish of the sponsor to turn the Independence Camp into a means to 'rediscipline' (*kitaenaosu*) sluggish youth by 'beating them into shape' (*tatakinaosu*). The head of the Health, Labour and Welfare policy council (*shingikai*) at the time – Mr Nagase Jinen of the Liberal Democratic Party who eventually became the Minister of Justice in 2006 – articulated a similar preference. Both of these actors were in their late middle-ages and their attitudes clearly reflected earlier mainstream thinking on the socialization of children and youth through the application of harsh discipline, as set out in the Preface to this volume.

However, the innovator firmly rejected such ideas due to feasibility and safety concerns. While he did not outright deny the potential benefits of disciplinarian training, the official argued that implementing such training would not be possible on a wide scale in the absence of a military draft system (*chōheisei*) that could be used to forcefully recruit participants. Who would voluntarily enrol in a disciplinary programme in the absence of such enforcement? In addition to the difficulty he foresaw with attracting enrollees, the innovator pointed out that harsh (so-called) Spartan education – that typically entailed corporal punishment (*taibatsu*) in one form another – always came with significant safety risks. The infamous Totsuka Yacht School incidents of the 1970s and the 1980s (in which a number of students had lost their lives) had, by the 2000s, helped to compromise the public image of disciplinarian varieties of 'education'.[4] The bureaucrat told me in several personal interviews that there was simply no way that the government could risk getting implicated in similar incidents.[5]

The innovator's solution was to define the Youth Independence Camp as a measure to 're-educate' (*sodatenaoshi*), rather than discipline, non-working youth. This term had a much more positive, open-ended ring to it than the tougher alternatives pushed by senior figures. The innovator anticipated that the Independence Camp could succeed only if it made its methods agreeable to young people and their parents. The same official never formulated in detail what *sodatenaoshi* was to mean in practice, though, but he did envision that it would comprise emphatic peer counselling in group settings, closely resembling his vision for the Young Job Spot (see Chapter 2). He also hoped that career consulting, that had long been a key item of interest for his section, would play a role in the Camp.

Importantly, the bureaucrat conceptualized the Independence Camp programme as consisting of two main stages. The first would see enrollees develop their attitudes and 'social orientation' (*shakaisei*) through communal living, while work trials and volunteer activities would help them to cultivate their 'work consciousness' (*shigoto ishiki*) in the second one. The outcome was that the initial disciplinarian leanings of the programme came to be significantly diluted, although an emphasis on a regular daily rhythm was retained. Ironically, the scheme would nevertheless come to be portrayed by government as a disciplinarian, correctional measure, for this was consistent with public understandings of *NEETs* as lazy and therefore undeserving of anything but punitive policy measures.

Once the disciplinarian leanings had been negotiated, the next hurdle the innovator had to face had to do with the scope and objectives of the Youth Independence Camp. Crucially, he needed to gain the approval of the Ministry of Finance in order to be granted a budget. It became very clear in late 2004 that finance bureaucrats were far less sympathetic towards the issue of youth support than MHLW officials and affiliated politicians. As we will see, the innovator was ultimately forced to compromise on three counts, having to revise the (quantifiable) achievement targets of the scheme, its main objectives, and the programme's total budget and therefore its scope.

The first two revisions – perhaps the most critical changes – meant that the Youth Independence Camp, on the level of policy design, became rather narrowly focused on employment as an end-goal and as the dominant criterion by which its performance was to be measured. The Ministry of Finance (MoF) threatened it would withhold any funding if the MHLW did not commit to guiding 70 per cent of Independence Camp enrollees to paid employment within half a year of completing the programme. This preoccupation with paid work (*shūrō*) – that was bound up with the popular image of *NEETs* at this point – later came under bitter criticism from young activists, practitioners and sympathetic scholars. The innovator also knew that, in light of the complex problems that many *NEETs* faced, having over two-thirds of Independence Camp participants secure a job after programme completion would be a tall order, but he had little choice but to comply with the MoF's requirements.

Furthermore, the MoF made it practically impossible to direct camp enrollees to educational institutions, pointing out that such an arrangement would require cumbersome collaborative policy-making between the MHLW and MEXT (the success of which the innovator conceded that he was highly sceptical about also). Making paid work the sole objective of the programme was not what the innovator had had in mind: he viewed employment as the 'final result' in a long process where underlying problems were gradually moderated, not as something that could necessarily be achieved right away. He also felt that, for youth who had fallen into an ambiguous zone between formal institutions, it should, in all fairness, be 'enough' if they broke away from the *NEET* condition (*nīto kara no dakkyaku ga daiji*) whether this was through education, training or employment.

A further blow was the MoF's decision to grant a budget that was a mere third of the sum requested by the MHLW (980 million instead of 2.7 billion yen). This meant that, instead of the planned 40 camps across Japan, only 20 could be opened in the first year. Such a drastic reduction disappointed the two bureaucrats who had designed the scheme: they had thought that requesting funds for just 40 centres had already amounted to a cautious strategy (they had indeed originally hoped to open many more camps). That the proposed budget was reduced despite plans to introduce an enrolment fee (which was to cover roughly 50 per cent of total expenses) further illustrates the magnitude of resistance to the Independence Camp from the MoF.

As for enrolment fees, key bureaucrats took it as a given that participants should bear associated housing and subsistence costs, even as training itself would be provided free of charge. Indeed, three leading bureaucrats whom I interviewed in May 2007 (after the innovator had left the CDSO) viewed user charges as 'hotel fees' rather than as fees for training per se. In the first two years, fees came to 280,000 yen per three months of training on the average, making enrolment practically dependent on parental sponsorship but, importantly, within the reach of many middle-class parents (see Chapter 5).[6] There is, moreover, no doubt that policy-makers had little choice but to attach a fee to the Independence Camp as they anticipated resistance not only from the MoF but also from the public: using taxpayers' money to provide free accommodation to 'undeserving', deviant *NEETs* who had paid little if any taxes was simply unimaginable due to the predominantly negative portrayal of this group at the time. That it was thought that *NEETs* mainly originated in affluent middle-class families instead of poverty-stricken households made the imposition of fees seem more or less 'natural' (see Chapter 3). The shape of the public *NEET* discourse thus had a pervasive effect on the kinds of policies and resources that could be targeted at this group.

However, it is worth pondering further why it was that the MoF's reaction to the Youth Independence Camp was indeed so negative. Why did it decide to give the scheme such a minimal budget, which amounted to just a tiny fraction within the total budget of the Youth Independence and Challenge Plan? One major reason was that the ministry saw the main target group of the Independence Camp as youth who 'had not worked properly' (*chanto hataraiteinai*) and who therefore had not paid into, and gained eligibility for support from, the Japanese special employment insurance account (*koyō tokubetsu kaikei*). It is this account from which employment training programmes have typically been funded in Japan. The only available alternative, in terms of funding '*NEET* support', was thus to draw on the general tax account (*ippan kaikei*), yet this was virtually unheard of in the realm of active labour market schemes. Consequently, the MoF was extremely reluctant to award a sizeable budget to the Independence Camp, a scheme it correctly suspected would arouse considerable criticism from various quarters. Had there been a viable way to draw on the employment insurance account, the Independence Camp might have enjoyed a much larger budget and, by extension, youth activation policy in Japan might have taken a very different direction on the whole.

Nevertheless, that a budget was finally granted to such an unprecedented programme for an unprecedented target group – youth with modest or non-existent work histories who would not normally have qualified for tax-funded public measures – was in hindsight viewed as something of a landmark achievement by the innovator and by pundits such as Genda. The key bureaucrats contended that, regardless of the modest scope of the programme they had enacted, a start was still a start, and hoped that they could later increase the number of Youth Independence Camps across Japan. They also wished to potentially expand the length of the training period that was at first set at only three months, partly for budget reasons.[7]

Before turning to the case of the Youth Support Station, the expert committee that was summoned in mid-2004 by the innovator to discuss how the Youth Independence Camp might be developed further deserves a brief mention. While at least three of its eight members – Genda Yūji, Miyamoto Michiko and Kosugi Reiko – were taking part in official government policy councils (*shingikai*) around the same time, this particular committee was intended for the more informal exchange of views on youth support (hence its name, *Wakamono Jiritsu Juku Setsuritsu Junbi Kondankai*, the 'informal study group for preparing for the establishment of the Youth Independence Camp').

In the absence of public records, it is difficult to ascertain the topics that it discussed, but three notable points are known. First, the expert committee included one young member, Kudō Kei, an enterprising youth support manager who was only 27 years old at the time. Since government committees tend to heavily favour senior or at least middle-aged experts, this was a highly symbolic development, demonstrating a certain understanding among key policy-makers that youth policies could benefit from incorporating young people's insights. Second, the bulk of policy-making had in fact taken place before this expert committee could be summoned; hence, the latter's influence remained limited to matters of detail. However, for the leading policy-maker, discussions with the committee led to a better understanding of the field of youth support, helping him to enhance the viability of the Youth Independence Camp. Third, the committee transformed in 2005 to the official Youth Independence Camp Expert Committee (*Wakamono Jiritsu Juku Senmon Kaigi*) to screen and choose actual delivery organizations (more on which is said below). This Expert Committee, just like the informal study group that predated it, was chaired by Sakaguchi Junji, a veteran of Japanese youth work who had played a key role in the field in the 1960s and 1970s (see Chapter 2). That his assistance was recruited in the 2000s can be viewed as a means to ensure a measure of continuity in policy. In addition to its formal role, the members of this committee became de facto patrons of the programme, penning notes of encouragement and advice for an array of pamphlets and handbooks as well as appearing at a range of youth policy events, from parents' meetings to large discussion forums and national youth policy liaison conferences (which typically were held under the banner of Wakachare, the 'state-society movement' to promote young people's independence and challenge-taking, reviewed in Chapter 2).

Despite the many constraints explained above, the policy-making process that produced the Youth Independence Camp reflected a small but non-trivial shift in Japanese social policy: there was now a tacit acknowledgement that not all *freeters* or *NEETs* were part-time workers or jobless out of their own volition. Through enacting new employment measures, the government agreed to take on some responsibility for supporting underemployed and non-employed youth, recognizing thus the limits of parental families who tended to be left alone with their workless offspring (Toivonen 2008). Although the shift in the public youth discourse from a preoccupation with the socially withdrawn *hikikomori* to a new focus on *NEETs* was a crucial precondition to policy change (Chapter 3), tangible policy-making efforts were spearheaded by two influential bureaucrats in this realm, the sponsor and the innovator. The next section observes how the same pair collaborated in the making of a second initiative of interest, the Youth Support Station.

The Youth Support Station: The promise of local support networks

While pleased with the successful launch of the Independence Camp in 2005, the proponents of this small programme quickly realized that it could not reach all young adults in need of support.[8] This is why, at the peak of the *NEET* debate in February 2005, the administrative vice minister of the MHLW (the sponsor) approached the innovator regarding what he would like to do as a 'follow-up'. The former was in haste to meet an internal ministry deadline for new proposals and insisted that his subordinate present him with a new blueprint by the following morning, immediately after which the latter was scheduled to leave town on an official trip. Fortunately, by this time, the innovator had already spent a great amount of time on developing a concept for a new youth support programme and, sure enough, his proposal was soon chosen over a competing design put forth by the Shokugyō Antei Kyoku of the same ministry (MHLW). It was based on this abruptly elicited blueprint that Japan's most extensive new youth inclusion measure, the Youth Support Station, was born in late 2006.

If anything, the policy-making process behind the Youth Support Station was bafflingly straightforward: once the sponsor (the administrative vice minister) had approved the original concept presented by the innovator, the rest was taken care of by the latter without aid from any internal or external committees.[9] Some might disagree with this account because it seemed, at the time, that the Cabinet Office Committee on Comprehensive Independence Support Measures for Youth (convened in 2004–05 and chaired by Miyamoto Michiko) had a strong hand in the development of the Support Station. However, reflecting the fragmented nature of the Japanese government and its various councils, this Cabinet Office committee indeed represented a 'parallel track' in youth policy deliberations, and thus its recommendations did not directly influence the making of the Youth Support Station. As of the mid-2000s at least, hands-on policy-making in the area of youth employment support was still the prerogative of the MHLW.

Before investigating in more detail the core concepts and objectives that the Youth Support Station came to embody, it is necessary to first address a key puzzle surrounding its origins. Indeed, from the moment it was enacted in 2006, the Youth Support Station came to be intimately and almost universally associated with the British Connexions Service for 13- to 19-year-olds who were 'at risk of social exclusion' (see Chapter 1).[10] But was it really the case that the Support Station was, in a substantive sense, a 'policy import' modelled closely on the Connexions scheme? Or were there other models, precedents and ideas that exerted an altogether stronger influence in the policy-making process?

In its country of origin, it may be pointed out, the Connexions Service had been the Blair Government's response to a perceived need for a more coherent and integrated service for 'at-risk' youth who were, or might become, NEETs. Launched in 2001, this programme intended to reorganize various existing services such as the Careers Service, the Youth Service and other specialist agencies. It was not, therefore, a completely 'new' policy innovation as such. Notably, Japanese actors organized several study trips, including a ministerial-level visit, to Connexions Service centres in London in the mid-2000s. The Cabinet Office moreover begun developing a 'youth advisor' training scheme based on the Personal Advisor system of Connexions (Cabinet Office 2008b).

In the Japanese context, that Connexions became so widely noted relates to its partial portrayal as the ideal '*NEET* countermeasure' by important policy entrepreneurs within and without the government. Most saliently, Miyamoto Michiko, a senior professor of family sociology at the University of Air (Hōsō Daigaku) in Chiba, promoted the 'Connexions model' (along with Swedish youth policies) relentlessly in her books, academic articles, on websites, at public forums, in newspapers and in government committees (see, for instance, Miyamoto 2002, 2004). A key figure in Japan's youth policy community, Miyamoto brought attention to what she viewed as an important concept, embedded in Connexions, of a 'comprehensive' and 'integrated' youth support policy. The act of highlighting Connexions within Japanese policy-making circles and claiming that it represented a highly promising, encompassing support scheme allowed Miyamoto to more persuasively argue that Japan lacked comprehensive youth services and that such services should be urgently enacted.[11]

It is ironic that, despite Miyamoto's energetic efforts and the ample media coverage that the Connexions received, it was ultimately not taken up as a main policy model by the innovator who was in charge of crafting the Youth Support Station. The reason he gave for this decision was two-fold. First, he could simply not imagine that a budget of anywhere near similar proportions could be secured in Japan as had been secured for Connexions in the UK under Blair (the innovator, 30 August 2008). Second, he had by 2005 located two attractive policy models of domestic origin that he thought were far more relevant to the development of new youth measures in Japan. One of these models was that of a comparatively large rehabilitation centre in Chiba for delinquent youth (*hikō*) that served several hundred young people at a time. The second was one developed by a private youth support organization for non-school-attending children and socially withdrawn youth that, as of the mid-2000s, boasted a history of around 30 years. The innovator noted how this second group had built close relations with small local enterprises and welfare services, leveraging a vast network for the benefit of its young supportees.

Instead of the more abstract-sounding concepts promoted by Miyamoto, it was precisely these concrete, domestic examples of linked-up local support initiatives that inspired the key concept of the Support Station as far as the innovator was concerned. In several interviews, he recounted how he had, in making and then explaining the Youth Support Station, consistently emphasized the building of new 'organic networks' that could make use of diverse and pre-existing, but still poorly connected, local resources.[12] His was thus an innovation, inspired by implicit precedents (that were never publicly stated), in social and institutional recombination. In a public presentation he delivered at Tokyo University in 2006, the policy-maker listed particular resources he wished to 'link up' through the Support Station, including the following:

1) public employment services such as Young Hello Work centres;
2) public occupational training schools (*shokugyō kunren-kō*);
3) private youth support groups, including, but not limited to, NPOs;
4) public health centres and mental welfare centres (*seishin fukushi sentā*) that catered to the *hikikomori* as well as those with mental health problems and developmental disabilities;

5) newly opened public support centres for the developmentally disabled (*hattatsu shōgaisha shien sentā*);
6) public work and livelihood support centres for the disabled (*shōgaisha shūgyō seikatsu shien sentā*; developed in collaboration by the ministries of Labour and Health and Welfare before their unification).

Taken together, these resources could furnish treatment for mental health problems; opportunities for engaging in group activities as well as in work trials; occupational skill training; and, finally, support in the job-seeking process. In the new scheme, referring young users to appropriate institutions would be the job of clinical psychologists and career consultants who would be hired as key staff. Local governments would be expected to play an active role in supporting the new programme, and eventually they would need to take responsibility for financing it. The Working Youth's Homes, conspicuously absent from the above list, could not be incorporated into this menu of support services – very much against the innovator's wishes – for reasons to be explained below.

It should not be missed here that the Young Job Spot (see Chapter 2), as the Youth Support Station's predecessor, acted as another implicit 'model' for the latter. Indeed, it is possible to retrospectively consider the former as a 'pilot programme' for the Support Station. According to the innovator, the Young Job Spot was ultimately unsuccessful because the majority of organizations that were charged with delivering it failed to build sufficient support networks beyond their own walls: they tended to 'hoard' work and attempt to 'do too much' by themselves. This failure to tap into various local resources convinced the key bureaucrat of the centrality of network-building efforts, prompting him to make it a more salient feature of the Support Station (other notable features that were added at this stage included mental health counselling by qualified clinical psychologists as well as more rigorous record-keeping practices). All of this had made the innovator highly sceptical of the 'one-stop shop' concept that (he thought) Connexions – as well as the Job Café – represented. In his mind, it was both impossible and inefficient to provide socially excluded youth with all necessary services at a single location due to the complexity of issues that needed attention.

A driving goal of the innovator was to institutionalize his policy ideas in the form of the Youth Support Station so as to catalyze the formation of organic local youth support networks across Japan. His implementation strategy was to first ask leading youth support 'veterans' (and some newer experts) to establish a handful of model centres in the Tokyo metropolitan area and in Yokohama that could then provide leadership and examples to Youth Support Stations established elsewhere (see below regarding the administrative aspects of implementation).

Viewed in the Japanese context, the innovator's network-based youth support concept, while not totally unique, was rather unconventional. It strived to overcome the formidable sectionalism of bureaucratic decision-making and social services and to harness the resources of a disorganized, and often discordant, private youth support sector. Chapters 5 and 6 will describe in some detail how network-building has proceeded at sites of youth support in actuality.

By way of a brief theoretical summary, it is possible to perceive of the policy-making process behind the Youth Support Station with reference to Kingdon's (2003) 'visible' and 'hidden' clusters of policy-making. External policy entrepreneurs such as Miyamoto and Cabinet Office committees clearly belonged to the first cluster, while bureaucrats operated within the second. In the Japanese context, these same dimensions are sometimes described as the *omote* (the outer surface or facade) and the *ura* (the hidden, implicit side) of bureaucratic decision-making. What this section has effectively uncovered is a situation where the policy ideas propounded by academics such as Miyamoto – who achieve high exposure through books, articles and the Internet – end up obscuring what unfolds in the less visible and perhaps more mundane realm of hands-on policy-making. Also obscured are power relationships which dictate that key decisions regarding youth employment policy are still taken by MHLW bureaucrats rather than scholars (or other experts), research centers or the Cabinet Office. One implication is that foreign policy models such as Connexions tangibly shape youth policy-making only when they are taken up by the MHLW officials directly in charge of crafting actual programmes.

Finally, it is worth highlighting that the Support Station (just like the Youth Independence Camp) was a case of 'solutions before problems'-type policy-making, also discussed in the classic work of Kingdon. The innovator had developed the key concept for the programme well before an opportunity finally presented itself, with the emergence of the *NEET* debate, to turn it into a concrete blueprint with a real budget. He had, in fact, presented a similar blueprint to the administrative vice minister some years earlier, but had been turned down, partly because the senior bureaucrat did not like the innovator's ideas about rejuvenating the old Working Youth's Homes ('sponsor', 26 November 2008), but also clearly because there was no youth discourse that could provide the necessary momentum. Reflecting on the process, the sponsor and the innovator acknowledged that timing indeed was crucial to the introduction of new policy ideas in their realm. This may explain why the Support Station, the second policy for non-employed youth, enacted amid the most intense period in the *NEET* debate, encountered significantly less resistance within the government than the Youth Independence Camp did.[13]

Because this section has focused on the key ideas behind the Youth Support Station, it has omitted important strategic and practical issues. These are taken up in the following section where I examine the justification of the new youth policies as well as the implementation of the Support Station and the Independence Camp.

Strategic dimensions of youth policy-making

Although policy-makers puzzle and seek solutions to tangible problems, they must also be highly strategic if they are to turn their ideas into actual programmes.

Strategy was indeed of tremendous importance to the innovator and sponsor as they sought to enact the Youth Independence Camp and the Youth Support Station. This was because youth activation policies for *NEETs* had no direct precedents in Japan (while not being devoid of historical roots; see Chapter 2) and targeted a group that was largely portrayed, in mainstream media, as undeserving of beneficial support measures. It was far from sufficient that the discourse had, after 2004, shifted from a focus on the socially withdrawn *hikikomori* to the issue of non-employed *NEETs*: policy-makers still had to justify the particular schemes they were promoting and explain why tax-payers' money should be spent on measures for youth who appeared 'lazy' and affluent. Here, it was necessary to engage in acts of justification within the government, while simultaneously making the new programmes more palatable to the media and the wider public. Finally, to move the two schemes towards the implementation stage, key officials needed to delegate duties to suitable external agencies, which, in turn, had to operationalize the considerably vague *NEET* category. This led to a contrasting and far narrower definition of non-employed youth who could be targeted by emerging activation measures. I briefly review each of these issues next.

How did the MHLW bureaucrats in charge of new youth activation programmes defend and justify their ideas within the universe of central government agencies? The main strategy was to lean on a strictly utilitarian argument: the officials consistently stressed that, without support measures, thousands of *NEETs* would inevitably fall into poverty in the future, thereby becoming a strain on government finances ('sponsor', 26 November 2008). In responding to my question on the extent of the government's responsibility for supporting *NEETs*, a leading bureaucrat at the Career Development Support Office offered to clarify that it was in fact budgetary imperatives that made such support necessary:

> That is indeed an extremely, or the most, difficult theme for us. And, well, the point is we use taxes to fund our various activities; taxes are their basis. We do use tax money but, put simply, if we leave NEETs as they are, it is likely they will turn into targets for livelihood assistance [*seikatsu hogo*]. Yes, we can expect this to result in a burden in the future. So, facing this, we are taking action so as to have such youth swiftly return to work, or to a place of work.[14]

Such reasoning resonated within the government at a time when it was deeply concerned over rising social expenditures amid population aging and low economic growth rates. But the same argument was not so persuasive vis-a-vis the wider society where most commentators thought less about the future expenditure implications of *NEETs* and more about whether this group of youth deserved tax-funded programmes to begin with. To counter the negative public image of non-employed youth, policy-makers and scholars alike chose to argue that new support measures would be directed not to all young people who were out of work, but only to those *NEETs* who had the motivation to find employment. In other words, they strived to carve out a 'deserving' sub-group within the main *NEET* category. Genda had already attempted this by creating sub-categories of *NEETs* such as the so-called *kibō-gata* and *hikibō-gata* – those who wished to find work and those who did not (Chapter 3). Kosugi, also, had supplied a culturalist four-fold taxonomy of non-employed youth which essentially achieved the same thing, distinguishing 'deserving' young people who were legitimately in need of support from morally suspect ones. In a presentation delivered in late 2006, the innovator drew on Kosugi's distinctions when he argued that it was surely the so-called 'yankee-type *NEETs*' – frivolous and trouble-making jobless young people – that the critics of new youth measures were talking about, and that the government was interested in supporting only those with legitimate needs.

There is another more implicit way in which key bureaucrats tried to make *NEET* support policies agreeable to the public: they made new programmes appear disciplinarian. Descriptions of the Youth Independence Camp, the first measure for *NEETs*, made it particularly clear that the government was to 'be tough' on such youth. The 2005 MHLW White Paper announced that they were to be reformed through 'camp-living' (*gasshuku seikatsu*) whereby they would gain 'the basic skills needed as a member of society and a worker' and improve their 'work-attitudes' (MHLW 2005a:274). The scheme was to target youth who had 'insufficient living habits and work motivation that are the precondition for social and occupational life, and due to being unable to break off their dependence on their parents, are not receiving education or training and are unable to work' (MHLW 2005a:274). Although the tone softened in the following year – the target group was now described as youth who had 'lost their confidence to work for various reasons', reflecting Genda's phrasing (Genda and Maganuma 2004) – there was no question that most people who heard of the scheme instantly associated it with correctional and rather harsh 'boot camp'-style training (see MHLW 2006:234). Moreover, official descriptions of the Youth Support Station began by explaining that *NEETs* needed to be taught basic 'human competence' (*ningenryoku*; see Chapter 2) in addition to cultivating their occupational consciousness (*shokugyō ishiki*). Also, although the nuances varied, in most policy descriptions and press releases, '*NEET* policies' were listed under measures for 'raising young people's work motivation' (*wakamono no rōdō iyoku wo takameru tame no torikumi*).

The symbolic message was thus clear: non-employed youth were dependent; lacked in work motivation; and needed fundamental, tough training to become 'proper members of society'. I argue that such a portrayal helped pre-empt, or at least to moderate, public resistance to new youth support schemes; it may have even been a necessary strategy considering the mood at the time and steep generational differences in attitudes to discipline and socialization (with those in the fifties and sixties expecting, on the whole, relatively harsh approaches). As Chapters 5 to 6 will illustrate, this disciplinarian image of youth support was, however, completely at odds with actual support practices that took on much softer, accommodating characteristics. It was, importantly, never the initial plan of the innovator to introduce disciplinarian youth support programmes, but he could see the benefits of pandering to lingering expectations that hard discipline was the best response to what seemed an alarming proliferation of young 'slackers'.

Towards implementation: Operationalizing 'NEET support'

The present chapter has so far focused on matters of policy ideas and policy-making strategy, but it is also vital to explain how the Youth Independence Camp and the Youth Support Station were taken towards the implementation stage. Though it remained ultimately responsible for policy implementation, the Career Development Support Office of the MHLW did not have the resources or time to deal with the day-to-day running and development of these schemes, so it decided to outsource important duties, to the following agencies and committees:

1) Japan Productivity Centre for Socio-Economic Development (JPCSED), a government-affiliated, semi-autonomous non-profit organization: runs national 'support centres' that take inquiries, promote policies, organize staff training and collect information on practical problems and solutions in youth support;
2) Civil society groups (NPOs) and other private organizations: deliver the actual services based on their pre-existing expertise and resources, hiring support staff and making efforts to locate support-seekers as well as local collaborators;
3) The Youth Independence Camp Expert Committee: chooses delivery organizations through formal screening procedures and monitors their compliance.

The delegation of the practical administration of social policies to semi-autonomous and professionalized not-for-profit organizations reflects an established practice of the Japanese government. Known as *gaikaku dantai* (affiliated organizations), such organizations are expected to act as extensions of the government, allowing the latter to control the size of the national civil service and to also generate post-retirement jobs for elderly bureaucrats (known as *amakudari*). On the other hand, the recruitment of civil society and other private groups as delivery organizations is part of a more recent trend that, according to Estevez-Abe, only fully began with the introduction of the Elderly Health and Welfare Law and the Gold Plan in 1990 and 1992, respectively (Estevez-Abe 2003:164). In the case of elderly people's services as well as new youth programmes, the reasons for creating partnerships with private groups were similar: their cooperation was sought because traditional partners – such as social welfare councils and welfare commissioners (*minsei-iin*) – were found to be either ineffective or simply unresponsive to new kinds of demands. In the case of youth policy, the most obvious 'traditional partners' in local communities had formerly been the Working Youths' Homes that were introduced in Chapter 2.

Although their reduced relevance was already noted, why is it that the pre-existing Working Youth's Homes could not be rejuvenated and tasked with delivering, say, the Youth Support Station scheme? In fact, this is exactly what the key bureaucrat (the innovator) had attempted: with around 500 Working Youth's Homes still in operation in the early 2000s, he had hoped that many of them could be converted into Youth Support Stations at the time that this new programme was being developed. One clear benefit of this would have been cost savings, and, although never mentioned by the innovator directly, the use of a pre-existing public scheme would surely have given the government more direct control over support activities. Yet, with their existence guaranteed by the Law Regarding the Welfare of Young Workers (1970), and with a limited number of staff – most of whom were elderly – efforts to recruit the cooperation of Working Youths' Homes were unsuccessful: only two out of the 500 centres eventually expressed interest. This, as well as the pessimistic attitudes of the sponsor to cooperating with the Working Youths' Homes, left the innovator little choice but to turn to NPOs and local governments to host what would become the new flagship youth policy of the Career Development Support Office.

The government also summoned a small Youth Independence Camp Expert Committee to help choose which private groups should be made into accredited delivery organizations of the Independence Camp. Observing how screening was conducted allows us to better understand why, despite certain disciplinarian tendencies in their designs, actual youth support practices took on an 'accommodating' character. First, the expert committee filtered out the 'least professional' and most 'risky' groups that were thought could produce deathly accidents which would, in turn, quickly tarnish the public reputation of the whole scheme. It was clearly safety and past achievements (*jisseki*) that made a successful applicant. Second, by putting in place certain requirements, the Expert Committee could engage in what amounted to the indirect regulation of a segment of private-sector youth support (Chapter 2), defined by diversity in history, philosophy and practices. This represented the first intervention of the state into this hitherto unregulated sector, although the subsequent monitoring of approved groups has not necessarily been very rigorous beyond the auditing of expenses. For the youth support groups themselves, government accreditation was important for the subsidies it brought, but it also acted as a vital 'badge of honour' that improved their standing and image in local communities (enabling them to build trust relations with various local institutions).

On the other hand, no external expert committee was called to oversee the choice of groups to run the Youth Support Station. Instead, interested organizations were required to seek the formal approval and recommendation of their local government before they could apply to deliver this scheme. Unsurprisingly, successful applicants have mainly comprised experienced youth support organizations, groups that already ran an Independence Camp and boards of education that had close relations with local governments.

Beyond the three types of organizations the government has utilized, it has pursued certain additional strategies in governing the variety of youth support groups that have chosen to cooperate with it. I argue that this has consisted essentially of creating a 'participatory feel' through the granting of prestigious prizes for 'exemplary practice'. On the first count, several national and regional meetings have been held each year since 2005 between government officials, the JPCSED, the expert committee and practitioners. Usually called *renraku kaigi* (liaison conference) or *zenkoku kaigi* (national meeting), these meetings have comprised explanatory speeches by leading bureaucrats, informational presentations of various public and private youth support initiatives and group discussions regarding practical conundrums that have surfaced in the course of youth work at Independence Camps and Support Stations. Thus, such events have opened a regular communication channel between practitioners and the government, making it easier for the latter to explain its policies to the former and to efficiently grasp what is taking place at sites of youth support.

In 2007 alone, youth support practitioners were given prestigious awards not only by the MHLW but also by Prime Minister Abe himself. The awards were conferred at formal, rather ceremonial events in central Tokyo and were typically covered visibly in the media. During Abe's rule, the conferral of such awards was part of his 'second challenge' (*sai-charenji*) agenda that sought to promote alternative routes to the labour markets for those who had 'failed' before. At the same time, their implicit purpose seems to have been to gently steer civil society groups towards practices desired by the government. Since the awards themselves did not entail large money prizes, they can be seen as part of a low-cost youth policy strategy where subsidies are kept small while promoting the prestige of youth support actors and organizations.

Before concluding this chapter, it pays to briefly observe how the *NEET* category came to be operationalized at the national level just as the Youth Independence Camp – Japan's first youth activation policy – was about to be implemented. The website of the national Youth Independence Camp Support Centre (run by the JPCSED just mentioned) stated, that as a rule, eligible applicants were those 15- to 34-year-olds who had completed compulsory education and been out of work, schooling and training continuously for over a year without (formally) seeking jobs in this period. Moreover, eligible applicants had past job-seeking experience and were unmarried (JPCSED 2007a).

This amounts to a significantly narrowed-down definition of *NEET*, which limited the number of potential Independence Camp enrollees, prioritizing those were are inactive but at the same time relatively 'close' to the labour markets. The requirement, imposed by the Ministry of Finance, to have 70 per cent of all participants enter paid work upon programme completion no doubt encouraged this focus on comparatively employable jobless youth and discouraged considering the needs of more 'serious' cases (where three months would be obviously insufficient for overcoming obstacles to employment).

By contrast, the Youth Support Station's target group was defined much more openly, partly due to its role as the 'first stop' for any youth aged 15 to 34 who sought support in progressing towards employment. Indeed, the official portal site operated by the JPCSED stated that one of the main roles of the Support Station was simply to identify the kinds of youth who needed support and the types of support that were appropriate for them (JPCSED 2007a). The hope was that, once various support-seekers were identified and their issues diagnosed, they could be referred to appropriate institutions in the local networks of each Support Station (such as psychiatrists, job training courses and local companies). This task, as documented in Chapter 6, was not to be completed as easily as policy-makers and the JPCSED had initially hoped.

One point that this leaves unclear is whether hard-to-access groups such as the socially withdrawn *hikikomori* were to be targeted by new youth support measures or not. Considerable ambiguity remained regarding this issue during my fieldwork period in 2007–08. The MHLW bureaucrats I interviewed took great pains to explain the position of their ministry which, at the time, appeared contradictory: policy was to target only those *hikikomori* who were able to leave their houses to actively request support as they strived to 're-enter society' (three leading bureaucrats, 30 May 2007). In other words, the new youth measures could not reach seriously withdrawn youth (due to lacking the capacities and rights to enter private houses and rooms that this would require). The bureaucrats did hope, though, that the programmes could offer a means of return to the labour markets for healthy young adults who had temporarily shut themselves in their rooms, having lost confidence (*jishin*) after having failed at numerous job interviews during the 1990s' 'Employment Ice Age' (*koyō hyōgaki*). So, in this sense a disconnect and plenty of confusion resulted from the shift in discourse from the *hikikomori* to *NEET*, though it can be concluded that withdrawn youth were partly included within the scope of the latter target group. It was, however, announced in fiscal 2008, that there would be a pilot 'outreach' programme that would make it possible for a number of Youth Support Stations to send staff for 'family visits' (*katei hōmon*) – just as Japanese schools used to routinely do – to invite withdrawn youth to sites of support (although it is hard to predict whether such initiatives will proliferate as they are associated with considerable risks).[15]

Much less surprising than the partial inclusion of the *hikikomori* in the target group was the implicit exclusion of delinquent youth, young homeless people and non-Japanese youth from the scope of the *NEET* category and indeed from 'youth independence support' altogether. It was perhaps assumed that juvenile reformatories (*kyōgoin*) and specialized NPOs would continue to cater for the first group. Homeless youth were largely ignored by policy until the emergence of the so-called *nettokafe nanmin* ('Internet café refugees') problem in 2007, which was constructed as a problem that was distinctive from that of *NEETs*. I never heard policy-makers mention young people of foreign or minority backgrounds as potential targets for youth policy, although a handful of practitioners said they hoped to help integrate such youth into Japanese society in the future. The exclusion of the above groups from youth inclusion policy designs makes apparent the middle-class, ethnically Japanese orientation of such policies although, in reality, actual users are not as homogeneous a group as official policy documents would suggest (see especially Chapter 6).[16]

Conclusions

This chapter traced in detail the policy-making processes that ultimately produced Japan's first activation programmes for non-employed young adults identified as *NEETs*. The focus was on the origins of key policy ideas as well as on the more specific, partly rhetorical strategies that central actors – mainly the two figures I have called the innovator and the sponsor – relied upon to negotiate against resistance to their plans. One interesting finding was that the frameworks for the Youth Independence Camp and the Youth Support Station were in fact developed well before non-employed young people appeared on the central government's policy agenda, but they could only be turned into concrete programmes with the fresh momentum delivered by the *NEET* discourse. Even then, the unfavourable public construction of this target group as 'lazy', affluent and therefore undeserving made it extremely difficult to argue for generous policies. The bureaucrats in charge maintained that the government had no choice but to 'invest' in support measures for this group to pre-empt a future increase in poor welfare claimants who might impose additional burdens on already strained state finances. Vis-a-vis the public and the mainstream media, they emphasized that their programmes would only benefit those sub-sets of *NEETs* that were 'truly deserving' and not those who were unemployed out of choice or who lacked appropriate morals.

The 'sympathetic bureaucrats' around which this account has centred were partly successful in tackling a climate that was predominantly hostile to youth policy-making, but in the end they could only receive paltry budgets. This, together with the demanding objective to have 70 per cent of enrollees find work at programme completion, subjected especially the Youth Independence Camp to a great risk of failure and ineffectiveness. A high degree of vulnerability was arguably built into this scheme, partly due to the effects of the undeserving image of *NEETs* and the lack of pre-existing policy frameworks and budget streams that could have been used to support non-employed young people (who have not paid into the regular employment insurance scheme). This helps explain why the Youth Independence Camp was suddenly abolished once the Democratic Party seized power and began aggressively cutting back government programmes under the banner of *jigyō shiwake* in 2009 (though, as Chapter 5 notes, the scheme survived in modified form).

The Youth Support Station, on the other hand, became something of an established youth policy in Japan towards the late 2000s. Yet it can in no way be said to offer a complete 'solution' to the *NEET* issue. A key reason for this is the fact that it lacks the capacity to financially support the more deprived groups among non-employed and precariously employed young people. This situation, once again, springs party from the negative public image of *NEETs*, which made it all but impossible to generously fund youth support policies in Japan. Nevertheless, the Youth Support Station, or at least the flagship centres, contain an important, sophisticated model for addressing youth inactivity and exclusion – that goes well beyond the salient features of 'symbolic activation' (Chapter 1) – in an age of ambiguity where youth marginalization is bound up with complex bundles of problems that concentrate on certain groups of young people. Chapter 6 will explore this model in depth and show that, rather than being rooted in the policy ideas set out above, it is, more than anything, an organic social innovation by grass-roots-level youth workers and youth support leaders. But first, the next chapter observes in detail the substance of the Youth Independence Camp and asks whether it provides a promising example of 'communities of recognition' that can, under certain conditions, point to further solutions to the post-industrial youth employment dilemma in Japan and beyond.

5 The Youth Independence Camp: Communities of recognition?

> Instead of pursuing vague ideals, Y-MAC [Yokohama Modern Apprenticeship Centre] puts first priority on 'concrete employment and independence support that fits the real society'. Helping our students to develop necessary work skills through workshops and training, we supply each individual with suitable suggestions regarding their future career. At the same time, we build ties with understanding companies at which our graduates can work without anxiety. Fostering a warm community where youth from similar circumstances can grow together, we offer a relaxed environment where our graduates, members of staff and families can live while supporting one another.
>
> From the brochure of K2 International's Youth Independence
> Camp programme (2007)

Very few among the observers of young people and social policy could have predicted that the first concrete activation programme for non-employed *NEETs* would, in the context of post-industrial Japan, assume the form of a residential 'life and work training' scheme. Yet this is precisely what transpired in 2005 when, as explained in Chapter 4, key actors within the Ministry of Health, Labour and Welfare developed and then successfully enacted the distinctive Youth Independence Camp (*Wakamono Jiritsu Juku*). Because the imagery of the *NEET* debate was strongly reflected in official descriptions of the Camp as well as in promotional posters such as that shown in Figure 5.1, it appeared, at first blush, that the programme was nothing less than the very embodiment of the desire of Japanese conservatives to punish 'lazy' unemployed 'slackers' who seemed to be putting their hard-working country to shame. So critical of jobless youth – and so evocative of Totsuka-style punitive training (see 'Preface') – was the official language around the Youth Independence Camp that even a sceptic would have been forgiven for viewing it as something of a disciplinarian policy-maker's dream.

Having begun the research project that ultimately led to this book with a tentative assumption that the Youth Independence Camp might indeed function as state-sanctioned 'boot camps' of some kind, the reader can only imagine my amazement as, through continued participant observation at several sites of support, a radically different reality gradually emerged. Individual young people were not dragged, resisting tooth and nail, to the affiliated facilities – which

Figure 5.1 An official promotional poster of the Youth Independence Camp by the Ministry of Health, Labour and Welfare

were located in both highly urban as well as rural areas – but instead often came out of their own initiative, or at least were gently persuaded to give the programme a try. Adopting what would to conservative pundits (if made aware of empirical realities behind the punitive image) seem a 'softly softly' approach, the staff (*sutaffu*) at the 30 or so Youth Independence Camps that existed in Japan as of 2007–08 (my fieldwork years) allowed their students (*jukusei*) to adapt at their own speed to varied training activities; no-one was forced to conform to any tight behavioural codes or undertake physically unpleasant tasks. Work training was conducted at a humane pace and came in diverse forms, from serving food to the homeless to harvesting tangerines and baking bread, with each activity addressing different local needs. Despite a general preference for early wake-ups at most Camps (encouraged, at one mountainous location I visited, through the beating of a *wadaiko* drum at 6 am each morning), it was understood that members did not always feel well enough to get up at the agreed time, and that sleeping in would not be severely sanctioned.

If not there to discipline unduly 'work-shy' 15- to 34-year-old *NEETs*, what were the Independence Camps really about? What was the more fundamental logic behind their relatively 'accommodating' approach (see Chapter 2) to youth employment activation, beyond a simple preference for a kinder treatment of young people? What was, in other words, the activation strategy that, notwithstanding superficial differences, was shared across the various Youth Independence Camps around Japan?

Based on fieldwork carried out over a period of one year, including repeated participant observation visits as a volunteer youth worker, I argue that the sociological significance of the Youth Independence Camp must be understood as deriving as much from its role as a community as from its designation as a site of employment support (*shūrō shien*). While embedded within the wider system of 'symbolic activation' that emerged in Japan in the mid-2000s, the Youth Independence Camp is indeed best viewed as a network of small but potent entities that may be referred to as 'communities of recognition' and that are open, rather than closed to non-members. While this concept should be read in terms of a Weberian ideal type, it nicely summarizes the finding that the Camps I visited foster *Gemeinshaft*-like but relatively egalitarian (internal) communities, while maintaining strong links with local (external) communities that they are located in. To address the dented self-esteem of their young members as well as the additional stigmatizing effects of labels such as *NEET* and *hikikomori*, they actively engage in various tangible practices of recognition that make it possible for individuals to establish a more positive sense of self and identity. These practices form a key element in a nuanced, multi-pronged process of activation that unfolds within local networks between Youth Independence Camp staff and various companies as well as not-for-profit organizations in the surrounding community.

To shed light on this contrasting logic of activation – quite different to that officially advocated by the Japanese state – this chapter first offers a brief analysis of the loose policy framework that underpinned the Youth Independence Camp between 2005 and 2009. A case study of a particular support organization called K2 International (located in Yokohama, Kanagawa Prefecture) forms the heart of this account, demonstrating how intricate youth support practices as well as communities of recognition have evolved in Japan under the guise of 'independence support' and behind the image of disciplinarian training.

The support process, as implemented by K2, is examined here in its entirety, followed by a crisp summary of main elements. Comparative observations of other similar organizations are provided next. While the primary focus throughout the chapter is on youth support staff and their leaders due to the fact that it is they who 'do' activation and largely determine key practices, a further section considers how supported youth themselves think of the goals of 'independence support'.

The chapter concludes with a consideration of the difficulties, despite relative success with social inclusion at the internal level, that the Independence Camps have faced with formal employment activation in a post-industrial, increasingly insecure labour market context. The tremendous further potential of the kind of 'open communities of recognition' that I believe Youth Independence Camps represent is a topic to which I return in Chapter 7. Together with Chapter 6, which highlights a second defining feature of youth support in 2000s Japan – that of youth work as a complex process of exploration – the present chapter forms the empirical core of this book. These chapters bring the larger story of symbolic activation forward by putting the spotlight, after an examination of the construction of *NEET* as a target for activation (Chapter 3) and of the policy-making process (Chapter 4), on actual youth support practices.

While at risk of slightly confusing the reader, in the following sections I employ not the past tense but the ethnographic present to describe my findings. This is despite the fact that the government-formulated Youth Independence Camp programme came to be suddenly abolished in 2009. This took place as the Democratic Party came to power and begun a high-visibility campaign known as *jigyō shiwake* to slash what it viewed as wasteful public spending commitments made under the Liberal Democratic Party. Yet, as is so often the case with media-friendly bids to abolish existing policies, the 'victim' survived in modified form under the title of *Gasshuku-gata Wakamono Jiritsu Jigyō* (Camp-type Youth Independence Programme). In practice this has meant that the more strongly established entities among those that delivered the Camp scheme between 2005 and 2009 still continue to run very similar programmes. The practices described in this chapter have thus not disappeared overnight, making it apparent that indeed they possess more continuity than Japan's highly changeable formal youth policy frameworks and youth problem debates (see Chapter 2 regarding the long roots of present-day youth support practices).

Youth Independence Camp as a government programme, 2005–09

> We started the Youth Independence Camp project in 2005 to target youth who have, for various reasons, lost their confidence so as to instil in them both work confidence and motivation through life training and work trials at collective camp-based living settings, and to so direct them to paid work.
>
> (MHLW 2006:174)

As set out in the previous chapter, the Youth Independence Camp came about as the Japanese government's first response to the '*NEET* crisis' in 2005, soon after the formulation of *NEET* as a target group for activation in 2003 and 2004. This section lays out its practical programmatic parameters. It needs to be stressed at the outset that these parameters amount to nothing more than a loose framework to support, and to some extent regulate, diverse practices at various sites of support. No new physical facilities were constructed, moreover, because it was thought more efficient to rely on existing private sector resources.

At its most basic, the Youth Independence Camp (*Wakamono Jiritsu Juku*) was officially intended as a three-month-long training programme during which participants are required to live communally and take part in various training activities. Descriptions of the scheme in MHLW white papers and elsewhere posit that the programme's key components comprise 'life training' (*seikatsu kunren*) as well as 'job trials' (*rōdō taiken*; see e.g. MHLW 2005a:274). The enrolment capacity of each Camp was set at roughly 20 individuals at any one time, with a total annual capacity of 1,200 in 2005, the scheme's initial year.

For reasons explained in Chapter 4, only 20 groups were initially appointed to deliver the programme in July 2005 under what was formally called the 'Project to Promote the Establishment of Youth Independence Camps' (*Wakamono Jiritsu Juku Sōshutsu Suishin Jigyō*). As the name implies, the Camp was intended as a time-limited measure, with the strengthening of self-sustaining youth support 'infrastructure' as its strategic objective ('innovator', personal e-mail communication, 21 February 2008). The key bureaucrat thus anticipated that, regardless of his own wishes for longer-term public commitment, the government would cease funding the scheme sooner or later. As of 2007–08, virtually all delivery organizations were acutely concerned over the survival of the Youth Independence Camp, feeling hard pressed to seek ways to ensure financial sustainability after the expiration of government support.

The official public objective of the Youth Independence Camp was set as 'teaching basic skills required of each member of society and of each professional worker', cultivating 'work-views' (*kinrōkan*), and guiding youth to paid work or occupational training while instilling in them 'work confidence' and 'motivation' (*hataraku koto ni tsuite no jishin to iyoku wo fuyo suru*; MHLW 2005a:274). These prescriptions are, however, decisively vague and (as argued in Chapter 4) should indeed be viewed primarily as strategic portrayals that respond to the negative public image of *NEETs*. In short, by relating the Youth Independence Camp so directly to dominant constructions of non-employed youth, actors within the MHLW thought they might be able to pre-empt some of the potential criticisms against government youth support measures.

In any case, all key bureaucrats were agreed that the Camp would comprise two main elements, developing, on the one hand, proper attitudes and sociability (*shakaisei*) through communal living while, on the other, also cultivating 'work consciousness' (*shigoto ishiki*) through concrete work trials and volunteer activities. This awareness was shared by Sakaguchi Junji, the chairman of the

Youth Independence Camp Expert Committee that developed the scheme further in late 2004. He framed the Camps as an initiative that aims to 'support the lives of young people who are trying to take one step forward [in their lives]', and that they are places where youth:

> *trust* one another and *learn* as they live together, *connect* with friends (*associate*), and gain communication skills as well as the courage to meet the *challenge* of work [italicized keywords emphasized in original text].
>
> (Youth Independence Camp Handbook Committee, 2007)

Sakaguchi's youth work philosophy, inspired by his exposure to British youth work ideas in the 1960s and 1970s, centres on the concepts (verbs) of 'trust', 'learn', 'associate' and 'challenge', thereby merging older pedagogical thinking with new concerns over communication abilities and employment (that characterized the *NEET* debate in the mid-2000s). In this philosophy, staff are expected to build trusting relationships with students and to study their concerns in the context of communal living; they are not 'teachers' (*sensei*) but rather facilitators who – through applying their whole characters and through their passion for youth work – act as the 'mediators' of growth and learning (Sakaguchi 2007:78). These ideas, as will be shown below, reflected actual support practices fairly accurately.

It should not be missed that, alongside these objectives and pedagogical underpinnings, the Independence Camp was, in the course of the policy-making process that led to its establishment, given one central (but publicly unannounced) achievement target that would heavily shape actual support practices: it was made into an official requirement that at least 70 per cent of support-receivers would find paid employment within six months of programme completion. This was the most important target ascribed to the Independence Camp, though it was not specified whether 'employment' (*shūrō*) was to be of permanent or temporary, or full-time or part-time, character, and whether it should lead to genuine economic independence. This resulted in some room for manoeuvre from the point of delivery organizations and key bureaucrats who, though initially concerned that having 70 per cent of Camp enrollees find paid work might prove an impossible task, were often able to introduce the latter to part-time work opportunities even as more stable jobs remained elusive.

There was one other, though less salient, requirement attached to the Youth Independence Camp. This second requirement obliged delivery organizations to work towards building a so-called 'cooperative system' (*renkei taisei*) with local public administrators and other relevant support institutions. This prescription is in line with the influential idea of creating 'organic' local support networks as the basis of youth support (Chapter 4), but it proved to be more relevant in the case of the Youth Support Station while the Independence Camps became preoccupied with meeting their more pressing employment targets.

All Youth Independence Camp delivery groups are expected to carefully screen potential enrollees. In light of the 70 per cent employment goal, it is a crucial task to find youth who have the readiness to enter paid jobs following a relatively short period of training. Although basic eligibility conditions are set by the government,[1] individual organizations must ultimately use their own judgement here. Short trial programmes are encouraged so as to confirm the suitability of prospective participants at the outset. However, not all Camps are very selective about recruitment due to the low number of applicants they have tended to receive. Expulsions, it should be added, are limited to only the most extreme cases where a student's presence is dangerous to others or too disruptive to training activities.

Actual Independence Camp programmes can be categorized broadly into 'urban' and 'rural' types (*toshigata* and *nōsongata*) based on location and key activities. The former operate in metropolitan suburbs such as Mitaka and Fussa (Tokyo) and emphasize business-related training and part-time work trials in service sector positions. The latter, meanwhile, are located in the countryside – between rice paddies or in mountainous settings – and they focus on agricultural work activities that can at times be physically demanding. This division is not absolute though, because a single organization may be running both urban and rural youth support programmes (that are organized separately or combined or merged in various ways). There are, moreover, groups that specialize in welfare-related training; others that are artistic and put on theatre plays to develop confidence and communication skills; and some that put their faith in nature and its healing effects (see JPCSED 2009).

Some of the visible features that Independence Camps across Japan share include early wake-ups (usually between 6 am and 7 am), cleaning and cooking activities, academic study for various vocational qualifications, and the provision of support towards job-seeking. All Camps are moreover required to carry out regular follow-ups (*afutā forō*, *afutā kea*) to see if 'graduates' need additional support or encouragement. Staff generally come from diverse backgrounds and include ex-teachers, social care workers, former company employees or dispatched workers, and some have themselves been support-receivers in the past. Instead of specific formal qualifications, they are expected to draw holistically on their know-how and character when conducting day-to-day youth support. With a few exceptions, core staff tend to be predominantly male. Many Camps are led by male youth support 'veterans' (see below), but also increasingly often by younger male and female leaders in their thirties, reflecting a generational change within this roughly three-decades-old sector.

All the Youth Independence Camps are small, training at most around 20 students at a time. The average male-to-female ratio is eight to two (JPCSED 2007b:11), and some centres train no women at all. The usual explanation for the predominance of males at Japan's youth support institutions is that, within a social context where males are still expected to act as the breadwinners, there is more pressure on young men than on women to seek respectable employment. This prompts parents to more actively direct male offspring to support groups. While these observations are valid, it is evident from my field research that the characteristics of particular support organizations also strongly shape their gender ratios. Out of the groups I visited, those with many female staff as well as 'female-friendly' work activities (such as bakery and restaurant work as well as social care work rather than, say, farm labour) had more female students. Female-oriented groups are nevertheless an exception, and thus there is a clear gender bias in the Independence Camp scheme as a whole in that it implicitly caters more to men than to women. This matches the gender assumptions implicit in the *NEET* debate which, as we have seen, influenced the design of the Independence Camp (see Chapters 3 and 4).

Unlike most youth support measures in the past – and indeed unlike the Youth Support Station that was established a year later – the Youth Independence Camp is not strictly speaking a 'local' youth service. While individual Camps are very much embedded in their surrounding local communities, a high share of students tend to arrive from afar, often even from other prefectures. This arrangement makes it possible to manage stigma and minimize shame, which is important because these factors can act as barriers to support-seeking in home areas. Since the delivery organizations tend to be diverse in terms of disposition and concrete activities, Independence Camps constitute a small 'youth support quasi-market' within which youth (and their parents) are able to choose from among various alternatives the programme that seems best to suit their individual needs and preferences.

Another key feature of the Youth Independence Camp, explained in Chapter 4, is the fact that it charges considerable enrolment fees. In 2007, fees ranged from a minimum of 180,000 yen to a maximum of 444,000 yen (JPCSED 2007a; Toivonen 2008). All Camps are required to make efforts to offer a lowered fee for those from households earning less than 4 million yen per annum (lowered fees ranged from 105,000 yen to 315,000 yen in 2007).

As a rule, the government pays the delivery organizations a subsidy of 300,000 yen per enrollee. But it is the parents, in the overwhelming majority of cases, who shoulder the enrolment fees. It is thus essential, first of all, that a young person has parents or at least one parent with a significant income and, second, that the parents consent to their offspring's participation in the Youth Independence Camp programme. The majority of inquiries about the scheme come from parents rather than youth themselves, though this does not mean that youth do not make the final decision to enrol by themselves. When parental understanding or financial support is not forthcoming, entering an Independence Camp usually becomes impossible (due to the absence of scholarship schemes). Although well within the means of middle-class families, the Camp fees are high enough to render the service inaccessible to youth from the vast majority of single-parent families in Japan, around two-thirds of whom have incomes below the poverty line. This underlines the programme's position as a middle-class-oriented scheme.

Table 5.1 Youth Independence Camp enrolment and subsidy data

Year	Number of Camps	Enrolment capacity	Number of enrollees	Occupancy rate	Government subsidies (yen)	Subsidy utilization rate
2005	20	1,200	506	42%	900 million	30%
2006	25	1,720	698	41%	970 million	33.5%
2007	30	1,584	–	–	1 billion	–
2008	28	1200	–	–	600 million (tentative)	–

Source: Wakamono Jiritsu Juku sōshutsu suishin jigyō no shōreihi nado no jōkyō (The Situation Regarding the Establishment of the Youth Independence Camp and Subsidy Expenses, etc.), a handout distributed by the MHLW to participants at the *Wakamono Jiritsu Juku Renraku Kaigi*, Tokyo, 28 September 2007

Table 5.1 tells us that the quantitative performance of the Independence Camp in its first four years was less than impressive, despite an increase in the total number of Camps from 20 to 28 between 2005 and 2008. Puzzlingly, the number of enrollees fell considerably short of total enrolment capacity in this period, which prompted a low subsidy utilization rate (i.e. the percentage of earmarked government subsidies that was actually used up). This, in turn, led to a decline in the overall budget to a mere 600 million yen in 2008. The recruitment of students has been a major challenge to Youth Independence Camps.

The poor enrolment rates, however, do not automatically suggest that the Youth Independence Camp's methods are altogether misguided or ineffective. Those who participate in the scheme often benefit considerably, and low enrolment rates seem to stem, in large part, from constraints within the policy design as well as from the disciplinarian image of the programme, which has been far less welcomed by young adults compared to their parents' generation (see chapter Conclusion). To understand in greater depth the nature of actual support practices and indeed the logic of activation at Youth Independence Camps, the next section turns to the case of K2 International, a youth support group located in Negishi, Yokohama that illustrates both the more innovative as well as the more challenging aspects of 'doing' youth support in post-industrial Japan.

K2 International: An urban Independence Camp in action

K2 International is a Yokohama-based social enterprise that was selected by the government to run a Youth Independence Camp in 2005.[2] It also operates other programmes that cater to school-refusers, who are generally younger than Independence Camp students, and to disabled young people aged between their teens and thirties. Based in Negishi, a metropolitan suburb roughly 15 minutes from Yokohama station by train, K2, with two decades of experience, is in many ways a cutting-edge youth support organization. Established originally as a small sailing programme in 1989, it has since grown considerably to the point where it had an annual turnover of roughly 200 million yen in 2008.

While its history is not without ups and downs, the first point to highlight about K2 International is the fact that it has developed an open approach to youth support, which is characterized by ongoing collaboration with various actors on the local, national and international levels. It should also be mentioned that K2's unofficial status as a 'flagship' youth support site in Japan is confirmed by the frequent visits it receives from Japanese TV stations and European OECD researchers who are keen to learn the secrets behind the group's impressive support outcomes. The group trains over 20 students from their teens to their mid-thirties at any one time, and its Independence Camp programme is called Y-MAC, short for 'Yokohama Modern Apprenticeship Centre'.[3]

In the following sections, I first summarize the history, organization and philosophy of K2. I then describe in detail the flow of the entire support process from the initial screening of students, to actual training, to 'next steps'. This I follow up by highlighting the extent to which K2's Youth Independence Camp relies on concrete practices of recognition as the foundation of its youth activation strategy, the key elements of which I clarify. Before concluding with a discussion on the challenges faced by residential training initiatives in 2000s' Japan, I provide comparative viewpoints and document how supported youth themselves think about the objectives of 'independence support' at a personal level.[4]

History, organization and philosophy

K2 International was originally founded in 1989 as the educational organ of a yacht company called Pacific Marine Project Co. Launched under the name of 'International Columbus Academy', teenage school-refusers (*tōkōkyohi*) were chosen as the primary target group. Such 'problem youth' of the day were taken on one-to-two-month-long sailing voyages during which they could rejuvenate themselves while experiencing 'true nature' (Kanamori 1999:9). However, after only a handful of sailing trips in Micronesia in 1990, the cruise programme was abolished due to intra-company strife and high operation costs. At this point, Mr Kanamori Katsuo, the employee who had overseen the programme, decided that he would run it independently. While possessing no formal background in education, having witnessed first hand how youth changed during voyages had left a strong impression on him, motivating him to keep the scheme afloat (Kanamori, 14 December 2007).

The International Columbus Academy was thus re-established in 1991 as a small volunteer organization (*nin-i dantai*) that subsequently grew into a complex grouping of small semi-independent units operating in Japan, New Zealand and Australia (see Appendix I and Figure 5.2). As of 2008, K2 consisted of K2 International Japan Ltd (the umbrella organization), NPO

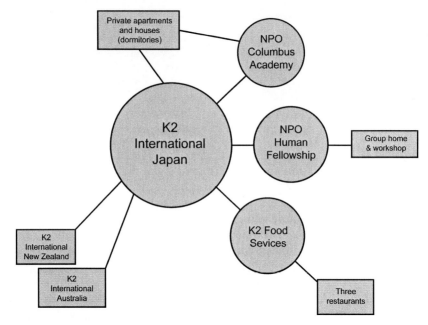

Figure 5.2 Basic organisational chart, K2 International (2007)
Source: Original chart based on interviews and the website of K2 International, consulted in November 2008 (http://k2-inter.com)

Human Fellowship, NPO Columbus Academy, K2 Food Services Ltd, and its two subsidiaries abroad. It also operated a number of dormitories to house members as well as three restaurants to provide training and revenue. This relatively complex organizational structure and the use of the status of a private company reflect K2's strong entrepreneurial side. According to staff, these arrangements have evolved as the group has sought new ways to cater to young people's needs. There is, importantly, no real boundary between the activities of the different sub-units.

As with so many of Japan's private youth support institutions, the philosophy and activities of this group depended initially on the efforts of a single man, Kanamori Katsuo – a resident *zainichi* Korean with a background in performing arts and business. After a fatal incident in New Zealand delivered a major setback to K2 in 2003, however, Iwamoto Mami emerged as a new leader figure (see Appendix I; Miller and Toivonen, 2010 describe the related circumstances in more detail). This shift in leadership appears to have been parallelled by a greater stress on safety and clearer admission criteria within the group, which in turn reflects a wider shift within Japanese education and youth support towards more 'accommodating' approaches (see 'Preface'). An enterprising Japanese female in her mid-thirties who previously worked for a securities firm, Iwamoto has taken over much of K2's overall management in Japan while Kanamori has concentrated more on the overseas branches.

K2 International employed altogether 20 staff in fiscal 2007, 16 of whom were full-timers. It is notable that those in leadership positions are over-whelmingly female; that over three-quarters are full-time employees (although four are hired as contract workers); and that ex-supportees account for the majority of communal living and restaurant staff. Although their ages range from the mid-twenties to the fifties, staff are on the whole youthful and mainly in their late twenties and thirties. The founder Kanamori Katsuo acts as an advisor and continues to provide a measure of leadership. There are also numerous external members, including a home doctor, two 'mentors' – a clinical psychologist and a psychiatrist – and several volunteers who lead various workshops. Such collaborators work on an unpaid basis, while core staff are said to be paid 'decent' wages with small differentials. Core staff are also provided with free shared housing, which is a major benefit in a context of high rents and house prices in the Yokohama area. Compared to many other youth support groups, there appears to be a comparatively low rate of turnover among K2 staff in general. This is partly explained by the considerable mobility that exists between K2's centres in Japan, New Zealand and Australia, which gives staff certain options and opportunities to progress to different types of positions. Working for K2 is viewed not as an 'employ-ment relationship' but as a 'mutual support relationship', distinctive from the hierarchical and bureaucratic work relations at most commercial com-panies in Japan. Leaders such as Iwamoto stress that the holistic working style of K2 requires such commitment that it cannot be managed by those who merely want a 'job' and a neat division between their work and private lives.

K2's philosophy is rooted in Kanamori's early views on teenagers who miss school for prolonged periods (the so-called *tōkō kyohi* or, more recently, the *futōkō*), his initial target group in the late 1980s:

> It is not that the children [we are dealing with] are sick. While they may be very close to being sick, they are in any case not sick. Instead, they are in a state resembling that of an empty car battery. Hence, they must first be 'recharged' – not through disciplinary training or persuasion but through complete relaxation in nature.

> (Kanamori, 14 December 2007)

Kanamori's original stance was thus that children were not to be blamed for their sometimes lethargic conditions, nor were they to be made into subjects of medical rehabilitation. If anything, it was society that was 'sick'. According to Kanamori, urban Japan suffered – and continues to suffer – from shallow human relationships; from the fact that children are brought up by their parents alone without the support of the local community as used to be the case; and from the custom of keeping all potentially shameful problems within the family (*kakaekomu bunka*) which prevents support-seeking and leads to vicious circles of hardship.

The younger Iwamoto – describing K2 students as 'normal young people' who for various reasons cannot find jobs – likewise criticizes her country's preoccupation with family responsibility. She contrasts Japan with other more 'publicly oriented' countries such as Australia where 'support for school non-attendants is consistent and well-organized' (MHLW 2007b:9). Iwamoto and Kanamori are both sceptical about Japan's public schooling system that 'causes children to feel formidable stress and is designed only to produce white collar salarymen', leading to the near-extinction of skilled craftsmen. What results is a 'majority society' where minorities – such as children who do not undergo mainstream education and those who suffer from various aspects of social exclusion – are given short shrift.

Kanamori perceives that this bundle of problems produces children who are unable to build trusting relationships or request help in times of difficulty. Iwamoto observes that, in the worst case, such children fall outside both formal and informal networks and thus experience complete isolation. Both agree that those who come to K2 typically suffer from a strong sense of inferiority and an extremely negative self-image, and generally feel that they are unneeded by others (Kanamori Katsuo, 14 December 2007; MHLW 2007b:9). Parents – especially white-collar fathers – are partly to blame, as they have neglected child-rearing, leading to an imbalance between 'maternal' (*bosei*) and 'paternal' (*fusei*) types of upbringing.[5]

Furthermore, K2 finds that the labour markets are particularly unforgiving to those not hired instantly upon graduation, and that those without technical skills and experience are forever doomed to manual service and factory jobs. Iwamoto laments labour market changes that have led companies to require 'instant competence' (*sokusenryoku*; see Chapter 1) of those not hired immediately upon graduation, which has meant that, even when labour markets improve, the situation will not change for K2's students who are 'behind their peers' in terms of communication skills and other basic competencies (Iwamoto, 11 May 2007). The demise of local communities – including their hitherto vibrant and cosy traditional shopping districts (*shōtengai*) – has left more young people with no place to go. Despite some recent improvements, Iwamoto contends that government policies have by and large failed to integrate socially excluded youth or to supply a real sense (*jikkan*) of 'community' and of 'connecting with others'.

To compensate for such inadequacies and problems in young people's social environment, K2 employs an array of support methods that have evolved over its two-decade-long history. While sailing remains, for Kanamori, the most 'dynamic' way to help students overcome their entrenched sense of inferiority, the same 'paradigm shift' can also be achieved via communal living on land. The essential requirement is simply to live in a social setting away from home, parents, school and one's regular environment for a significant period of time – this by itself can solve a great deal of problems and reduce the pressures being exerted on youth. Kanamori first opened a communal living facility in Yokohama at the start of the 1990s, but in 1993 he transported his activities wholesale to New Zealand, where there were great opportunities for sailing and other outdoor activities and where he had prior (business) connections.[6] This decision and K2's continued operations in both New Zealand and Australia reflect the group's interesting belief that 'life in Japan does not suit all youth' and that many who suffer as outcasts in Japan flourish abroad (MHLW 2007b:9).[7]

K2's historical legacy lives on in its current mission, which is simply to 'live together with various kinds of youth who struggle in their lives'. The organization's activities continue to be grounded in communal living (*kyōdō seikatsu*), although more emphasis has been put on employment training since the launching of the Youth Independence Camp in 2005. The following four basic principles, elicited through participant observation and interviews, guide K2's activities:

1) Tolerance. Staff stress that they do not force their organization's ways of doing things upon new enrollees, but instead try to adjust themselves to newcomers' personalities and interests. Diversity and individuality is appreciated based on the Christian view that every human being is invaluable and equal before God (see Miller and Toivonen, 2010).
2) Mutual support. K2 makes active efforts to build a positive community where youth can 'grow together' (*sodachiai*) based on 'mutual support' (*sasaeai*), which also involves former students, staff and family members. Staff view themselves as mere facilitators who give the leading role to the youth themselves. These ideas as well as the notion that 'interdependence' is the genuine meaning of 'independence' have close affinities with Buddhist and Confucian thought.
3) Openness. The study and sports facilities of K2 are actively shared with local citizens, parents and other interested people who are invited for visits on a daily basis. There is active cooperation between K2 and local psychiatric clinics, welfare authorities, youth support institutions across Japan, Yokohama city officials and domestic as well as foreign researchers.
4) 'Learning by doing'. K2 places tremendous importance on diverse hands-on training and social participation activities which it thinks can act as springboards (*kikkake*) for motivation and career planning; a key part of its approach is allowing students maximum choice over their next steps.

These principles are not elaborated in length in any formal publications, but they are internalized by staff who articulate them in various meetings and through their daily activities. Perhaps most importantly, there is a simultaneous emphasis on the fostering of interdependence and individuality. Instead of 'living and working by yourself', interacting with others and supporting one another comprise, according to the founder Kanamori, the 'true substance of independence' (Kanamori, December 14, 2007). Indeed, there is a consensus that 'independence' – a central concept in the youth policy discourse that K2 finds less than helpful in practice – should never imply 'isolation' (*koritsu*). It is the ability to request help from others that characterizes an independent person. At the same time, Kanamori places a high value on autonomous action and originality, exhorting students to 'not do what everyone else is doing' and to never turn into stereotypical people.

The support process and the characteristics of support-receivers

In this section I analyze the intricate process through which K2 implements its youth support philosophy. The support process necessarily begins with parents and/or non-employed young people first learning about K2 in one way or another. Indeed, there are several routes to this organization: some of the parents whom I encountered at guardians' meetings in 2007 and 2008 said they had first learned about the organization from newspapers, while others had been led to it through the Yokohama Youth Support Station, other public consultation services or relatives. Many of the students I met told me they had discovered the organization on the Internet.[8] Comprehensive records of how guardians and youth learn about K2's programmes are not kept, but it is evident that media appearances as well as the Internet have great influence, and that introductions from other affiliated institutions are exceedingly important. It is estimated that in up to half the cases it is the guardians who first make contact and encourage or persuade their offspring to consider enrolling at K2.

Yet this does not mean that youth can simply be forced or coerced by their parents to join the programme: staff stress that it is imperative that the youth themselves are sufficiently motivated and committed, for otherwise the prospects of progress are very low. In practice, however, establishing an individual's level of motivation can be extremely tricky – especially when a youth is shy and unable to fully express his or her thoughts – so staff are to some extent required to rely on their past experiences and intuition when making admission decisions.

K2 is surprisingly selective – perhaps more selective than the majority of Japan's residential youth support institutions – about who it enrols. While its target group is defined broadly as 'youth who struggle in their lives' (*ikizurasa wo kakaeru kodomotachi*), it is understood that organizations that believe they can help any young person inevitably fail. K2 is hence said to have no choice but to impose certain minimum enrolment conditions. First, K2 asks parents to confirm whether their son or daughter has a background of risky or indecent behaviour, and whether a psychiatrist has agreed he or she can join the organization. Second, the group ensures that there is sufficient 'emotional compatibility' (*aishō*) between K2 and the prospective enrollee, and that he or she will find at least one suitable mentor among the staff. In case the first condition is not fulfilled – for instance when serious mental health or disability issues arise – K2 directs the young person to professional psychiatric services or to its affiliated care home. If, on the other hand, it is deemed that K2 and the applicant are not a good fit, staff are happy to direct him or her to another, potentially more suitable, support group such as the Children's Life and Culture Association (CLCA) in Odawara, south-west of Yokohama

City. Kanamori, for one, is proud of his group's 'creative', even 'artistic', spirit, but acknowledges that not all prospective enrollees feel comfortable with this orientation.

The formal government-imposed requirements of the Youth Independence Camp scheme mean, furthermore, that applicants must be unmarried 15- to 34-year-old *NEETs* who have been out of employment and education for at least a year, and they must have had some prior job-seeking experience (see Chapter 4). Importantly, like other Independence Camps, K2's Y-MAC programme is charged with guiding 70 per cent of the enrollees to paid employment within six months of 'graduation'.

Finally, the ability to shoulder the programme fees is another de facto enrolment condition. Youth Independence Camp (or Y-MAC) students are charged 105,000 yen per month for the duration of this programme. If they desire to stay at K2 for longer, they may do so, but since government subsidies apply to only the first three months, the fee increases to 136,500 yen for subsequent months.[9] Fees present an obvious barrier to prospective students from low-income households (including those headed by single parents) – something which Iwamoto and other staff acknowledge and regret – but at the same time K2 stresses that such costs must be seen in context. Many enrollees have previously attended other more expensive educational institutions but have nevertheless failed to launch careers. Not many parents hence perceive K2's fees as unreasonably high, and they see it as offering good value compared to letting their offspring spend their money in 'reckless' ways.

What are the typical characteristics of those youth who meet most of the above conditions and successfully enrol in K2's Youth Independence Camp? Aged 25 to 26 on the average, all have experienced joblessness for a significant length of time, from months to several years. In most cases, this has led to some degree of social withdrawal where youth have few friends, stop talking to their parents and simply 'get bored' at home, and where some become suicidal or develop an obsessive interest in their hobbies (Guardians' meeting, 8 December 2007). The longer such conditions last, the more worried parents tend to become. Beyond simply being disappointed with their children's failure to conform to the 'standard life course' (entering a good school, then a great university and finally a prestigious company, after which marriage is expected), they realize that they themselves will inevitably grow frail and die, making it imperative to ensure their offspring's independence before too long.

Direct causes behind K2 students' joblessness are said to include their repeated failure at job interviews and frequent job changes due to what parents see as lack of 'adaptability'. Both tend to result in a profound sense of personal discouragement. Even before such setbacks, many students have suffered from collective bullying at school (*ijime*) and, more often than not, from extended periods of school non-attendance (*futōkō*). Another common problem among enrollees is work exhaustion and burnout, for instance from social care work or from temporary dispatch labour (*haken*) where an employee may be sent to a different company every month or even every week.

Parents and staff alike describe most K2 enrollees as 'good kids' (*ii ko*), 'sincere' (*sunao*) and 'sensitive' (*sensai*), the connotation being that they have tried hard to do what their parents and teachers have told them, and that lack of effort is not why they have wound up in a standstill. Puzzlingly, a considerable share of K2 enrollees are said to suffer from some variety of mental illness or developmental disability. Such conditions tend to become apparent some days or weeks after admission as staff spend time in close interaction with new students and begin to explore their challenges in depth. At this stage, one of staff's key goals is to help youth as well as their parents to gradually come to terms with the presence of an illness or a disability. Although labelling is generally disliked, official diagnoses are often sought from affiliated psychiatrists. This sometimes makes it possible for students to become eligible for state disability benefits, which is recognized as an important complementary source of income.

Whatever their background or condition, the first few weeks at K2 tend to be the hardest for new entrants: they sometimes find it difficult to 'enter the group' and may become prone to emotional outbursts. It can be stressful for many to constantly interact with others after long periods of withdrawal. For some, living at K2 may be the first time they talk to members of the opposite sex (e.g. where they have previously attended boys-only or girls-only schools). Here, the staff strives to strike a balance between being highly flexible – 'adjusting to the pace of each student' – and teaching basic rules of conduct, which may occasionally involve scolding. Yet, even as they struggle to adapt to their new environment, it is a major positive shock for new students to meet others at K2 who struggle with similar challenges as themselves. The significance of such a peer-support effect cannot be overstated and it is cited as one reason why new enrollees gradually 'emerge from their tunnel', become more 'energetic' (*genki*) or 'cheerful' (*akarui*), and generally come to enjoy their time at K2.

For new and old students alike, communal living (*kyōdō seikatsu*) is the basis of daily activities. While there are a handful of commuting students, most dwell in nearby dorms – private houses where rooms are shared between two or more youth – from where they walk or are shuttled to K2's activity centre ('Atorie K2') each morning. In addition to generally waking up early, each student is in turn required to undertake breakfast shifts (*chōshoku tōban*). That at least half of the four students assigned to this shift on a given day arrive late speaks of a certain latitude in K2's approach to training, but the first meal of the day is in any case provided to all students without fail. Apart from breakfast shifts, it is a rule of thumb that all students follow the same daily schedule as others, except when they take part in voluntary or part-time work outside or when they dash out in business suits for job interviews. It should be noted that K2's routines resemble the group-based activities carried out at regular schools, but instead of having students function as part of a 'chain of command' – as LeTendre argues is common in lower-secondary school clubs in particular (LeTendre 1996:278–79) – K2 is marked by a far more egalitarian and relaxed atmosphere. Appendix J provides an example of a typical weekly schedule for Y-MAC students.

Y-MAC students frequently take part in employment-related workshops that range from CV-writing lessons and self-introduction drills to mock interviews and group discussions. Such sessions are typically carried out by external facilitators who may be experienced school teachers or career coaches, or even students or foreigners who are invited to freely share their experiences with K2 enrollees.[10] Engagement in volunteer work at small workshops or plants, disabled children's centres, elderly care homes and poor people's canteens (such as the Sanagi Shokudō in the Kotobukichō district of Yokohama, known for its high concentration of day labourers) is another essential component of job training at Y-MAC. Just as important in terms of support outcomes, however, are K2's 'internal training' and 'restaurant training' programmes (which are referred to as 'on-the-job-training'). By working closely with staff at the office or at the three self-owned restaurants,[11] students are able to acquire basic skills and test their abilities in a safe, relatively low-stress environment. Such training is crucial also from the staff's perspective, since observing students while they work makes it significantly easier to guide them to appropriate post-support destinations later.

K2's work-oriented training is embedded in a rich variety of other social activities that are, one the one hand, meant to build a strong sense of community and, on the other, to provide students with the chance to enjoy 'normal' life experiences that they have missed due to prolonged periods of absence from school and social isolation. Birthdays are celebrated enthusiastically at the *tanjōbikai*; Christmas parties are held before the end-of-year holidays; fun sports events are organized with youth from other support groups; students contribute to local festivals as well as flea-markets; some play in a band or sing in the choir; and trips are made to skiing resorts, camping sites and even foreign countries. Enjoyment is thus viewed as being just as important as hard work, and as a way to make K2 a more motivating and interesting place for students and staff alike. Voice training and yoga are some of the other activities that are used to strengthen students in both a mental and physical sense, very much as is done at many Youth Support Stations (see Chapter 6).

One of the direct benefits of joining K2's Y-MAC programme is that it marks the end of a 'blank period' (*kūhaku kikan*) in most students' lives as well as in their CVs. 'Becoming busy' at various new activities is said to remove them from the trap of excessive dwelling on counterproductive, negative thoughts. Gaining good friends is another benefit that students often mention. However, the staff harbour no illusions about the effects of their scheme and admit that most students do feel a degree of stress at K2, in most cases because they 'cannot see a way forward' (*saki ga mienai*). In order to minimize feelings of anxiety and frustration staff strive to focus students on concrete action and to gradually bring into view motivating but realistic future options.

In terms of quantitative outcomes, K2 appears to be an exemplary performer: by April 2008, it had trained a total of 114 students in its Youth

Independence Camp programme, and Iwamoto reports that 70 per cent of enrollees have progressed to paid work (Iwamoto 1 April 2008, 28 August 2008). This does not necessarily take place within the time limit imposed by the government – only 12 of the 31 students who completed the Youth Independence Camp programme in fiscal 2006 found work in the same year – since many students are said to require a longer period in support. The majority thus stay at K2 for 6 to 12 months. JPCSED statistics show that not a single youth quit K2 in fiscal 2006, which (if accurate) may be the outcome of selective admissions practices along with programme effectiveness (K2 itself clearly has few incentives to dismiss students since this would incur a loss of income). According to Iwamoto, enrollees can be divided into two groups according to their support needs and the duration of support they require. First, there are those who have just finished school or are recovering from illness and who possess basic skills. Their problems are easy to identify and thus the support process is quick. Second, there are those who do not know what they want to do and whose problems are harder to pin down. It makes no sense to hurriedly push such youth into jobs (as they would only quit soon) and so staff must spend much more time with them to look for ideas regarding suitable next steps.

Although it used to prefer having its enrollees hired as 'regular' workers (*seishain, seiki*), K2 has noted that students do not always do well as regulars because this can involve great pressure (due to high expectations and demanding duties). Part-time work at an 'understanding' and well-matching workplace can thus be a more viable first step. Employers vary from small shops and agricultural enterprises to volunteer and welfare organizations, and K2 itself hires a few of its former students at its own restaurants and sometimes also as support staff. (As of April 2008, eight youth were hired as restaurant staff and at least three as 'communal living support staff' in Yokohama).

It is suggestive that K2 does not operate through standard routes in securing its students' post-support paths. Indeed, directing youth to the Hello Work public employment offices to browse job advertisements is rejected in favour of introducing them to employers via direct face-to-face linkages. Like many other youth support institutions in Japan, K2 is actively striving to build relations (*kaitaku suru*) with 'understanding' companies (*rikai no aru kaisha*) to ensure its users will be able to work in a sustainable fashion and without major anxieties. The reason why Hello Work as well as private job-brokering services are not usually used by K2 has to do with their anonymity: without a prior relationship, it is next to impossible for staff to explain the special circumstances of particular students to a potential employer, and it is similarly very difficult to ensure there is a good general match between the student and the company. K2's supporters feel that, after months or even years of close interaction, they know their students and their capabilities very well, and at the same time they feel great responsibility over their students' futures. This is why – unlike Hello Work and even the Youth Support Station – staff at K2 say they simply cannot direct students to workplaces where they have only a slim chance of long-term success.

Since the transition to work, including the first months at a new workplace, is challenging to most support-receivers, K2 has developed ways to provide continuous care to help youth overcome this difficult stage. One of these consists of voluntary follow-ups (*afutā forō*) that can be carried out through regular phone calls or consultations at K2 or when the need arises. The other more substantial method is called the 'Step House system' where students are accommodated at K2's dormitories after they have completed their training and sometimes even after they have started working. Living close to staff and old friends is considered to be an advantage in the process of getting accustomed to working life. Beyond these two methods, efforts are made to stay in touch with the broader K2 community through encouraging 'graduates' to return for special events or whenever they are in the neighbourhood.

K2's activation strategy and recognition

We are now in a position to more concisely grasp the key elements of what may be called K2's activation strategy, i.e. the key approaches and methods it applies in re-engaging young adults who have spent considerable time without work and without much social contact. It needs to be stressed that this strategy does not, despite my use of numerical ordering below, unfold in a strictly linear form, but is of iterative nature. Neither does K2's definition of 'activation' accord perfectly with the official government stance that the only appropriate goal of youth support is turning formally inactive youth into 'regular' full-time employees (see above regarding how K2 defines 'independence'). In any case, the main components of K2's approach can be summarized as follows:

1) Initial consultation, screening and matching: the group holds meetings with parents and prospective students, guides those with mental health conditions to other professionals, selects appropriate youth (amounting to 10 per cent of all prospective students) and pairs them with 'mentally compatible' (*aishō no aru*) staff members, using staff diversity as a key resource.
2) Adjusting to/adjustment by new enrollees: new entrants are involved in daily group activities and training; they discover 'others like them'; staff detect any obvious (but previously undiagnosed and undisclosed) mental health and disability issues; and they identify two main types of students.
3) 'Exploring the student': staff gradually gain a deep understanding of each individual's characteristics, abilities and motivational patterns through prolonged daily observation; low-risk training at the group's own work sites facilitates this.
4) Negotiating rigid middle-class expectations: staff liaise patiently with students and especially parents to 'loosen up' rigid expectations that students should conform to the standard life course and work for large corporations; alternative, more feasible opportunities are introduced; and mental health issues are addressed.

5) Preparations for job-placement: appropriate job opportunities within K2's network of organizations as well as within its own labour markets are considered; students are taught how to write CVs and take interviews; and employer introductions take place.

6) Continued community support: even after placement, some students continue to live in K2's shared housing to facilitate mutual support and gradual adjustment; 'graduates' are invited to various events to maintain the K2 community.

The process of activation is, as we can see from here, altogether more nuanced and multi-dimensional than official blueprints – or even K2's own descriptions (such as the one placed at the top of this chapter) – would lead one to believe. What stands out is the idea that staff diversity is a crucial resource in youth support as it makes it possible to find 'emotionally compatible' mentors for more applicants. That staff thoroughly 'explore' their students is a surprising finding which contrasts strongly with typical short-term and essentially impersonal activation consultations at Western employment services. It is only through in-depth exploration (i.e. long-term observation and interaction) that staff become aware of the complex challenges that each individual support-seeker faces, and it is in parallel with this long process that they are able to negotiate unhelpful middle-class expectations (that tend to be extremely rigid) among the support receivers' parents in particular. Importantly, job place-ment takes place in the context of face-to-face networks rather than through anonymous employment services, re-establishing the kind of protective 'social closure' (in this case, between K2 and employers) that Brinton (2011) points out once encapsulated youth transitions in Japan but is now endangered.

It is the final point – that support indeed continues beyond job placement – that drives home the fact that what K2 provides through its Independence Camp scheme is not just a time-limited 'programme' of employment support, but membership in a community of mutual support, or a community of recognition. Even as students find positions in the surrounding society, whe-ther within a few kilometres of K2 or in the wider metropolitan area extending from Yokohama to Tokyo, Saitama and Chiba, they are invited to remain close to the support community and continue to attend various social events. Hardships and pressing personal issues are therefore shared with others, and staff is still available for consultations on an informal basis. The various practices of recognition that begin when a student enters K2 – allowing entrants to develop at their own pace, telling each that they are valuable and unique, promoting diverse free-time activities and celebrating special days together – are therefore extended into the future. Those who view the Youth Independence Camps through the orthodox lens of activation rooted in an efficiency calculus will find this troubling, because for them the ultimate goal is to 'return as many *NEETs* to work of any variety as quickly as possible'. Yet for those who accept that economistic theories and official political dis-courses on how activation is supposed to work remain far removed from the practical realities that confront youth in today's post-industrial societies, K2 presents a thought-provoking alternative model. This model is particularly potent precisely because it merges a concern with job placement – the official priority of activation policy – with a method for embedding young people in enduring (open) communities amid increasingly unstable labour market conditions. Chapter 7 further considers the potential of such arrangements.

Contrasting K2 with other residential youth support organizations

As of March 2009, there were altogether 28 organizations in Japan that were running a Youth Independence Camp, 18 of which were registered as not-for-profits (the rest had the status of a private company, association, school, social welfare institution or enterprise union; JPCSED 2009). Three groups were located around the Tokyo metropolitan area, while the others were scattered all across Japan from Okinawa to Hokkaido. During my fieldwork, I was able to pay short visits to altogether six groups in addition to K2 International, conducting three-day stays at two locations. I will dedicate a few paragraphs here to introducing these two Camps in order to set K2 into a larger context.

The NPO Hokuriku Seishōnen Jiritsu Enjo Sentā 'Hagurekumo' (The Hokuriku Youth Independence Support Centre 'Stray Cloud'), located near Toyama city in Toyama prefecture, is an agricultural youth support group with a substantial history. Its activities are organized around a steady daily schedule where members wake up at 6.30 am, take a walk outside, study after breakfast (if needed) and then head out to the fields to plant or harvest various crops. Lunch is served at midday and afternoons are spent in the fields or doing sports. Dinner is followed by roughly three hours of free time, after which lights go out at 10 pm. A farmhouse serves as the headquarters and as the hub for daily activities, and some students also reside there.

Over his 20 years of running Hagurekumo, its director, the jovial and down-to-earth Kawamata Nao, has come to trust the effectiveness of a simple and unchanging daily routine that ensures that students get physical exercise, eat healthy food and acquire good living habits. Farming is a good initial training method precisely because 'it does not demand too much intelligence', and because it 'yields a sense of achievement' (Kawamata Nao, 15 June 2007). However, Kawamata and his half a dozen staff members do not force new students to participate in particular activities or to engage in discussions if they do not feel like it, allowing them to gradually adjust to the new environment. The atmosphere at Hagurekumo is generally very relaxed, friendly as well as familial, with Kawamata's wife acting as the house mother who oversees cooking and housekeeping. Since staff believe that it is a crucial formative experience for youth to learn to live away from their parents, frequent visits by parents are not encouraged and, partly to limit child-parent communication during training, cellphones are likewise prohibited.

In terms of results, up to half of the students are said to eventually find employment, but this generally takes much longer than three months (the official length of the Independence Camp programme). Hagurekumo's students – most of whom are in their early-to mid-twenties – are allowed to engage in part-time work and to take courses for computer and welfare-related qualifications, in addition to developing their farming skills (such training is, however, not intended to prepare students to become independent farmers).

Compared to Hagurekumo's relatively unadorned and loose approach to youth support, the Independence Camp run by the NPO CLCA in Odawara is more pedagogically oriented. While it, too, emphasizes physical activity and early wake-ups, CLCA creates many opportunities for discussion during weekly meetings, daily meals and various work activities. Indeed, most students are intensely talkative and contemplative to a degree that would be highly unusual even at regular Japanese secondary schools, let alone at other Independence Camps. Interaction among enrollees is further facilitated by the sheer absence of distraction at the 150-year-old traditional mountain house that serves as the main Independence Camp facility.

The founder of CLCA, Wada Shigehiro, is an ardent educator who has, since the 1970s, run a 'free school' called Hajime-juku for teenagers who have stopped attending mainstream schools. Its students tend to be proactive and highly inquisitive, with not a few coming from elite families. The Independence Camp programme of CLCA is run by the sub-leader Fukumori, a former Buddhist monk in his late thirties who is a prolific conversationalist. A graduate of Hajime-juku, he echoes Wada in stressing the need for students to reach 'genuine mental independence' by learning to also do things they do not want do, and by developing an emotional, intuitive sensibility to enable 'organic' mutual support relationships with their peers (Fukumori, 4 December 2007). Although Fukumori says youth need to cut their emotional dependence on their parents – especially mothers – and to develop perseverance, at the same time he admits that 'true' independence has never existed in Japan, and that it can not exist in any human society. In any case, Independence Camp students are encouraged to make their own decisions, take responsibility over them, and gradually develop confidence in their abilities based on practical work experience.

80 per cent of the students at CLCA come from a background of prolonged social withdrawal, and according to Fukumori's estimates, 20 per cent suffer from a mental illness while a fifth have intellectual handicaps. Enrollees are recruited mainly through CLCA's consultation centre (Kitemiru) that is located conveniently in downtown Odawara. In the majority of cases, parents appear to be unaware of their offspring's illness or impairments, so when Fukumori raise these issues they display great resistance. It often takes months for parents to accept that their son or daughter may suffer from a mental health problem or disability. Due to their close involvement with individual youth and their links with psychiatrists, Fukumori believes that CLCA staff come to know their students extremely well – sometimes better than the parents – and are thus able to more objectively grasp and report health problems (although Fukumori is not sure if this is supposed to be the Independence Camp's role).

That potential health issues are tackled is considered to be vitally important from the point of view of the enrollees' future livelihoods.

On average, it takes a student six months to 'graduate' from the CLCA Independence Camp, although some of the students I met had stayed as long as two years. The organization is not as well-structured as K2 in terms of its employment support strategy, but it, too, makes use of its links with local companies in the Odawara area. Fukumori finds that 80 to 90 per cent of the students, even when they find jobs, return to their parental homes upon finishing at CLCA. Yet this is not necessarily a problem since Fukumori believes the most important thing is that youth are able to have the experience of living away from home. The staff try their best to conduct follow-ups through e-mails and through inviting graduates to visit later, but with only four staff members this can be challenging.

In sum, both Hagurekumo and CLCA differ from K2 in terms of their rural setting and farming-focused activities, but they share a similar emphasis on a regular daily schedule as well as a relaxed, accommodating approach to youth support. As with K2, various subtle practices of recognition form the basis for their activities. Since both organizations have long histories, they have had time to develop extensive local and national networks upon which the two organizations can draw when seeking employment opportunities for their students (although unlike K2 International, they sometimes make use of public employment services or private recruitment agencies also).

Young people's views on activation and 'independence'

The perceptions of the supported youth themselves have so far been absent from this account. Although hard to survey comprehensively or in a representative way (due to issues of ethics, access and different levels of talkativeness among youth), one way in which I probed the thinking of supported youth was through group discussion. On 13 March 2008, I conducted a workshop with six K2 International students aged 21 to 34, including five males and one female. I asked this group to draft impromptu mindmaps on the theme of *jiritsu* ('independence'), of which one is illustrated in Figure 5.3. This was a helpful method as students created their mindmaps before any group discussion took place, therefore presumably minimizing the direct influence of others on how students conducted this exercise.

Like the author of the mindmap in Figure 5.3, all the six youth who participated in the discussion agreed that a central aspect of independence was the ability to 'live by one's own strength' (*jibun no chikara de ikiteiku*). For four students, this included learning how to live alone away from their parents, while all wished to earn their own money through paid work. 'Independence' was viewed by everyone as a means to a happy or meaningful life, rather than as an end in and of itself. Dimensions such as learning communication skills and seeking support from others as well as 'self-affirmation' (*jiko kōteikan*) and positive human relationships were also raised in varying

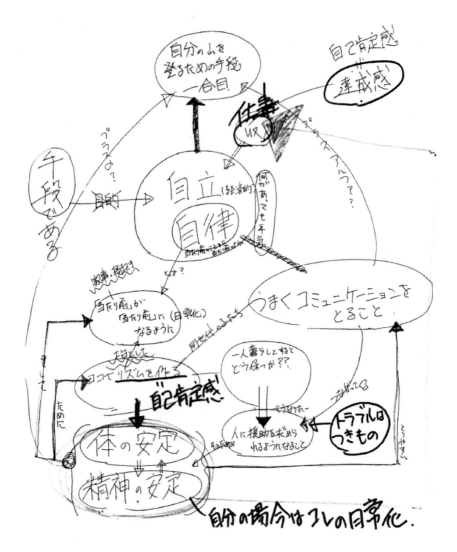

Figure 5.3 A mindmap on the topic of independence by a 24-year-old male Independence
Camp student at K2 International (2008)

combinations, appearing to reflect Japan's youth support discourses as well as
K2's own philosophy. The male student who drafted the mindmap in Figure 5.3
put emphasis on *jiritsu* as 'self-regulation' (pronounced identically, in Japanese,
with 'independence' but written differently), which to him amounted to sus-
taining a regular daily rhythm and maintaining mental and physical stability.
Surprisingly, only one of the students was enthusiastic about getting married
in the future, but all wished to work as permanent workers (*seishain*), if possible. A 34-year-old male student felt that it was more realistic for him to first

gain experience through part-time work (*baito*) and then consider applying for a more stable position.

Although elicited from only six students, the above views appear to be widely shared by others at K2 as well. Most aspire to find employment and to thereby gain a degree of economic independence. That half of the students who drafted mindmaps explicitly articulated their wish to live by themselves 'without borrowing the strength' or the money of their parents also reflects an understanding that they have been a 'burden' on their family and have 'caused them trouble' (*meiwaku wo kakeru*). So the desire to fulfil parental expectations or to relieve parental dissatisfaction appears to be just as important a component of 'independence' to many students as the achievement of autonomous living per se. What is less clear is how the perceptions and ideas of K2 students change over the course of their training: this was hard for me to analyze systematically due to K2's rolling enrolment system (whereby students enter at different times) and due to the general difficulty of interviewing students consistently while remaining unobtrusive. My impression, however, is that most students gradually internalize K2's general discourse of 'interdependence', while many continue to desire more autonomy than can be enjoyed during their programme (or indeed as long as they remain without socially recognized jobs).

The challenge of residential youth support in post-industrial Japan

This chapter has surveyed the Youth Independence Camp scheme at the level of actual support practice, with a focus on the specific case of K2 International. Although the name of the scheme was revised in 2009 (see Introduction), the nuanced and locally-grounded approach to activation that was analyzed here, the key elements of which are shared across various delivery organizations, remain highly relevant. I conclude the chapter with an overview of the difficulties that have characterized residential youth support in post-industrial Japan, starting with the specific case of the Independence Camp and moving to more fundamental labour market-related issues.

From its inception, the Youth Independence Camp struggled with recruiting enough enrollees. This is striking because the total capacity of the scheme was set extremely low and never exceeded 2,000. The underlying reasons include the newness of the scheme (it was never given sufficient time to 'bed in' and become widely known); the less than positive public image of the scheme (many viewed it as a dangerous Totsuka-like disciplinarian project); and limited recruitment activities (staff were few in number and too busy to carry out such activities). Perhaps more obviously, a residential programme that appeared to be offering 'correctional' training to 'lazy' *NEETs* was not exactly something that appealed to many young people in Japan. It is likely that very few non-employed youth fully identified with this target group, and probably quite few were willing to give up their privacy to live in a communal setting away from home. This was partly an issue of packaging, however: the Independence

Camps could, in theory, have been 'sold' as comfortable, safe and even entertaining places for various kinds of young people with no place to go.

The inability of the Independence Camps to attract more participants only aggravated the in-built instability of the entire scheme, making managers and staff acutely worried about the immediate future of the programme. That the government never made it perfectly clear whether the Camps would be funded beyond the initial five-year limit added to this sense of insecurity. This, in turn, added to the difficulty in recruiting and keeping able staff members. While K2 constitutes an exception, most Independence Camp staff have indeed comprised unmarried males, and it has been clear that, with the insecurity of their youth support jobs and low salaries, they could expect to marry only after moving on to more stable jobs. A related worry that was expressed during my fieldwork year was that this situation would prevent the development of highly experienced youth workers and the passing-down of professional knowledge (as youth supporters of around 30 years of age ended up quitting their positions without time to train their followers). As Chapter 6 will go on to show, this has been less of an issue for the Youth Support Stations that have been staffed to a higher extent by married women and pensioners not burdened by expectations to act as main bread-winners.

Beyond these programmatic challenges, several dilemmas of a more fundamental nature have affected residential youth support in post-industrial Japan. By far the greatest of these has been the combined problem of locating suitable work positions for young trainees and ensuring that these lead to sustainable incomes. To be sure, data given to me by the Ministry of Health, Labour and Welfare indicate that, as of the end of 2008, 86 per cent of those who had completed the Independence Camp programme six months before or earlier had found jobs, entered education or become job-seekers. Yet a more detailed, slightly earlier survey conducted by the Japan Productivity Centre for Economic Development suggests that over two-thirds of those hired entered 'irregular' (or non-standard) jobs and that the average income of all employed Independence Camp 'graduates' came to about 100,000 yen per month on average (JPCSED 2007b:13). This amounts to little more than half the income required for single living in Japan's metropolitan areas.

There is thus a vast gap between the official aspirations of government-affiliated residential training schemes – to provide support towards economic independence – and the actual outcomes of the support process. The essential backdrop here is a low-wage post-industrial economy where stable manufacturing jobs have decreased significantly and where 'flexible' service-sector work proliferates. The wider picture of symbolic activation that was set out in Chapter 1 and that suggests *NEETs* are being activated predominantly to low-paid labour thus remains in place. Indeed, small schemes such as the Youth Independence Camp can be expected to have only the slightest direct influence on this broader structural situation. Still, the kinds of communities of recognition that the Independence Camps represent offer one attractive alternative model for youth activation and inclusion. Further social innovation and programme expansion, if supported at a wider scale and with long-term subsidies, will make it possible to enhance the impact of this emerging model. The strengthening of support communities needs to go hand in hand with substantial labour market reform that will make it more realistic for the formally inactive to (re-)enter diverse work positions which contain genuine potential for career advancement. In practice this will require the abolishment of the separate labour market that exists for new graduates and which disadvantages young people who are not hired immediately upon graduation.

6 The Youth Support Station: Exploring the user

Only a year after the launch in Japan of the Youth Independence Camp in 2005, a second programme for formally inactive young adults was established. Called the 'Youth Support Station' (*Wakamono Sapōto Sutēshon*), this was an initiative that, in contrast with the residential Independence Camp scheme, comprised easy-to-access drop-in centres that were said to offer various kinds of counselling services at a single location. In this chapter, I analyze the Support Station in a similar fashion to the way I examined the Independence Camp in Chapter 5, relying primarily on long-term participant observation as a volunteer youth worker as well as on extensive staff interviews, while also highlighting the complicated conditions of the supported young people.

Once again, despite official descriptions that stated that the Support Station was a 'job-seeking support service for non-employed youth' (*jakunen mugyōsha no tame no shūrō shien torikumi*), it was not at all obvious from the outset what it was that it would do in practice. This chapter makes it clear that the portrayal of this scheme as an employment support measure is an act of necessary but misleading self-labelling, whereby certain explanations are given of the programme's activities to the outside world while concealing and indeed protecting a nuanced 'inner logic' of youth support that does not easily lend itself to such explanation. This inner logic, while resisting the wider dynamic of symbolic activation (see Chapter 1), does not differ essentially with that of the Youth Independence Camps, despite the ostensibly different format. The Support Station, too, relies on trusting communities of recognition as a basis for its activities. But there is another alternative methodology of activation that the Youth Support Station demonstrates particularly well: that of youth support as a fascinating process of search. By creating a space where stigmatizing labels and value judgements are largely suspended and where there is time for repeated consultations in a sympathetic atmosphere, the staff at Youth Support Stations engage in what I call 'exploring the user'. The former get to know particular support-seekers and their circumstances at a deep level in the course of several months or even years (while also consulting with parents as well as potential local employers). The result is that staff members, as individuals but also as teams, come to acquire such a wealth of information about the young people they support that they become able to negotiate complex bundles of issues with considerable delicacy, intuition and tact. They engage in a process of search and exploration without knowing, at the outset, what it is exactly that they are looking for, but recognize critical information and opportunities when these present themselves.

The following section of this chapter introduces to the reader in greater detail the Yokohama Youth Support Station, which served as my main field site in 2007 and 2008 (I also paid short visits to several other Support Stations located in Tokyo, Okinawa and Kyoto). I have sketched a brief history of this particular support organization, which contains some important lessons about the development of youth support in Japan and is placed in Appendix K. In the second main section, I set out the support process as it was explained and acted out in the first three years that the Yokohama Support Station operated (2006–08). I then move on to describe the diverse members of staff at the Yokohama centre. They are the protectors of their service's support logic, explaining and justifying it to the outside world and doing what they can to reduce the impact of various stigmatizing labels such as *NEET* on users. I also discuss the staff's own sources of work motivation briefly. I then shift the focus onto the supported young people themselves, beginning with an examination of the staff's understandings of the causes of youth non-employment and exclusion in post-industrial Japan. The narratives of four individual support-receivers are set out next, to demonstrate the sheer complexity of the factors that contribute to their joblessness (which is something that is hard to grasp sufficiently through usual social surveys). The chapter concludes with a brief recapitulation of the challenges as well as considerable benefits of youth support that is informed by the principles of exploration, non-linearity and diversity.

An overview of the Youth Support Station

The 17 December 2007 was a day invested with special meaning for the Yokohama Youth Support Station. At this centre, which lies by a small canal a mere ten minutes' walk from the bustling central train station of Yokohama city (which had 3.5 million inhabitants at the time), an anniversary event was held to commemorate the opening of the still gleaming facility – a bright, almost living-room-like space with only a few partitions – exactly one year earlier. By this date, the initial ramblings that inevitably accompany the launch of a new service were a thing of the past, and the representatives of the 20-some staff explained with some pride the progress made – as well as the most pressing challenges encountered – over the preceding 12 months. Theirs was not just one among the 50 or so Support Stations (or *saposute*, as the centres are called more casually) in operation across Japan at the time, but something of a flagship version of the central government's most prominent support scheme for *NEETs*.[1] An unprecedented programme in flesh-and-bones form in a convenient location, the Yokohama centre had begun attracting keen attention from the widest range of domestic and international observers from its inception in late 2006. The staff told many such guests that they aspired to make their facility the 'first point of call for employment support in Yokohama'.[2]

What this unconventional centre of youth support had achieved over the course of its first year was quite impressive: it had been visited nearly 7,000 times by youth in highly diverse situations, for whom a dazzling menu of activities was offered around the core functions of career and psychological counselling. The uncomplicated sign-up procedure as well as the absence of user fees ensured that the Support Station was substantially more accessible to more youth than the Youth Independence Camp. Hence, with a high number of visits from a range of young adults falling within the formal definition of *NEET*, the chief of the centre could credibly pronounce that 'a layer of youth that had previously been invisible is now gradually coming into view at our Support Station'.[3] There was a shared understanding, however, that the problems the supported youth faced were starkly different from popular perceptions of *NEETs* in Japan at the time, which staff saw as discriminatory and largely unhelpful.

In any case, the staff found little reason for complacency, at the anniversary event, regarding the future of their Support Station. The reports given by each staff member of the parts of the programme they were in charge of – from career and psychological counselling and guidance for guardians to basic skills education, networking with related institutions and job training – contained long explanations of severe difficulties on each count. Not unlike the Independence Camps, this particular *saposute* faced the formidable challenge of securing alternative career paths for youths who had been excluded from mainstream society for long periods of time and hence tended to have minimal job experience. Moreover, against the expectations of key policy-makers within the MHWL (see Chapter 4), youth with a variety of developmental disabilities and mental problems appeared to be flooding in. That the service was delivered free of charge meant that youth from comparatively deprived families could also readily consult the Support Station if they knew about it. Being called upon to respond to such a complex set of issues, the staff, while generally adopting an upbeat, even hopeful tone in their presentations, openly admitted that they at times felt overwhelmed and confounded.

These observations capture many key elements of the complex situation that the Yokohama Youth Support Station faced in its initial years. With the aim of gaining a thorough understanding of its activities, I started paying weekly visits to the centre from the autumn of 2007 onwards after a series of prior visits and interviews with key staff members. On regular days, I arrived at the Support Station in the afternoon, finding a handful of students engaged in consultations with members of staff, one or two waiting for a consultation or a workshop to begin, and a few sitting on the bar chairs, working on their study assignments or surfing the Internet (see Figure 6.1 for the physical layout of the centre). The atmosphere was always friendly and nearly always calm. Occasionally, however, there were male users who were in an obviously

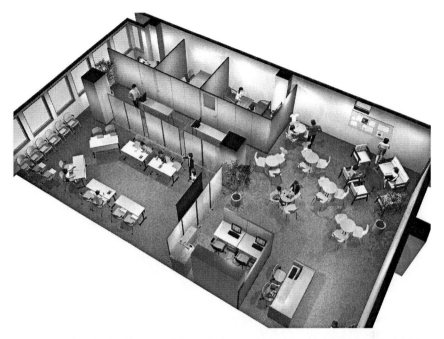

Figure 6.1 The physical layout of the Yokohama Youth Support Station in 2006–07
Source: Totsuka Yumi

disturbed, anxious state and females who were sobbing as they poured out their worries to the staff. Many (but not all) of such clearly more challenging consultations were carried out in a sealed-off cubicle which nevertheless had an open top. There would always be a half-a-dozen-strong group of frequent users whom I met whenever visiting the centre and several of whom kept going back and forth between the Support Station and the Young Job Square located two floors below. This is one example of how the Support Station sometimes functions as a community space – or an *ibasho* – for some youth, although it does so on a limited scale.

Despite the relaxed air, it was rare to witness two users engage in spontaneous conversation. This was in line with the staff's descriptions of their clients as being in too anxious a state to independently interact with others (see below). The majority simply received counselling, sat quietly and patiently through any workshops they attended, and went home soon afterwards. Fortunately though, there were many youth who were willing to talk to me directly either out of their own initiative or after a brief introduction by staff. The fact that I was made into an official volunteer staff member in the autumn of 2007 was of great help, as was the fact that I visited the centre repeatedly over one year. This way I could build trust and rapport with many users and became better known to them (my bright self-introduction card was also attached to the notice board alongside those of other staff). It was my utmost priority to act as discreetly as possible and to be unobtrusive. Hence, I did not try to aggressively make contact with anyone I did not already know without a staff introduction or without the user approaching me first. This inevitably led to a bias in data collection, but I was nevertheless able to gather substantial information on a number of cases that illustrate the sheer complexity, obscured in ordinary survey data, of the circumstances of support-seeking young people and non-employed young people more generally.

The support process

Since its launch, the Yokohama Youth Support Station has, in broad terms, strived to provide employment-related support to youth in an 'individualized' (*kobetsuteki*), 'comprehensive' (*hōkatsuteki*) and 'continuous' (*keizokuteki*) fashion, as set out in official explanations of the programme. The actual support process, however, is more nuanced than this would seem to suggest, and it is underpinned by important principles nowhere to be found in official publications. I shed light on this process in the present section, beginning with a few notes on the physical dimensions of the Yokohama centre. As in Chapter 5, I employ the ethnographic present when describing my findings despite the fact that the programme has continued to evolve and undergo certain changes after the end of my fieldwork period.

Spatial dimensions

Located conveniently near the Yokohama Station and the surrounding shopping area, the Yokohama Support Station is housed in the fourth floor of a typical medium-sized office building. It is easily accessible, although not necessarily noticeable to most passers-by. In the hallway outside, there is a friendly notice board that welcomes visitors to the centre (which, as of early 2008, frequently announced that there were no more personal appointments available for the day). As shown in Figure 6.1, a receptionist's desk is located at the entrance, next to which there is a café-like open area that covers roughly half of the centre's total floor space. Here, staff hold informal consultations with users between 11.00 am and 19.00 pm although the same space also serves as a venue for larger staff meetings and events. Room plants and the brightly coloured but comfortable furniture – together with ample lighting – help to create a cosy atmosphere distinct from most pre-existing counselling or employment centres in Japan (with the possible exception of the Job Café and Young Job Spot described in Chapter 4). Two notice boards inform visitors of upcoming events and the weekly programme. Past users' hand-written accounts of their time at the Support Station and their subsequent life paths (which include 'success stories' by youth who have found employment or made other achievements) are also presented. On a wall near to the reception desk hangs a collage of hand-written staff profiles with smiling photographs. Occasionally, newspaper articles that discuss youth support and

NEETs – for instance, critical statements by scholars such as Honda Yuki and explanations of developmental disabilities of interest such as ADHD – can be found too. The remaining half of the centre consists of two booths for private counselling; a staff rest area; a middle-section with bar stools and narrow tables for chatting, studying and using laptop computers; an open area by the window for various workshops and sports sessions; and another small booth behind the reception desk that serves as the staff's work room (this was expanded and fully partitioned in the spring of 2008 to provide more desk space).

Although some activities do take place elsewhere, the Youth Support Station's main site is where most of its functions, from individual counselling to workshops for family members and basic skills teaching, are carried out.

Individual counselling, the sorting of users and psychological support

Remarkably in light of the history of Japanese social services (see Goodman 2000),[4] the Support Station gives priority not to collective training but to individualized support. Staff contend that 'each youth is different' and that each face unique circumstances. This assumption is reflected in the forms of support offered at the Support Station, with one-on-one counselling forming the essential foundation. Next, I examine how such individualized support operates in practice, starting with the sorting of prospective users, followed by psychological counselling and parental engagement.

When a youth first makes contact with the centre, an initial appointment is arranged with the purpose of getting to know the youth and his or her basic support needs. Rather than 'checking boxes' or covering particular facts in a routine manner, the staff's ultimate goal at this stage is to make the support-seeker feel at ease and to establish a trust relationship with him or her. The terms used to express these two objectives – *anshinkan* and *shinraikan* (a sense of comfort and a sense of trust) – indeed appeared frequently in staff's speech.

At the first counselling session, the staff adopt a soft, non-judgemental approach and essentially focus on listening. Excessive guidance or 'lecturing' is consciously avoided at this stage as well as over the whole support process so as to maintain trust and to develop the users' confidence. The support-seeker is invited to voice requests regarding the types of support he or she would prefer and the activities he or she would like to partake in. The youth might prefer a staff of particular sex, age or background, or ask for an appointment with the clinical psychologist at the centre. Here, in a very similar fashion to K2 International and other organizations that run the Youth Independence Camp, the notion of *aishō*, or 'emotional compatibility', informs the matching of new users with particular staff. The goal is to find an 'emotionally compatible' member of staff so as to make the youth feel as comfortable as possible and thereby lower the threshold for visiting the Support Station. As was seen in the preceding chapter, such a stress on *aishō* motivates the hiring of diverse staff members with varying personal histories, life experiences, interests and qualifications.

Those who contact the Yokohama Support Station are sorted into broad groups and guided into appropriate directions (see the second half of this chapter regarding how users learn about the Support Station). In accordance with the networking concept that informs the centre's activities (see Chapter 4), the Support Station does not provide direct and continuous guidance to all youth who pay a visit, but instead strives to refer them to associated services, including many NPOs. Between April 2007 and March 2008, over one-fourth of registered users (of whom there were 415) were directed to affiliated institutions.

Figure 6.2 illustrates how new users are sorted into those who fall directly within the ambit of the Support Station and those who are referred elsewhere. According to data distributed by the Yokohama centre in February 2008, 10 per cent or more are deemed capable of taking independent action toward finding employment and are hence swiftly forwarded to public and private employment agencies such as Hello Work and the Young Work Plaza. A further 10 to 20 per cent are found to possess mental illnesses or disabilities that are likely to qualify them for a handicapped person's card (*shōgaisha techō*) that will give eligibility for certain public benefits and services. Such youth are directed to public health and welfare centres (*hoken fukushi sentā*), to psychiatrists, or, if they already have eligibility, to employment services designed especially for the handicapped. Those with 'milder' conditions are, however, not disqualified from attending the Support Station if this is not considered risky. The remaining three-fourths or so fall into those who face

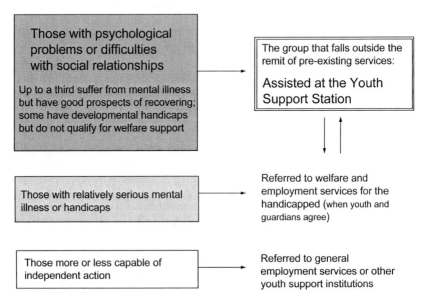

Figure 6.2 How new support-seekers are sorted by the Youth Support Station
Source: Summary based on original interviews and Yokohama Youth Support Station documents

psychological problems or difficulties with social relationships. A significant portion of youth in this category are found to suffer from mental illnesses and/or developmental disabilities, but are nevertheless considered to be in good enough condition to attend the Support Station. They are, however, typically recommended to also begin consulting psychiatric or other medical specialists.

While this is generally how incoming youth are channelled by the Support Station, it is acknowledged by staff that it is not always possible to neatly categorize users' problems and conditions: there are often multiple and overlapping difficulties with complex antecedents. It is at this point that the principle of search, or practices of 'exploring the user', become more important. Here, decisions on how to sort and treat particular youth become a matter of staff judgement, and ambiguous cases are typically discussed during staff meetings and workshops on a case-by-case basis.

For those who are deemed to benefit from the services of the Support Station and agree to attend it regularly, general counselling is continued. Here, five broad 'steps' or 'stages' and corresponding objectives are said to guide the counselling process though, as hinted in the Introduction to this chapter, these should be read as a loose guide to a complex process and as convenient explanations of the support process for the outside world. Table 6.1 presents a word-for-word translation of these steps as reported in the Yokohama Youth Support Station's report for the fiscal year 2007 (YYSS 2008:18).

Although fresh users have various needs and conditions and can thus begin from any of these stages, we see that a 'soft landing' strategy is offered to those who are seen furthest from entering paid employment. In step 1, communicating with staff while gradually engaging in various internal activities is stressed. Step 2 introduces 'social experience programmes' (*shakai taiken jigyō*) that aim to accustom the particular youth to interacting with other people. In this way, confidence (*jishin*) is slowly built up and activities become more work-related, culminating in job-seeking activities and, ideally, in becoming employed. It should be recalled that no formal guarantees of employment or other favourable outcomes are given, however, although staff are generally dedicated and try to make the most of the means available to them.

Another table in the same annual report illustrates how the services of the Support Station are to progress from information dissemination, at-centre activities and mental health counselling to programmes run by external organizations, job training, and, eventually, employment (YYSS 2008:16). This is facilitated by an iterative process that begins with the identification of problems, moves to the planning of solutions and their execution, and ends with reflection.[5] In reality, support activities usually do not follow such clear formulae, and complex bundles of issues are discovered only very gradually through a process of continued search.

While it is difficult to gauge the performance of general counselling activities at the Support Station, the users of the centre appear to very much like the members of staff they talk to and rarely voice a critical word about

Table 6.1 The Yokohama Youth Support Station's principles according to stage

Target group(s)	Objectives
Step 5 Those who wish to attach themselves stably to a job and those who wish to change jobs.	Continued counselling according to need for users to stay on in jobs they have found or for users who wish to change jobs. Responding to labour problems while referring users to affiliated agencies.
Step 4 Those who are writing their work histories and CVs, taking steps to locate job openings and beginning job-seeking activities with the goal of attaiing occupational independence.	Assisting users with locating information on job openings, preparing for employment examinations and drafting application documents with the goal of having the user find employment.
Step 3 Those who take part in work trials while striving to cultivate their work consciousness and decide about a future course (*shinro*).	Administering short-term work trials once users have improved their levels of confidence and work consciousness in steps 1 and 2. Also, simultaneously helping users acquire information on vocational aptitude tests and concrete occupations.
Step 2 Those who wish to take part in activities (including social experience programmes) to improve their communication and self-expression skills prior to finding paid work.	Having users gradually take part in social experience programmes by other NPOs while regularly consulting with staff and engaging in activities at the Support Station.
Step 1 Those whose goal is to commute to, and get used to, the Support Station, and those who are recovering after a period of social withdrawal. (Those who wish to achieve occupational independence in the future.)	Having users visit the Support Station to talk with various members of staff and to participate in activities (Support Station acts as the base for all activities at this stage).

Source: Yokohama Youth Support Station (YYSS) (2008)

counselling sessions per se. Thus, insofar as trust and rapport is built and maintained between users and staff, the centre can be said to be successfully fulfilling one of its basic goals. As Chapter 7 will point out, this makes the Support Station dramatically different from most youth employment services in Europe where distrust (between support-seekers and counsellors and the employment offices they work for) appears to characterize the activation process.

It should be noted that, even though general counselling forms the backbone of the Support Station's programme and acts as an interface for participation in other activities, it is not mandatory for youth to take counselling every time they call in at the centre. Rather, since it is acknowledged that many are recovering after months or even years of social withdrawal, users are allowed to freely spend time at the centre reading, leafing through pamphlets, using computers or chatting with others if they feel like it. It is presumed that in this way fresh users will gradually get used to the 'atmosphere' of the Support Station and reduce their feelings of anxiety. During my visits, there were typically one or two youth sitting around reading, doing their study assignments or waiting for appointments. It appeared that, instead of the most socially insecure youth, it was mainly the talkative and sociable ones who regularly 'hung around' at the centre, but even such youth only numbered two or three at a time.

The other form of personal support that is offered to users consists of psychological counselling (*shinri sōdan*). This is carried out by a qualified clinical psychologist (*rinshō shinrishi*)[6] – a young female enrolled in a graduate school at one of the most prestigious universities in Japan – as well as by a newly hired part-time male staff with the same qualification. The role of psychological counselling is to provide professional help whenever general counselling is not going smoothly due to mental health problems or when staff members are not able to ascertain a particular user's mental condition (YYSS 2007:7). Users are free also to independently request a meeting with the psychological counsellor whenever they wish to. Due to growing demand, the number of days on which psychological counselling is provided was increased to four in April 2008 from two or three in the previous year. As a rule, 50 minutes is allocated to each session. Consultations take place in a cubicle by the window that serves as the psychologist's office. The sessions are typically one-on-one but occasionally another member of staff (who is typically the main personal counsellor of the user in question) may attend as well.

The three most common issue areas that users sought psychological counselling for in 2006 and 2007 were 'mental health', 'anxiety regarding human relationships' and 'uncertainties about work' (YYSS 2008:41). In contrast to these categories that are based on concerns self-reported by the users, according to the clinical psychologist, the three most important underlying factors were, in order of prevalence, family relationship problems, past school-refuser (*futōkō*) and/or social withdrawal (*hikikomori*) experience, and mental illness and/or disabilities (including developmental disabilities). These issues will be discussed in more detail below.

A considerable proportion of those who receive psychological counselling at the Support Station do so continuously. According to the clinical psychologist, the majority of individual users received counselling once in two or three weeks, although most of them would like to do so even more often; however, the Support Station did not have enough resources to further increase counselling hours at the time of my field research.

While I was not able to observe psychological counselling sessions directly, I carried out several interviews and informal talks with the main psychologist at the Support Station to understand the methods employed and the problems that had emerged. In her practice, she mainly draws on cognitive behavioural therapy (CBT) which aims to raise patients' level of self-understanding and therefore alter entrenched patterns of thought and action. During the first appointment, the psychologist asks a broad range of questions and occasionally employs psychological tests to establish a particular user's personal background and mental condition. In Japan, clinical psychologists are not permitted to prescribe drugs such as anti-depressants so, where medication is deemed beneficial, she directs the support-receiver to a qualified psychiatric or another type of doctor (e.g. of internal medicine).

What the psychologist at the Support Station can do, however, is to arrive at a better understanding of the mental condition of the youth she counsels and to determine more accurately what kind of support is appropriate for them. She frequently finds that many users suffer from multiple conditions, having for example developed a secondary mental illness in addition to pre-existing developmental disabilities. Here, the psychologist performs pioneering (if small-scale) survey work as she analyses and records the mental health problems of youth who have previously received little coordinated support through public welfare or medical care services. At the same time, she participates in the sorting of users as she directs those with serious mental disabilities or illnesses to external services and those with milder conditions to internal programmes such as 'mental training' (discussed below) that aim to systematically improve the psychological health of participants.

Albeit not considered an illness or disability, according to the Support Station psychologist as well as other staff, the most common shared condition among those who seek mental counselling is that of a 'low sense of self-affirmation' (*jikō kōteikan ga hikui*). This term is frequently employed both at the Yokohama centre as well as in the wider youth support community, essentially to denote a chronic lack of self-esteem and confidence (which is related, in Chapter 7, to a structurally rooted denial of recognition to young people outside 'standard' employment positions). A large proportion of Support Station clients are seen to be unable to make progress in their lives and careers due to an acute fear of failure and a frail belief in their abilities. Such entrenched frames of mind are said to be associated with extended periods of school-refusal and/or social withdrawal, traumatic experiences such as bullying or abuse, and 'excessive interference' (*kakanshō*) from parents. Accordingly, psychological counselling is deployed so as to undo negative self-images and to help users restore (or build up) their sense of 'self-affirmation'.

'Self-affirmation' is a concept closely linked to the less specific theme of 'confidence' (*jishin*) that runs through all the Support Station's services. Indeed, a healthy degree of confidence is seen by the staff as a fundamental prerequisite for success in social activities and job-seeking. Easily confused with these two terms is the psychological concept of self-efficacy (*jiko kōryokukan*) that is used (in the context of Japanese youth support) for theorizing and understanding the preconditions of high 'self-affirmation'. This concept is appealing for the psychologist at the Support Station because it helps to explain how an individual's belief in his/her capacity to succeed in particular social situations is constructed and conditioned (see Bandura 1997). It also supplies a rationale for providing users with 'success experiences' (*seikō taiken*) through structured activities.

At the Yokohama centre, one other less individualized kind of psychological service is offered that goes by the name of 'mental training' (*mentaru torēningu*). This type of training is provided in the form of short courses that consist of six classes held once a week. The basic objective is to prompt trainees to shed their 'negative' or 'backward' (*ushiro-muki*) thought-patterns and acquire a more positive way of thinking (*maemuki na shikō*) conducive to a higher level of confidence. This is done progressively through learning about basic psychological mechanisms; becoming aware of changes in one's mental state through exercises and keeping a diary; acquiring strategies to positively influence one's mood; and through creating small goals to translate improvements in one's mental state to constructive action. These strategies draw primarily on Western cognitive behavioural therapy.

In sum, though still in somewhat limited supply, psychological counselling has an integral place in the Support Station's overall programme. This may lead to the hiring of more (part-time) psychologists in the near future. Significantly, the Support Station is one of the first public services in Japan at the time of writing that provide mental counselling free of charge to youth without access to school or company-provided services (counselling is not covered by the National Health Insurance in Japan and it is only provided at elementary and secondary schools). This represents a notable change to the status quo since the only other way for the kinds of youth who use the Support Station to receive counselling is to purchase it privately at up to 5,000 yen per hour (roughly five times the hourly wage of a part-time worker). The downside is that those young people who do not identify as *NEETs*, or who do not feel that exclusion from employment is a grave problem for them, are extremely unlikely to benefit from free counselling.[7]

Job training, remedial education and other activities

Supporting the job-search activities of users in appropriate ways is one of the main official objectives of the Youth Support Station. Where a user is considered physically and mentally capable of some kind of work activity, the staff take gradual steps towards directing him or her towards employment (as outlined in Table 6.1). While general counselling is the first method for getting to know the needs of each user and giving them concrete support with job-seeking, job training (*jobutore*) provides an important method for moving from discussion to practice. According to interviews with members of staff, such practical training is one of the most promising tools in the support process. This is because doing a trial at an actual workplace gives users a hands-on feel regarding work and because it can provide psychologically important 'success experiences'. It also teaches basic skills similar to those promoted by the Youth Independence Camp, requiring participants to report to work at an agreed time, take responsibility, ask for assistance when they need it, and to communicate spontaneously with superiors and workmates (YYSS 2008:130). All of this, it is believed, strengthens confidence and clarifies the skills a trainee needs to improve. In the process, more useful information is generated that staff can utilize as they continue to support a given young person.

What has made job training particularly attractive are its reported outcomes: in 2007, 73 per cent of all job training participants were able to find employment or enrol in a vocational training course shortly after their training periods. Many staff consequently have high hopes regarding this support measure and wish to expand the availability of suitable job training opportunities. However, if we look at this more closely, we find that only a total of 23 (out of 415 registered users) actually took part in job training in 2007, giving us less reason for optimism. It may simply be that those who are generally doing well at the Support Station – and who are 'closest' to employment from the start – get selected for job training. Moreover, no job trainees were subsequently hired as full-time workers: some stayed with the NPOs and small businesses they trained at, while others became contract, dispatch or part-time staff at other organizations.

The Yokohama Support Station's staff are, of course, acutely aware of these challenges. They do not view job training as a 'quick' solution and find that most users require considerable time to prepare mentally so that they are able to function in a work situation. To this end, a field trip (*kengaku*) system has been set up where youth can observe the workplace beforehand to alleviate their feelings of anxiety. Social Skills Training (SST) is also being developed with the same goal in mind.[8]

Starting in April 2008, the MHLW agreed to pay a subsidy to all employers and organizations that provide training opportunities to Support Station users (who themselves receive no compensation for work performed during training periods). This has slightly increased the potential scope of the job-training scheme but, as of August 2008, the staff complained that there still was an enormous, pressing shortage of suitable training places. 'Suitable' in this context means, more than anything else, workplaces with a degree of willingness to accommodate youth with special needs, from chronic anxiety and fear of failure to learning difficulties and developmental disabilities. It is argued by staff that the demand for 'understanding' job training sites will increase as the number of Support Station users grows.

Because staff need to ascertain just how understanding potential training sites are, they strive to establish personal links with many relevant organizations in advance (instead of searching for training sites anonymously, say via the public employment services). Such personal relationships are often based on the pre-existing connections of Support Station staff. The Workers' Collective Association, the earlier workplace of a member of staff, has been among the most important partners so far.[9] There are efforts to greatly expand the volume of partnerships with relevant organizations to increase the number not only of training sites but also of potential employers, or 'exits' (*deguchi*). However, it has proved especially challenging to find commercial enterprises that are willing to accommodate special needs and to discuss individual cases directly with the Support Station. That few staff have previously had careers in the mainstream business sector further limits the building of such cross-sector partnerships.

The Yokohama Support Station's approach to job training thus turns out to be broadly similar to that of K2 International, which runs a Youth Independence Camp nearby. Clearly, the former has had less time to expand its local network to maximize training opportunities, but it speaks in similar terms about how hands-on trials help youth to understand their capabilities, skill development needs and interests, allowing them to build confidence in the process. It remains to be seen whether the resources needed to increase training places can be amassed and whether the private sector will be more cooperative in the future.

That the Yokohama Support Station has begun offering remedial tutoring in basic academic skills is also notable. It is not that the centre is growing into an educational institution – with no more than one weekly tutoring session, this much could not be expected – but these supplementary tutoring activities speak volumes about the challenges faced by supported young people as well as their mentors.

Under the banner of 'relearning' (*manabinaoshi*), half a dozen volunteers and Support Station staff provide tutoring in Japanese, arithmetic, geography, economics and politics in two small groups that convene biweekly. The meetings take place around a table in a relatively quiet area towards the middle of the centre. In 2008, one of the sessions ran for six hours and was provided for roughly 10 participants, while another smaller group met for two hours at a time. The rationale for the programme is based on the observation that a significant proportion of youth who come to the Support Station possess insufficient reading and writing skills along with poor knowledge of mathematics. This not only weakens their ability to land jobs, but also causes them to resign (or be dismissed) quickly when they have found one. It is said that employers often lose patience with 'slow learners' or those who make frequent mistakes and that such youth, in turn, tend to lose their confidence in the process. Problems that clearly relate to gaps in basic knowledge, learning difficulties or disabilities are typically not understood as having such origins, and employers consequently treat ill-performing young workers harshly. Staff at Support Stations and other youth support institutions find that this pushes the concerned youth into a negative spiral of low confidence, self-blame and, at worst, towards depression. The goal of *manabinaoshi* is to break such a negative spiral by providing individually-tailored tutoring. For many users, engagement in such 'relearning' is a useful way to relieve feelings of anxiety and insecurity ahead of job training. In cases where a user is a lower-secondaryschool graduate, tutors assist him/her with getting admitted to an upper-secondary school. This is quite vital because an upper-secondary school leaving certificate is required by the vast majority of jobs available in Japan today (it is also a condition for entering various professional training programmes).

In addition to counselling, job training and remedial tutoring, the Yokohama Support Station runs various other complementary activities. These include stretching and yoga classes, self-expression workshops that make use of visual arts, occasional social parties (that are facilitated by a handful of interaction rules), voice training and work camps. In addition, day trips to famous sights in Tokyo or to rural locations outside metropolitan Japan are sometimes made. Support Station users are also invited to plan their own events and take part in the planning and running of parties and trips.

These kinds of complementary activities, while no doubt enjoyed by many participants, are important for what they symbolize. First, the inclusion of physical exercise and voice training expresses a holistic conception of the person and the support process. For someone who has been withdrawn and excluded for as long as several years, full recovery is seen to require not only mental but also physical improvement. Learning how to strengthen and project one's voice is based on a similar conception of the person as a 'bodymind' and is something taught at many support institutions across Japan (several of which place special emphasis on mastering vigorous *aisatsu* – basic daily greetings – that are viewed as part and parcel of good manners and proper conduct at the workplace). That work camps are also organized shows that the staff at the Support Station do not reject the value of residential group-based support either. They endorse such forms of support and even sometimes collaborate with Independence Camp delivery organizations, provided user participation is made voluntary.

Services for guardians

The active and positive involvement of parents in the support process is increasingly seen as important by Support Station staff.[10] We have seen above how parents in Japan often act as 'gatekeepers' when youth may want to access support measures. Unlike in the case of the Independence Camps, however, families are not required to act as financial sponsors for users of the Support Station as this is mainly a feeless service, but they nevertheless play a crucial role. Guardians are, after all, often the only link between support services and socially withdrawn youth. Hence, the Yokohama Support Station is acutely aware of the need to reach out to parents of inactive young adults of various types and strive to give them some means to overcome their difficulties. In practice, guardians are catered for via family counselling (*kazoku sōdan kai*) and seminars (*hogosha saron* and *hogosha seminā*).

In fiscal 2007, the Yokohama Youth Support Station received 825 visits from guardians, amounting to a tenth of the total number of visits to the centre. Around 80 per cent of the guardians who accessed the Support Station were mothers who came alone without their husbands or children. The Support

Station's yearly report noted that, in the vast majority of such cases, the mothers who visited were puzzling over what to do with their socially withdrawn sons or daughters who would not talk to them or interact with non-family members (YYSS 2008:37). By contrast, there were very few visits from parents whose children were already using the Support Station or in the process of job-seeking, suggesting that those who did visit felt they were in an extremely difficult situation. Support staff observe that parents tend to be socially quite isolated and unable to discuss their problems with acquaintances due to feelings of shame; that in many cases they are emotionally exhausted and stressed; that they harbour grave worries about their offspring's future after they themselves have become frail or deceased; and that they often forcefully take their children to support centres, which typically leads to negative results (YYSS 2008:38). These points are consistent with my own observations and with the interviews I held at other support institutions across Japan, and similar issues are also reflected in Horiguchi's discussion of private *hikikomori* support groups (Horiguchi 2011).

At the Support Station in Yokohama, family counselling is seen as one of the primary methods of reaching out to concerned parents. Provided as a once-a-month service, it is hoped that one-on-one counselling for parents will function as the first step in a process of continuous support that will eventually lead their children to sign up for regular counselling. Another aim of this service is to reduce the psychological stress that many parents feel by allowing them to freely air their grievances. However, the capacity to supply parental counselling at the Support Station remains low and only a handful of families are counselled each calendar month. Therefore, a 'guardians' salon' (*hogosha saron*) is held once a month with much the same aim of relieving stress and providing fresh perspective on problematic situations through peer counselling and support.

The guardians' seminars (*hogosha seminā*), in turn, are more-organized workshops run once in three months by different members of staff. Their objective is to relieve parents' anxieties regarding their children; to help parents to better comprehend problems such as youth unemployment and the changing labour markets; and to teach them how to more effectively communicate with their offspring. For guardians who take part in the seminars, discovering others in similar situations is a liberating and comforting experience. This is said to relieve the intense sense of shame that many parents harbour over having 'failed' as guardians.

All of the dozen or so participants at the *hogosha saron* that I attended in September 2007 were females in their fifties and sixties. The theme of the particular session was parent-child communication and the main teaching method was free discussion and role play. The staff member who facilitated the session invited participants to identify their concerns regarding their families and then convey them clearly and succinctly to husbands and children. A variety of sensitive issues was brought up: many mothers reported that their children were no longer talking to them or even greeting them in the morning, and several had offspring that had withdrawn socially and physically for as long as two years on end. The facilitator noted that, even in such circumstances, it is common that especially sons adopt a 'stronger' or 'superior' role vis-à-vis their parents, who correspondingly become weaker. To address this problem, the facilitator invited participants to divide into small groups and practice voicing their concerns and wishes to each other so that they could later voice them more forcefully to their families. There was thus a desire here to help activate withdrawn young people through 'empowering' their mothers.

Activities such as the *hogosha saron* reflect both the dire, emotionally exhausting circumstances of many parents with socially isolated youth as well as dominant ideas regarding the role of parents. There is currently still an overwhelming emphasis on parental responsibility over the perceived failures or problems of children (including youth aged up to 30). Predictably, as the *NEET* debate erupted in the media, many began calling for parents to change themselves in order to change their children. A book by Genda Yūji and Kosugi Reiko that essentially amounts to a parents' manual for coping with 'children who had turned into *NEETs*' is but one example here (Genda and Kosugi 2005). Youth support services, in a social context focused on parental responsibility, provide a degree of relief to many guardians by showing that they are not the only ones who are struggling with their offspring's situation.

The staff: Protecting the inner logic of support

It is the staff members of the Youth Support Station who are in charge of delivering this programme in practice and who serve as a concrete link between state policy, various local institutions and employees, parents and supported youth themselves. As suggested at the top of this chapter, their practices are characterized by a certain inner logic which is not obvious to outsiders. In this section, I review the backgrounds of the staff members at the Yokohama Support Station while also discussing what motivates them and how they relate to the government.

Staff backgrounds

Although Japanese youth workers in general come from a variety of backgrounds, the staff of the Yokohama Youth Support Station are a particularly diverse group. They include members who have extensive work experience in the voluntary sector, some who have previously built careers in IT, and others who have taken up their positions following a period of social exclusion and withdrawal. Indeed, it will become clear below that, while there is a growing emphasis on professional qualifications, hiring a great mix of staff with rich personal experience is viewed as crucial to making the Support Station effective. At the same time, youthfulness is stressed: the average age of staff is well below 40, which means that, in some cases, a member of staff may be younger than the 'youth' he or she counsels. Appendix H provides a summary of basic information on the support staff, including their positions, backgrounds and formal qualifications at the beginning of the fiscal year 2008.

From this appendix one can observe that, first of all, 12 of the total 20 staff members are female, and that 70 per cent are either part-timers or volunteers. However, the bulk of work at the Yokohama Support Station is shouldered by the seven full-time employees (of whom four are female) who take care of management, scheduling, networking, overall programme coordination and mental counselling services. Around half of the part-timers work two to three days a week and are in charge of specific programmes such as guardians' events (although they routinely engage in general counselling also). The remaining half turn up more rarely, sometimes only once or twice a month, but they nevertheless bring important expertise to the centre – e.g. on the labour markets and workers' protection – and connect it with other youth support organizations, various social enterprises and wider society. There are, for example, dispatched workers from NICE, a youth organization that organizes international and ecological work camps across Japan, and from the Temp Workers' Union as well as from a local self-help group launched by parents of socially withdrawn youth (Tsuki Ichi no Kai). It is notable also that two of the volunteers are university lecturers who assist not only with counselling but also with the collection of statistical data on the Support Station's activities.

Despite considerable diversity, the core staff at the Yokohama Support Station have many important characteristics in common. First, only the chief has had significant experience in the corporate world. Others have prior work experience in the youth support, welfare and NPO sectors, or come from backgrounds of social exclusion and withdrawal. The lack of young full-time staff with a corporate background is, of course, common across the field of youth support in Japan and other civil society groups, and is hardly surprising. With the mainstream employment system emphasizing rigid, one-track career paths, it is virtually unheard of for a company worker to move flexibly between the for-profit and non-profit sectors. Hence, the decision for someone to work in the NPO sector is 'final' in the sense that it forecloses the opportunity to return to generally much better paid full-time jobs at corporations. The wages being drastically lower and employment generally more insecure in the former, few material incentives exist for full-time company workers to transition into not-for-profits. The notable exceptions are, needless to say, female workers who have retired from their jobs on giving birth, and retirees who have completed their formal careers.[11]

Increasingly, as their numbers rise, irregular workers may also become relatively more interested in joining NPOs since this does not necessarily imply a loss of income for them. Naturally, for youth who have a background of social exclusion, there is little to lose and much to gain (both socially and economically) from joining the not-for-profit sector, for example through working at the Yokohama Youth Support Station. This partly explains why former support-receivers are well represented among the staff of youth support organizations in Japan.[12]

These tendencies, of course, do not explain why the Yokohama Youth Support Station has recruited the particular members it has. Although Kudō Kei, the founding chief of the Young Job Spot in Yokohama (the Support Station's direct predecessor), is highly explicit about his recruiting principles, this is not the case with the managers of the Support Station. Most recruiting seems to take place rather spontaneously and through existing networks. Two of the managers are board members of the NPO that runs the Support Station (along with a few youth support organizations), one used to be a support worker at the now closed Young Job Spot, two are former social withdrawees (*tōjisha*) and one has long years of experience in the not-for-profit sector. Recruitment routes appear more varied in the case of part-timers, some of whom had applied without prior connections after having discovered the Support Station online or through other support services. That it can have several part-timers who do not aspire to become full-time staff derives from the fact that two-thirds of such employees are females in households where the husband is the main breadwinner.

Although formal qualifications are not yet an absolute requirement for staff, they are being actively promoted by the government. The most common qualifications held by the Support Station staff in Yokohama are those of career consultant, industrial counsellor, clinical psychologist and mental health care worker. As of March 2008, just under half of the staff had acquired one or more of these qualifications, but the government was putting pressure on them to get qualified as career consultants (see below). In addition to formalized competencies, efforts are made to improve the staff skills through monthly training sessions. These consist of 'case study circles' where particular users and support situations are discussed and debated between staff, sometimes with the involvement of outside experts; of lectures by guest speakers from affiliated or related organizations; and of workshops on particular topics such as mental health, disability and sexual discrimination. Here, most is made of the know-how of individual members of staff who are asked to teach others about their areas of expertise.

Three further points should be made about the Support Station's staff. First, the organization they form is remarkably flat: there is a sense that the members are on an equal standing with one another, and terms such as senior (*senpai*), junior (*kōhai*), superior or subordinate are never used. *Dōki*, the word used by Japanese company workers to refer to colleagues who were hired at the same time as them, is also absent since the Support Station clearly does not hire its staff at steady intervals. Moreover, although the chief – an energetic female in her early thirties – displays leadership at meetings and typically represents the organization at important events, other staff do not feel restrained from airing their own views in her presence (as would certainly be the case at the vast majority of commercial companies). There is a distinction, however, between the level of influence that full-time and part-time staff exert, but this is more due to a difference in the level of involvement in the centre's activities than to active discrimination between full-timers and part-timers, which is something the staff strive consciously to avoid.[13]

The second point is that staff are, on the whole, very young. Their average age is just below 40, but several are in their late twenties and early thirties. This state of affairs relates to a widely shared belief within the Japanese field of youth support that stipulates that supported youth feel more at ease when talking to young rather than middle-aged (or older) members of staff, and that support staff must be *genki*, i.e. full of vitality and positive energy. Complex reasons underlie this belief, beginning with the vast generational differences in life experiences – including labour markets experiences – between many youth and their baby-boomer parents. Moreover, since one of the purposes of the Support Station and other youth independence support policies is to prompt young people to establish their own 'independent' lives separately from their parents, it would appear contradictory if most supporters were in their fifties or older. This does not, however, mean that older support staff are altogether absent or undervalued: the oldest volunteer I met during my fieldwork at the Support Station was 70 years old, and his contributions were greatly appreciated by both other staff and users. Indeed, having senior counsellors is often indispensable, since they may wield more influence over status-conscious guardians.

Third, unlike many private non-government-affiliated youth support groups, the Yokohama Support Station (which has been largely supported by subsidies from the central and city governments from the start) employs very few mothers of excluded or isolated youth. As of March 2008, only two of the ten volunteers were females with socially withdrawn and/or non-employed offspring, both being in charge of guardians' services. Being a mother was not seen as a sufficient 'qualification' for a support worker. Indeed, it was implicitly viewed as counterproductive due to the stark generational divide in values and attitudes. Since the Support Station emphasizes non-judgemental interaction and equality of standing between staff and users, having many staff from the users' parents' generation might endanger these priorities.

Sources of work motivation

What motivates the Support Station staff to remain in their line of work despite its potential stressfulness, lack of public recognition and relatively low wages? Low wages are, as suggested above, tolerated partly because most staff come from previous jobs with relatively similar pay levels or enter the field after having been socially excluded for significant periods of time. Many female part-timers can manage paltry wages due to their bread-winning husbands. What are some of the other sources of the motivation that drives the staff?

At the Independence Camps and in the wider residential support sector, staff frequently point out that witnessing their students change and grow is, for them, a major source of joy and motivation. There were times when, during some of the interviews I conducted, such staff had tears in their eyes as they shared past 'success stories' of youth who had risen from desperate, dismal situations into meaningful and relatively stable lives under their guidance. Such emotions are sometimes expressed by staff at the Yokohama Support Station also. A middle-aged part-time member of staff who engages with both young support-receivers and guardians says that nothing motivates her more than observing positive changes in her clients (Planner for guardians' services 1, 28 March 2008).[14] However, personal change is in general emphasized far less by staff at the Support Station than by their colleagues in the residential sector. This may reflect the more limited chances of the former to observe their supportees (since they only meet them intermittently), a 'less intensive' programme that has less scope for 'changing' individuals, or simply a different philosophy regarding youth support altogether.

The last of these reasons is, in fact, very important. A male administrative member (who had himself experienced a family member's suicide and a period of non-school attendance in the past) says his humble wish is to 'make this society liveable for people like him' (*shakai wo jibun no yō na hito ga ikiyasuku shinai to*). This staff member is of the view that youth who are excluded from formal education and the labour markets constitute a type of minority that faces particular hardships while living in today's Japan. Such a perception of 'society' instead of individuals as the fundamental cause of youth exclusion is common to virtually all staff at Yokohama Support Station. While the staff's immediate duties consist of running their centre and attending to users, they are thus keen to help change the surrounding society and dominant understandings of youth exclusion. It is telling that the Support Station's yearly reports for 2006 and 2007 are entitled *Empowerment* (in English) and contain a number of short essays that lament what are perceived as negative changes in Japan towards more inequality and strong-eat-the-weak-style competitive employment practices. Many staff members are clearly driven by an underlying sense of dissatisfaction, even anger, towards what they see as blatant injustices in current Japanese society – feelings that are, no doubt, strengthened by past personal adversities and daily encounters with disadvantaged young people.

The staff at the Yokohama Support Station do derive a sense of meaningfulness and motivation simply from interacting with their clients also. A part-time counsellor with a mental health welfare qualification (*seishin fukushi-shi*) says she feels a tremendous sense of fulfilment whenever a user books an appointment with her. This makes her feel rather special and needed (Professional counsellor 2, 1 April 2008). According to the same counsellor, it is not uncommon that a bond (*tsunagari*) develops between a member of staff and his or her young client, and she hopes that, in the severest cases, this will keep the latter from committing suicide. More positive examples of progress – if not of dramatic personal change – are at times mentioned as well, for example at larger meetings such as the anniversary events in December. A degree of pride is felt over the fact that the centre is working hard to provide new opportunities to those who have once 'stumbled' or 'failed' in society. Although an air of modesty and self-effacement is generally maintained, the vast majority of staff essentially believe that the work they do is important, and that there are potentially hundreds of thousands of youth in need of the kind of help that the Support Station provides (see the concluding section regarding trends in Support Station user figures).

Resisting changing government agendas ('external logics')

The government's promotion of career consulting qualifications within youth support provides a fruitful example of conflict between youth policy bureaucrats within the MHLW and youth support staff. Although it is not possible to survey the history of Japanese career counselling here, it should be noted that, incidentally, the very same bureaucrat who engineered Japan's new youth policies (the 'innovator') has also been one of the central developers of the government's recent career consulting schemes. Such schemes strive to strengthen the position of career consulting as a profession by working towards the creation of a national qualification and by advancing the training of counsellors.

Viewing youth support and career consulting as two complementary and closely interlinked projects, the MHLW stepped up its efforts to promote the role of career consulting qualification at sites of youth support in 2008.[15] The Yokohama Support Station, however, did not think much of increasing the role of such counselling at this point. Rather, many of its staff were actively protesting against the government's moves: they argued that over-emphasizing career counselling would be counterproductive and that, if anything, there was a need for more welfare-related know-how at the Support Station (since a large share of users were said to face mental illnesses and disabilities). Moreover, prioritizing one qualification over others was said to run squarely against the Yokohama Support Station's principles of employing staff with diverse backgrounds and skills. Many thought that career counselling was promoted by the government simply because it wished to secure more jobs for the swelling ranks of qualified career consultants that it had produced.

This disagreement between policy-makers and youth policy practitioners is symbolic of tensions that go beyond individual skirmishes. First, although many Support Station staff do hold formal qualifications, they by and large give much higher value to the role of experience, both the kind gained in their personal lives and careers and the kind accumulated through youth work practice. The government, on the other hand, sees a need for the professionalization of the sector, largely because it wishes to create jobs for career counsellors. There are, of course, advantages that qualifications confer on youth workers apart from any professional skills they involve, as such formal recognition may boost the occupational prestige of their holders and the whole sector of youth support. Japanese youth workers – still largely not recognized as an occupational group – are aware of such benefits. What matters, for them, is having the 'right' mix of qualifications represented at a given support centre, and the 'right' balance between formal and informal kinds of experience. Furthermore, there is, among some parties, a strong desire for an exclusive youth worker's qualification that could substantially improve youth supporters' skills and legitimize youth work as an occupation.

Managing the NEET *category and its consequences for youth support practice*

Alongside observing the characteristics and the thinking of Support Station staff, it is equally crucial to examine the strategic elements of youth support. Importantly, how do staff manage the negative associations of the *NEET* category so as to protect the inner (accommodating) logic of their support service, creating a secure space for exploring and addressing their users' circumstances?

Chapter 3 has examined how *NEETs* were constructed by the mass media as youth without work motivation and Chapter 4 showed how this construct influenced the making of youth support policy. It is vital to also examine the significance of the social category *NEET* and associated stigma in the practice of youth support.[16] In fact it turns out that this term has many negative and some positive effects on support practice. Also, the associated stigma are being managed in distinctive ways on three levels: at actual sites of youth support; by youth support staff when they look for potential partners and employers for their clients; and by the youth support community when it strives to improve its legitimacy and recognition in the wider society. In addition, it will be noted that *NEET* appears to be affecting support-seeking behaviour in some unanticipated ways.

The assistant chief of the Support Station made it clear during our first encounter in April 2007 that staff indeed consciously avoid using *NEET* to describe their users because they passionately reject the assumption that non-working youth have no jobs due to their own laziness or lack of motivation (Assistant chief, 18 April 2007). Instead, the Support Station staff argue that their clients want to work but are not able to do so for some reason, echoing the views of Genda in his trend-setting (though in many ways contested) book (Genda and Maganuma 2004; see Chapter 3). They also often describe users as 'youth who face hardships in their lives' (*ikizurasa wo kakaeru wakamono*), perhaps owing to the influence of K2 International and the labour activist Amamiya Karin. At the same time, the assistant chief and other members of staff recognize that *NEET* is nevertheless a convenient means of self-identification for many socially withdrawn youth. A typical first-time visitor to the Youth Support Station would introduce himself or herself as a *NEET*, or as 'doing *NEET*' (*nīto wo yatteiru*) in the same way as an employed person would say they are working as salaried men or office ladies (*salarīman wo yatteiru, ōeru wo yatteiru*). So, even if they harbour complicated feelings about the label, *NEET* provides many youth with a useful shorthand for identifying themselves that is not quite as specific or negative as *hikikomori* (socially withdrawn youth). On a different note, that many users employ the *NEET* label in this way demonstrates that there is a strong empirical link between the *NEET* category and actual support-seeking behaviour, with the symbolic label implicitly guiding inactive young people to sites of support, precisely as illustrated by the schema of 'symbolic activation' (Chapter 1).

According to a formerly withdrawn young staff member in his late twenties, *NEET* has some real utility as a colloquial expression, since the only term that had previously existed to describe non-employed youth, *jakunen mugyōsha* (literally, a non-employed youth), is highly formal and cumbersome to pronounce (Networker 2, 22 October 2007). This partly explains how *NEET* could become part of the general vocabulary so quickly. The downside is that the term renders non-employed youth much more visible than before, subjecting them to (media) bashing by those who view them as indolent and work-shy.

On the other hand, the same young staff member underlined that the youth who frequent the Support Station do not necessarily give very much thought to the deeper social meaning of *NEET* or to how it locates them in the social hierarchy. They may well recognize that they are in a disadvantaged position, but it is likely that much of the negative commentary and disparagement escapes them. This is especially the case with those who remain withdrawn and hence have little contact with mainstream society or media. At this stage, it is more often the case that the *NEET* discourse affects the parents who feel ashamed and may as a result be mobilized to seek outside support (if they are aware that such support exists; this element is also considered in the discussion on symbolic activation in Chapter 1). Ironically, *NEET* becomes more consequential to the identities of non-employed youth precisely when they re-engage with the outside world through seeking work or support, i.e. precisely when they try to 'exit' the *NEET* category.

It is here that the implications of the *NEET* discourse to support practice become acutely felt: non-employed youth are faced with the need to repeatedly explain their social status to others (who implicitly do not give the former recognition). For example, they are required to confront the suspicions and dismissive attitudes of conservative employers. These factors have significant influence over and above fragmented or blank CVs which were mentioned before. Insofar as those responsible for hiring new staff at a given workplace have bought into the dominant construction of *NEETs* as lazy and low on work morale, they tend to adopt a negative stance towards any job applicant falling into this category, no matter what skills or potential he or she might be shown to have.

Accordingly, most support institutions for non-employed youth feel the necessity to change employer attitudes regarding youth issues and to promote general societal understanding of youth. Carrying out public educational activities (*keimō katsudō*) is indeed heralded by the Support Station staff as an important goal. Their centre is now also gradually building direct relations with manufacturing firms and other companies. Such direct relations can be seen as a way for youth support organizations to manage the *NEET* stigma at an institutional level. Another strategy employed by many support groups is to strip off the 'otherness' and negativity of the *NEET* category by reframing supported youth as 'local young people from the community' or by using other types of disarming linguistic strategies.

It is of course not uncommon that people who are negatively constructed within mainstream society decide to actively confront unfavourable portrayals by criticizing them or even by actively appropriating them (see Thoits 2011). Indeed, there are some Japanese youth who playfully call themselves 'neo-*NEETs*', others who aspire to become 'the number one *NEET* in Japan'; and many relatively affluent youth who joke about living as a *NEET* as they travel or seek for better jobs. But the types of youth who frequent the Support Station are by and large not in a position to confidently appropriate *NEET* in these ways due to the economic and mental hardships (including low self-esteem) they experience. Such youth tend to casually, but often grudgingly, use it for self-identification, ignore it or, at most, criticize it as unfair.

Still, Support Station users are not simply passive targets of labelling by the mainstream society: some of them covertly choose to be labelled as *NEETs* over other more stigmatizing categories. One and a half years into the operation of the Yokohama Youth Support Station, the staff were discovering that such implicit management of stigma was having a real impact on support-seeking behaviour: the influx to the centre of youth with various types of developmental disabilities seemed to stem from the fact that such young people would rather consult a 'youth' service than consult services explicitly targeted at the 'disabled'. Apparently, it felt much less stigmatizing for them to identify as *NEETs*. Chapter 7 briefly revisits this point, but the important thing to note is that *NEET* had the merit, for young people with complex, potentially highly shameful situations in particular, of making it possible to process such situations in an open-ended and partly destigmatized manner.

This dynamic helps explain why so many youth with developmental disabilities and mental illnesses are found at the Support Station and other youth support sites across Japan, suggesting that they may be guided there by a 'hierarchy of stigmatizing labels' that prevails in Japan (though within a context of few alternatives in terms of social services). It thus becomes difficult to make assumptions, based on data gathered at places such as the Support Stations and Independence Camps, about the overall prevalence of such young people within the larger population of *NEETs*, as they are almost certainly over-represented at current sites of support.

The users: Facing complex circumstances

While they have already been described in some detail, it is important to analyze further the types of users that the Yokohama Youth Support Station receives and their perceived problems. I begin here by discussing typical routes to the Support Station.

In fiscal 2007, it is reported that nearly one-fourth of the Support Station's registered clients were referred to the centre by other related institutions and organizations (YYSS 2008:21). The most salient of these were employment support facilities located around Yokohama station such as Hello Work (public employment services), Kanagawa Wakamono Shūrō Shien Sentā (Kanagawa Youth Employment Support Centre) and Young Work Plaza, as well as ward offices and closely affiliated NPOs. The importance of direct referrals had surpassed that of the Internet and other media compared to fiscal 2006 when the latter were relatively more significant as routes to the Support Station. Furthermore, in fiscal 2007, a tenth of users had heard about the centre from parents and another tenth from personal acquaintances. Slightly fewer had read about the Support Station in leaflets distributed widely in the Yokohama area.

While not captured by statistics, whenever the Support Station featured on TV or newspapers, there was usually a sudden bulge in the number of visits during the subsequent weeks. As of mid-2008, there was a puzzling increase in referrals to the Support Station from professional psychiatrists. This was unexpected, since referrals had hitherto taken place in the opposite direction, i.e. from the Support Station to psychiatric services. The staff find that many psychiatrists as well as other related institutions often misunderstand the role of the Support Station – some viewing it as a 'day-care' for mentally ill or disabled young people – which leads to difficulties with organizing support. However, the centre's policy remains to welcome all types of prospective clients since it positions itself as the 'first stop' in Kanagawa Prefecture and Yokohama City for youth who seek independence and jobs.

As we have seen, the role of parents is slightly less significant in the case of the Support Station compared to the Independence Camp. Since parents are not required to act as financial sponsors, youth are freer to take initiative and consult the service even without explicit parental consent. However, this does not mean that parents are unimportant. They can, in many cases, positively encourage (or exhort) their child to seek support. Conversely, they may sometimes act as a major barrier to effective support delivery. (Dozens of parents consult the Support Station monthly regarding their problems without their children showing up at the centre.)

The number of monthly visits to the Support Station grew from 508 in December 2006 to 778 in March 2008 (peaking at 882 in November 2007). Since these figures include repeat visits by the same individuals, it is instructive to consider the number of registered users, which has grown slightly less impressively from 303 in fiscal 2006 to a total of 415 in the fiscal year 2007.

The ages of registered clients ranged between 15 and 34 in 2007. One-third was aged 27 to 30, while nearly as many fell into the 23 to 26 age group (the data do not distinguish between the average ages of male versus female users, but my observations suggest that these are similar). Only 18 per cent were aged 19 to 22, which is surprising considering the large increase in non-employment among those just out of upper-secondary school.[17] Those aged 31 and over, at 15 per cent, were also a significant group that generally seemed to face more severe, aggravated problems than younger support-seekers. These findings are in line with the results of an official survey of 418 supported youth conducted in January 2007 (at both Support Stations and Independence Camps across Japan), in which a third of the respondents were aged 25–29, a fourth were between 20 and 24, and a further fourth were aged 30 to 34 (JPCSED 2007b:Appendix). This confirms that the users of the new Japanese youth support services are indeed relatively old.

In terms of gender, males were heavily over-represented, comprising 70 per cent of all visitors in fiscal 2007. Somewhat unexpectedly, slightly over one-third of registered users were graduates of universities or two-year colleges, while nearly a fifth had completed upper-secondary school. This suggests that many users of the Yokohama Support Station come from middle-class or lower-middle-class backgrounds. Lower-secondary school graduates, on the other hand, were extremely few, but the share of those who had dropped out of upper-secondary school, university, two-year college or vocational school was, at 5 to 10 per cent, not insignificant. Over four-fifths of users had at least some work experience, but over two-thirds of this previously employed group had laboured only as irregular workers.

For support-seeking youth and parents alike, the single most common stated purpose of visiting the centre was 'consultation' (*sōdan*) followed by 'observation' (*kengaku*). Observation visits help make potential users acquainted with staff so as to lower the threshold for starting regular consultations. As for the stated reasons for consultations, 'uncertainty regarding one's career' came at the top with 'identity-related confusion' closely trailing it (YYSS 2008). The third most prevalent recorded reason was 'inability to work for the time being' (due to family reasons or illness, etc.).

More revealing than this are the 'background factors' assessed by staff (Table 6.2). That nearly 40 per cent of all registered users in fiscal 2007 were thought to suffer from a mental illness, mental disability or developmental disability (or overlapping illnesses and disabilities) is a notable finding. This can be partly explained with reference to the 'hierarchy of stigmatizing labels' that was mentioned in a previous section.

Equally significantly, a further third had a record of social withdrawal and/or school non-attendance. The clinical psychologist at the Support Station observes that those with illnesses and/or disabilities are indeed far more likely than others to have experienced withdrawal or school non-attendance (YYSS 2008:45). Failure to gain admittance into an educational institution, the inability to find work, and problems stemming from human relationships (*ningen kankei*) were also common issues. Albeit rarer in overall terms, some Support Station users are also said to have been victims of bullying, abuse and economic hardship.

Table 6.2 The most important background factors that relate to consultations (may include several items per individual)

Category *(explanation to parenthesis)*	Total
1 **Mental illness, mental disability, development disability**	**163**
2 **Past *hikikomari* and/or school non-attendance experience**	**141**
3 Failure in passing entrance examinations or in finding work	90
4 Human relationship-related difficulties in the past	72
5 Other family problems (religion-related trouble, economic hardship, divorce, problematic upbringing, etc.)	68
6 Experience of being bullied at school	46
7 Experience of excessively heavy labour	36
8 Physical illness or disability	32
9 Experience of being bullied at workplace	17
10 Receives livelihood assistance (and/or struggles economically)	14
11 Intellectual disability	14
12 Experience of abuse	12
13 Has never experienced human relationships and/or friendship	9

Source: Yokohama Youth Support Station (YYSS) (2008:31)

The staff's views on users' problems

In section I offer an overview of the staff's perceptions of their clients' problems based on interviews conducted over the course of one year, organized by theme. As might be expected, the staff's views are not always consistent and they vary considerably between different staff members. In any case, these perceptions are extremely important as they guide the support process and also reflect some of the information that staff have elicited through practices of exploring the user.

Labour market issues

1) The 'fresh graduates first'-hiring system (*shinki gakusotsu saiyō seido*): those youth who are not employed at graduation face tremendous disadvantages. As prospective 'mid-career recruits', they are treated very differently to fresh graduates and face strict expectations of 'instant competence' (*sokusenryoku*) as well as communication skills (see Chapter 1). Youth who have gaps in their work histories find such requirements hard to meet.
2) Low salaries: those supported youth who manage to locate jobs suffer from low pay regardless of whether they are hired as 'regular' or 'irregular' workers.

3) Harassment: sexual harassment and 'power harassment' causes many youth (some of whom are said to suffer from 'light' developmental disabilities) to resign and become socially withdrawn.
4) Health damage from excessive work: young employees are often forced to labour prohibitively long hours which causes some to get depression or other serious ailments, after which some seek for help at the Support Station.

Educational issues

1) Educational exclusion: school non-attendance is increasing as schools are pushed to their limits (due to large class sizes and teachers' heavy teaching loads). Such weakening of schools is accompanied by widespread bullying and ostracism that causes victims to become socially withdrawn and traumatized.
2) Weak basic skills: many youth have not mastered basic language and arithmetic skills. School non-attendance and the neglect of learning disabilities are two important underlying reasons.
3) The gruelling examination system: examination pressures make it hard for students in Japan to learn to think for themselves, and thus they often arrive at a dead-end when they are required to independently look for jobs and work.

Family issues

1) Parents as a barrier to independence: many parents still treat children as their 'property', imposing outdated ideals on them and denying their independent choices and preferences. In many cases, parents forcefully resist their offsprings' wishes to move out and live by themselves.
2) Lack of communication within families: excessively long working hours and an undue emphasis on education have led to a drastic decline in discussion time within the family. Hence, many children fail to learn communication skills that they need in order to find jobs and stay in employment.
3) Uncooperative parents: parents frequently disagree with Support Station staff and obstruct the support process, especially when their children are said to require help with mental health and disability issues. Parents, especially those from a middle-class background, typically resist their male children's involvement in any other than regular types of employment.

Cross-cutting issues

1) 'Light' disabilities: those who suffer from undiagnozed, 'light' developmental disabilities fall into a grey zone as they can find neither employment nor welfare support, and as their parents do not understand or recognize their problems.
2) Lack of 'self-affirmation': a high proportion of excluded youth are incapable of 'self-affirmation' (*jiko kōtei*), suffer from low self-esteem and are moreover unable to build relationships with other people.

3) Lack of energy and direction: many youth do not have the energy to craft dreams for the future and they do not know what they want to do.
4) Bureaucrats' lack of understanding: officials from the MHLW do not understand the practical realities of youth support well enough. This is one reason for misguided policy choices.
5) The 'self-responsibility' discourse: excluded youth are often caught in a negative spiral of self-blame which is reinforced by the government-promoted self-responsibility discourse (*jikosekinin-ron*). Youth policies are designed in line with this discourse.

The above points show that the staff of the Yokohama Youth Support Station attribute their users' problems to a number of complex factors. A high level of consensus exists regarding these problems, although emphases differ quite clearly between different members of staff: full-time employees overwhelmingly stress labour market and educational issues, whereas most of the part-time counsellors are more focused on family concerns, reflecting both their different personal backgrounds as well as their roles at the Support Station.

The issues I have listed above form a type of a practitioners' discourse which is distinctive from, and indeed critical of, government discourses (especially that on independence 'self-responsibility').[18] The Support Station's discourse puts far more emphasis on social structural issues of which labour market barriers are a key example. This is one of the central exclusion mechanisms that the staff discern, but it is accompanied by other pressing issues, most notably that of mental and developmental disabilities and mental illnesses. The language around such perhaps more puzzling issues is reviewed next.

The language of 'light disabilities'

None of the staff at the Yokohama Support Station are trained in medicine (though two hold the formal qualification of clinical psychologist). Yet, since up to two-fifths of their support receivers are suspected of suffering from a mental illness, mental disability or a developmental disability of one type or another, the staff increasingly find themselves grappling with psychiatric terminology. The most general way to refer to potentially ill or disabled users is to call them 'youth with mental problems' or 'mental-type' (*mentaru-kei*) users. The generic categories of intellectually or mentally 'disabled' and 'mentally ill' are also used, but the more curious term of 'light developmental disabilities' (*keido hattatsu shōgai*) features equally often. This is a somewhat confusing non-scientific social category under which a wide range of learning difficulties and other established disabilities (most of which are defined with reference to American diagnostic criteria[19]) from dyslexia, ADHD and Asperger's syndrome to high-function autism are subsumed. The more recently recognized conditions (such as ADHD) are called by their English names and abbreviations, which staff learn through self-study, training or newspapers. The influx of new psychiatric language into the realm of youth support is part of wider movement in Japan towards the expansion of 'special needs' education (indeed, the *manabinaoshi* classes discussed before can be viewed as the Support Station's own 'special education' initiative).

Intellectual disabilities are not uncommon among users either, but they can be hard to notice since there tend to be many 'borderline' cases (*bōdā*). This term refers to youth who have levels of IQ that are low but not necessarily low enough to qualify them for the disabled people's card (*shōgaisha tecchō*) that gives access to welfare benefits. In other cases, a young person's IQ level may be well within the range of eligibility, but the youth in question may not be fully aware of this. Mental disabilities such as schizophrenia (*tōgō shicchō*) and illnesses such as depression (*utsubyō*) are discussed often as well, not usually in sophisticated medical terminology but in casual terms and with regard to the broad symptoms of these conditions. In serious cases youth are referred to affiliated psychiatrists after consultations with the in-house clinical psychologist.

Four narratives of Youth Support Station users

While the Support Station staff's views revealed some key features that users appear to have in common, there is no substitute for examining particular cases of young people to understand how individuals experience their lives as well as the complexity of the hardships they face. The diverse and complex circumstances that the following four narratives reflect are hopelessly lost in quantitative surveys as well as in short-term, shallow interview studies that helped to construct the *NEET* debate (see Chapter 3).

Makoto

Makoto, a 17-year-old lower-secondary school graduate, is the Support Station user I got to know best during my research.[20] We met roughly ten times between the autumn of 2007 and the late summer in 2008. Usually donning a baseball cap and dressed in black wear as a skateboarder might, Makoto was not especially talkative but nevertheless was quite happy to chat about hobbies as well as foreign languages and countries with me (although he had never been abroad). I quickly found out that he had experienced some unhappy family-related incidents in the past few years: his father had physically abused both Makoto and his mother, which eventually led to the parents' divorce. Makoto traced the origins of his father's violent behaviour back to the bullying of the father by his workmates and to the consuming (repetitive manual) work that he eventually failed to withstand. Throughout the period we interacted, the financial circumstances of Makoto's family – now headed by his mother – appeared to be dire, and the boy was unsure whether he had the motivation to ever enter upper-secondary school.

Makoto had one dream though, and that was to acquire a licence to operate a forklift so that he could work independently once he turned 18. He also had a strong interest in video games, but was most of the time too short on cash to visit a gaming arcade (he had no cellphone – a must-have item for youth of his age – for the same reason). Visiting the Yokohama Youth Support Station was nevertheless one thing he enjoyed, and he strongly felt the staff members were 'good people' (*ii hito*).

However, during our final discussions, Makoto appeared more apathetic than before and had all but lost interest in acquiring a forklift driver's qualification and even in playing video games. My impression of the situation was that his parents' divorce and past experiences of abuse had had a numbing effect on Makoto, and that a chronic lack of pocket money had made him feel like there was nothing he could do and nowhere he could go besides the Support Station. To my surprise, however, I later heard from a member of staff that Makoto had been diagnosed with an intellectual handicap, which turned out to be something of a relief as he subsequently qualified for public welfare and employment support. Makoto's story demonstrates just how difficult it is – even for professional counselling staff (for whom it took one and a half years to reach the above, rather surprising conclusion), let alone outside researchers – to accurately grasp the situations of support-seekers since they often lack crucial information and access to home environments.

Keiichi

A 19-year-old son of a well-to-do family in Kanagawa prefecture, Keiichi had been visiting the Support Station intermittently for nearly one and a half years by the time I learned of his case in March 2008. Due to his volatile condition, I was never able to interview Keiichi personally, but since his case was extensively discussed at a staff study meeting (the facts of which I later confirmed through staff interviews) I am able to provide an overview here.

Keiichi began receiving counselling at the Support Station upon finishing upper-secondary school. Since the very beginning, he appeared highly restless, finding it hard to concentrate for even a few minutes at a time. The staff member who talked to him most regularly – a soft-spoken female in her thirties who held the qualification of a mental health welfare worker – gradually began noticing signs that suggested the boy may have had schizophrenia. She grew more concerned when she found the boy had acted violently towards his mother and had even wielded a knife before his father. Later Keiichi reported that he was afraid he might end up killing someone during one of his emotional bursts.

So, it was clearly imperative to have Keiichi consult a professional psychiatrist, and the mother who had eventually also visited the Support Station consented to this after some persuasion. Soon thereafter, however, the previously uninvolved father made an abrupt appearance at the centre and overruled this decision, effectively removing the mother from the picture as 'she would only make things more complicated'. Keiichi's father was apparently sceptical of any medical solutions due to an earlier disappointment with medical treatment.

He preferred his son to instead develop through 'mixing' with various other people in social settings.

It became obvious to staff at the Support Station that, in Keiichi's family, the businessman father who worked for a large company exercised absolute authority over both his wife and son. Due to his negative attitude towards professional treatment and lack of awareness regarding mental health issues, the support staff wound up at a loss over how to proceed with Keiichi – it was not an option for them to bypass the father. At the case study meeting where Keiichi's case was discussed, it was suggested discreetly that perhaps his father, being of the patriarchal type, would more readily take advice from a senior male staff member than from a soft-spoken female counsellor with relatively low social status (owing to her gender and young age). Something would have to be done as it was becoming simply too risky to allow Keiichi to continue visiting the Support Station in his current condition.

Saori

The case of Saori, a 35-year-old female whom I interviewed in February 2008, illustrates several important problems quite different from those faced by Makoto and Keiichi. She had exceeded the formal age-limit for Support Station clients but was thankful that the staff were willing to counsel her regardless. However, Saori regretted that she could not attend workshops or other events at the centre because of her age.

Because Saori had earned a music degree and worked for a Suzuki piano school in the USA, she was highly fluent in English. Thanks to her language proficiency, she had landed a job at an English conversation school upon returning to Japan, but had eventually quit after some years. This decision was partly due to work stress and partly it was due to a past relationship trauma that she struggled to overcome. However, recently Saori had realized that the anxiety she felt derived largely from how she had been brought up by her mother. Her mother had, she now recalled, been excessively strict and pushy, demanding that Saori undergo intensive daily piano practice in her early years. She came to understand that her overeating problem, too, was related to such childhood experiences.

Residing with her parents and little brother, Saori said she hoped to engage in volunteer work before finding paid work to try out something new. Upon discovering the Support Station, she had been both surprised and relieved to find just how many young people in Japan were in a similar position to hers, i.e. out of work and not quite knowing what to do next in their lives.

Nakano

The story of Nakano, a male aged 28 at the time of our talks in February and March 2008, is extraordinary although not completely dissimilar to the above cases. An extremely bright young man, keen to discuss politics, Nakano's past was dominated by illness and unlikely family-related misfortunes that had led to a chequered personal and career history. In his teens, Nakano had developed an atopic rash which often prevented him from attending school for significant periods of time. Although not a condition without available treatments, Nakano's mother – a dedicated member of a religious sect – resisted the use of pharmaceuticals due to her faith and related beliefs. Things got much worse when, shortly before his upper-secondary school graduation, Nakano's father collapsed due to cerebral haemorrhage, leading to an inevitable drop in the family's income. This made it unrealistic for Nakano to enrol at an art school or at any 'decent' university. Throughout his adolescent and adult life, Nakano's feelings towards his parents had remained mixed as his father, a public servant who used to work long hours, had treated him 'like a stranger' while his mother had always seemed to put her religion before her son.

The first real job that Nakano had entered was at a factory run by a subsidiary of a large manufacturing firm. There he had received low pay despite harsh work conditions and was granted no holidays, which made Nakano feel like he was being 'treated like a thing'. After 18 months, he had eventually quit and became depressed again. After months of withdrawal, Nakano had begun a four-year career at a bookshop where he was treated much better and was given many responsibilities. However, just as Nakano had made plans to produce a picture book with a co-worker, his rash resurfaced and, not wishing to create a burden for his employer, he quit soon thereafter.

After another difficult period and a frustrating family conflict, Nakano discovered the Support Station's predecessor, the Young Job Spot, in early 2007 through information he received at the city hall. After the Job Spot was temporarily closed down, he began to attend the Support Station where he felt relieved to be able to discuss politics and movies with members of staff (but not with other users who, according to Nakano, were unable to hold conversations on such topics). This provided him with valuable intellectual stimuli and made him feel alive mentally. On medication to alleviate his atopy, Nakano dreamed of authoring a high-quality movie script and winning a script competition. However, he acknowledged this might not be realistic right away. He was thinking of opening a coffee shop as a second option. The staff at the Support Station have not made any concrete career recommendations to him, although he has benefited from the 'mental training' courses at the centre. For the time being, Nakano's priority was on recovering from a recent period of depression and a difficult family past: he hoped to regain his confidence and then make concerted efforts to build his future.

These four cases of individual users at the Support Station illustrate powerfully both the diversity in support-seekers' backgrounds as well as a critical shared factor: neither Makoto, Keiichi, Saori nor Nakano face a single problem, but rather a complex bundle of interwoven disadvantages. Makoto's case is especially important since it shows how challenging it can be for both youth support staff and researchers to accurately grasp the circumstances of socially excluded youth at sites of support (let alone the circumstances of those who never access such sites or respond to surveys). This is one reason why statistics collected by youth support institutions and researchers in Japan must be regarded as highly tentative as well as partial – and in many cases as methodologically flawed. Interview-based accounts, if not based on rigorous and longitudinal research strategies, must be given a similar treatment.[21] Such studies artificially disconnect factors that are intimately related, ignore critical personal events and also gravely underestimate the difficulty of eliciting reliable data from vulnerable, stigmatized populations.

The above cases share another important dimension, namely that of family-related social exclusion. Where Makoto had faced parental abuse in addition to poverty, and where Saori had been treated exceptionally harshly by her mother, in Keiichi's case, the father of his affluent family was barring him from receiving the psychiatric services that Support Station staff were recommending. Nakano, on the other hand, had suffered from his mother's religious pursuits as well as from his father's sudden illness that had led to a dramatic slump in the family's income. All of these stories speak of the grave consequences of 'family failure' in Japan and of the vulnerability of youth who are made to depend solely on their parents – sometimes up to their thirties – in the absence of other social and economic resources to draw upon. Parental families, even when economically stable, can in fact contribute to exclusion by keeping their offspring in a 'grey zone' outside the labour markets, education and welfare services. In such cases, the Youth Support Station and other support institutions can provide important moral support and promote self-understanding. Yet, when it comes to delicate issues, the Support Station can usually not bypass parental authority, and it cannot provide economic support in cases where such support would be critical.

Conclusion: Exploration, diversity and youth support

This chapter has illustrated in some detail how the Youth Support Station – Japan's second tangible policy response to youth non-employment – functions in practice. At first blush, the Support Station would appear to constitute a 'modernized' youth programme that, in contrast to the Youth Independence Camp, makes far more use of professional counselling than of practical job training or other group activities. This is true up to a point but, as the above account made clear, the underlying logic of support here (insofar as the Yokohama Support Station is representative of the entire scheme) differs in no essential sense from the logic that guides the activities of residential training centres.

First, Youth Support Stations also rely on communities of recognition where stigmatizing labels and judgemental views are suspended, and where trusting relations between staff and users facilitate the support process. Second, within such a secure setting, staff engage in practices of exploring the user to unravel complex bundles of problems that cannot be accessed through short-term interviews or one-time self-reports. In the course of these rather profound processes of search, staff members creatively and patiently utilize the 'thick' information that they elicit from users so as to find solutions to their problems through mediating between the users themselves, their parents and potential employers. In a sense, what youth workers do is therefore not that different to what teachers at Japan's upper-secondary schools did in the country's affluent post-war years when they mediated between students and prospective employers that existed within their schools' networks. Yet the very complexity of the task of the youth worker is distinctive from the task of the teacher who provides employment guidance to 'normal' students entering the labour markets as 'fresh graduates'. Also, the relatively modest networks that Support Stations have of 'understanding' employers (who are willing to hire non-employed youth, branded as *NEETs* even when engaging in training initiatives through the Support Station) distinguish the work of youth supporters from that of upper-secondary school teachers, although, as Brinton (2011) has demonstrated, an increasing proportion of teachers also now grapple with limited employer networks.

Another important aspect of the Support Station's activation methodology – which can be viewed as a substantial alternative to the orthodox activation paradigm (see Chapter 7) – is the way in which it makes use of diversity as a key resource in the support process. There is a strong preference for recruiting staff of various backgrounds and various ages. This is seen to be vital to finding 'emotionally compatible', effective mentors to the widest possible range of prospective users. It is partly for this reason that the government's efforts to 'professionalize' youth workers by requiring all of them to acquire the same career counselling qualification have been vehemently resisted. The positioning of diversity as an indispensable resource by the Support Station is at odds with current mainstream organizational practices in Japan and can therefore be very hard to explain to outsiders. This is true of the dimensions of exploration and recognition also, which is why the staff find it convenient to simply explain their activities with reference to established symbolic categories such as 'employment support' and 'youth independence support'.

Soon after the end of my fieldwork at the Yokohama Youth Support Station, it became clear that, while the Independence Camps continued to serve fewer than 1,000 individuals a year (hosting only 594 trainees in 2009, a slight increase on previous years), the Support Station had managed to reach a much larger clientele throughout Japan. Having received 35,000 visits in 2006 when there were only 25 centres in operation, data provided to me by the MHLW shows that in 2010, young users and their parents paid altogether 274,000 visits to the 100 Support Stations that were in service that year. While these figures must be read critically as they indicate the number of individual visits rather than individual users, it is becoming easier now to argue that there is a certain demand – unmet until recently – for services such as the Youth Support Station in post-industrial Japanese society.[22] This, in turn, may well (as Chapter 7 will go on to suggest) reflect a yet greater unmet demand for social recognition and diversified ways of working among Japan's heterogeneous youth citizenry.

7 Beyond symbolic activation: Scaling up the alternatives

In the preface to this volume, I emphasized that the main purpose of this inquiry is not to explain the supposed decline, or the 'unravelling', of some aspect of Japanese society – whether its economy, demographic health or so-called school-to-work transitions. Had I taken the circumstances of the 1970s or the 1980s as my normative standard and functionalism (or institutionalism) as my theoretical lens, such a story of depression and decline would not have been very hard to tell using youth employment data. Instead I chose to highlight, with the help of a 'three-dimensional' constructionist approach, a set of phenomena that suggest a far more upbeat picture of (quiet) innovation in the area of youth, work and policy. This partly explains why the main title of this book is not *Japan's Youth Policy in Crisis* or *The Plight of Japan's Insecure Workers*, but *Japan's Emerging Youth Policy*. By selecting such an open-ended, even positive, title, I wished to convey to the reader that something new was indeed brewing amid all the 'gloom and doom' over the loss of the supposed past paradise of (male) life-time employment and corporate-centred identities.

It is worth noting at this point that 'to emerge' means to come into view, to become apparent or to rise into prominence. An 'emerging economy', therefore, is not quite yet a 'leading' economy in the world, but it is thought to be well on its way towards global prominence. More relevantly for this book, an 'emerging (policy) model' implies something slightly different. An emerging model does not (yet) represent a complete or coherent entity, and there are no guarantees that it will ever come to fully displace a currently dominant system or reality. This is why evolving entities which are 'incomplete' (i.e. not yet institutionalized or scaled up) present a challenge to social scientists, who would much prefer to wait until they can, with some confidence (and plenty of hyperbole), declare the dramatic 'shift', the wholesale 'transformation' or indeed the 'end' of a previously taken-for-granted hegemonic social configuration.[1] Piecemeal changes and trends around the periphery of a mainstream society and/or its policy systems, no matter how interesting, are hard to place in scholars' theoretical universe and even harder to dramatize in book and article titles. Nevertheless, despite their fragmented, unarticulated nature, it is exactly the new creative elements and innovative recombinations (which typically exist on the boundaries of established domains and fields) that have the potential to offer genuine alternatives to prevailing models and practices. In this sense, what the present book has attempted to set out is not a coherent new policy system or some kind of an 'equilibrium' that has somehow already displaced an older, declining regime, but the seeds of a future social order around youth, policy and work, the specific shape of which is still unknown but the ingredients of which already exist. The arrangements behind symbolic activation (which I revisit below) do not amount to such a new order but capture a moment in an uneasy transition from an old employment paradigm towards another, as yet unknown, but almost certainly more diversified conception of work and employment. The development of such a new paradigm is proceeding gradually, but it seems likely that the tragic events of March 11, 2011 may have accelerated – and indeed created a greater openness to – the search for alternatives to what many quietly understand are bankrupt societal and employment models.

I am personally in great favour, especially in the case of books that inevitably introduce many potentially confusing side-plots just as the present volume has done, of succinct conclusions where the author finally spells out in clear language what it was he/she was meaning to say all along. The concluding chapter is especially important here because it is the only place within this volume where I explicitly critique the phenomena under inspection (for, in the previous chapters, normative criticism was suspended, as far as possible, to let the empirical realities around Japan's emerging youth policy, and especially the voices of key actors, speak for themselves). By way of a brief overview, the following three sections explain the fundamental flaws embedded in symbolic activation, the label *NEET* as well as the very idea of activation itself; two attractive alternative methodologies of activation ('communities of recognition' and practices of 'exploring the user') as well as related theoretical threads to promote further scrutiny of these patterns; and finally, the ways in which alternatives to an outdated employment society can be 'scaled up', in Japan and beyond, so as to bring forth a new, quite possibly healthier, relationship between youth, work and wider society.

Critiquing symbolic activation and *NEET*

How did the government, experts, the media and youth support leaders respond to the rise of youth joblessness in early twenty-first-century Japan? This was the central question that this volume began with and around which subsequent chapters were organized. It was argued that the main response evident at the level of government policy and the labour markets amounted to something called 'symbolic activation'. At a basic level at least, it is fairly easy to critique this variety of activation. It clearly constitutes a subtly coercive arrangement whereby universally diffused, negatively constructed labels such as *NEET* are deployed to prompt formally inactive young adults to 'activate' themselves back into work. In practice, in a deregulated post-industrial labour market setting where stable jobs, including skilled and semi-skilled positions in the manufacturing sector, are increasingly scarce, this overwhelmingly amounts to pushing more young people into the low-paid, low-skilled service sector labour markets. With few bridges between 'irregular' jobs (that come with little training) and 'regular' positions (that are supplied with on-the-job training with a view to developing complex skills), the future career prospects of many activated young people remain limited. This is the essential architecture of symbolic activation, an intervention that has done little, at the macro-level at least, to rectify the deep inequalities in terms of social protection, skill development and career prospects that characterize Japan's labour markets.

It should not be missed here that, instead of uncritically accepting this state of affairs, Japan's youth support leaders and their staff, despite receiving government subsidies, have in fact embodied an active critique of symbolic activation. For this reason, Chapters 5 and 6 of this volume can be read as cases of implicit resistance to government-endorsed, internationally hegemonic ideas of activation, featuring examples (based on staff accounts) of the damage done to a particular layer of young people amid rapidly changing, destabilized labour markets and an educational system that does not equip students with useful occupational competencies (also see Honda 2009). Though they have inevitably had to operate within the far less humane wider terrain of post-industrial labour markets, sites of youth support have offered a small but potent alternative methodology for involving young people in diverse forms of activity. We will return to the substance of this methodology below.

Unlike the symbolically driven activation pattern just described, various scholars have quite thoroughly critiqued the particular category of *NEET* ('not in education, employment or training', denoting 16- to 18-year-old young people in the UK context, but 15- to 34-year-olds in Japan; see Chapter 3; Furlong 2006; Honda, Naito and Goto 2006). For this reason, I will merely offer a brief overview here, informed by existing research and my fieldwork data, of the drawbacks of the *NEET* category, organized under three perspectives, while also noting a few potential merits.

1) *The policy perspective*: to the extent that the label *NEET* has helped to make the case for the enactment of new youth support programmes, it has been indispensable to their development. Yet, in the Japanese case, the predominantly negative valence of the category has also severely constrained the making of effective policy (see Chapter 4). More generally, *NEET* aggregates a fundamentally heterogeneous population, limiting its analytical value (Furlong 2006:554); it draws an artificial line between the non-employed, the unemployed and non-standard workers despite the fact that individuals tend to zig-zag between these social locations, obscuring the nature of the underlying employment dilemma (Chapter 6); it focuses attention, in the Japanese context, on males who are said to be in need of work, at the expense of neglecting the circumstances of formally inactive

women and the role of education as another way out of social exclusion; and the label creates a bias towards helping young people to merely 'exit the *NEET* condition' instead of seriously considering their long-term prospects. Because there has been such a strong moral accent on this category, it has not been sufficiently clarified when being a *NEET* is, and when it is not, a genuine economic welfare problem to individuals and families. Moreover, since *NEET* grew into a mildly stigmatizing category in Japan in the mid-2000s, many young people probably never identified with it, reducing their keenness to consult youth support services (which were, at least at first, framed as '*NEET* support services', not as services that any 'normal' youth could consult). Paradoxically, while *NEET* has carried a stigma in Japan, for those threatened by less desirable social classifications (mentally ill, intellectually handicapped), it has offered a more 'open' way to process complex problems related to work, welfare and identity (Chapter 6). It is partially thanks to the *NEET* category that support-seekers are not labelled as 'occupationally disabled' when accessing Japan's youth services, which could have had a strong 'disabling effect' on them (see Holmqvist 2009 for an important discussion on how this problem plays out in Sweden). While it may sometimes be useful to conceptualize the inactive youth who use Japan's youth support services as marred by 'social incapacities' (owing to a disabling labour market context that favours certain kinds of skills and communication abilities), not using disabling labels is preferable. This way supporters can create a space for exploring support-seekers' preferences, motivations and abilities much more productively, without imposing artificial, paternalistic limits on what the latter 'can' and 'cannot' do. Genda, the main proponent of the *NEET* concept in Japan, must be given credit for appreciating the need for such 'leeway' (*yoyū*) for exploration in the field of youth support (Chapter 3).

2) *The humanistic perspective*: from a humanistic and social citizenship perspective, there is little good that can be said about *NEET*: it defines young citizens by what they are not, reflecting an underlying 'deficit model' (which brings attention to the presumed deficiencies and weaknesses of targeted youth). Because the connotations attached to *NEET* imply that non-employed young adults are morally inferior compared to those who engage in formal work, it violates the principles of equality and social citizenship (see Chapter 1) that position all citizens as deserving the same degree of basic respect and social support. Singled out as deviants, *NEETs* are likely to suffer from low self-esteem, for they receive little recognition from peers, parents and the representatives of public institutions (not to mention most employers, who, at least in Japan, are rarely interested in 'hiring *NEETs*'). Because low self-esteem appears to be a major impediment to positive, systematic action at the personal level – including job-seeking action – here (symbolic) activation works against itself and does unnecessary damage. As with so many social policies, activation measures, therefore, would appear to lead to unintended consequences. Anyone taking a

humanistic, democratic perspective to youth activation must thus begin by defining jobless young people as 'normal youth' with various characteristics who happen to be in a situation where they are out of work (which is exactly what organizations such as K2 International have attempted to do; see Chapter 5). This, as the reader must by now realize, is a perilously difficult balancing act in any work-centred society that offers few alternative bases for personal identity and worth.

3) *The academic (research) perspective*: the introduction of *NEET* prompted a great volume of research within Japan, the UK and OECD countries more broadly. However, the problem here is that this category contains a profoundly misleading 'explanation' of the origins of non-employment. Perilously, it puts the spotlight on individual-level factors and conditions researchers to look for the personal characteristics that put a young person 'at a high risk' of becoming a *NEET*. While I recognize that carefully conducted psychological studies (that refrain from reducing non-employment to an individual condition) can be extremely valuable, there is a persisting danger that the vital role of social structural factors is neglected. As demonstrated by Brinton (2011), it is through the interaction of labour market changes (post-industrialization) and a sharply hierarchical educational system that jobless youth are 'produced' in the Japanese case. At the pre-university level, it is students at non-academic schools with the weakest employer networks that send the highest proportion of graduates into unemployment and labour market disengagement. Kariya (2011) has shown that institutional hierarchies remain decisive to employment outcomes also at the university level. For those of a critical Marxist persuasion, the category *NEET* therefore emerges as a tool for upholding a false consciousness where unjust social hierarchies are obscured and where exclusion as well as poverty are framed in terms of personal failure (and not as genuine public concerns). Clearly, researchers are now required to pay serious attention not only to individual-level skills and qualifications, but to the wider educational system and its hierarchical organization, and they need to more forcefully define non-employment as the product of underlying social forces instead of individual attributes. New accessible concepts that denote these social forces (instead of artificially delineated target groups) need to be highlighted. A final, more subtle, research-related issue is the specific 'framing effect' of *NEET* (which also affects policy-makers): in the Japanese setting at least, it has overwhelmingly focused analysis on the supposed problems of middle-class (and lower-middle-class) male youth. The consequence is that the issues of potentially more deprived and excluded layers of the population (the children of single-parent families, the homeless, children who need to work from an early age, the children of organized criminals, etc.) are given less attention. Scholars will thus benefit from a more reflexive treatment of social categories that portend to be about 'social exclusion' but that do as much to conceal important aspects of marginalization as they do to reveal them.

For anyone who has digested these critiques (even while appreciating the partial merits of the category), it will become quite hard to recommend *NEET* for any serious scholarly or policy-related usage in the future. By the same token, it will be imperative to avoid generating any social classifications with a similar slant lest the very same problems emerge again. Because symbolic activation has been driven by the *NEET* category and similar labels in the Japanese context, it is an arrangement characterized by deep flaws at its root. How about the very idea of 'activation' itself?

The limits of the West European and North American idea of 'activation'

As of the writing of this volume, scholars worldwide appear to be growing more aware of the drawbacks of the very idea of activation (granted, the more critically oriented ones have challenged it from the beginning). In an important recent contribution, a range of authors reflect on the ill effects of activation and related policies on individual autonomy and social citizenship (Betzelt and Bothfeld 2011). Also, Jaana Lähteenmaa, a leading youth researcher in Finland – a Nordic country frequently idealized in Japanese educational discourse for its supposed schooling successes – observes how increasingly heavy-handed activation practices by public employment authorities are taking their toll on young people's motivation (Lähteenmaa 2010). Holmqvist (2009), as noted above, provides an important ethnographically-grounded cautionary tale of how activation programmes, by labelling their clients as 'disabled' or otherwise deficient, do damage to both human motivation and capabilities. One of the most comprehensive critiques of activation is offered by Standing (2009) for whom activation amounts to paternalistic control, or a type of government panopticon for the surveillance of the precariat. Of great practical relevance to policy-makers is the important finding that young people in European countries such as Denmark, Finland, Italy, Greece, Portugal and Austria do not trust the public employment services and/or their activation counsellors (Walther and Pohl 2005).

The defects of the dominant concept of activation and related governmental practices are thus so serious that few sensible policy scholars could recommend countries such as Japan to implement it more thoroughly through further measures. There is a coercive, demotivating edge to orthodox activation measures which, as explained in the above discussion on the *NEET* label, almost without exception lead to (undesired) unanticipated consequences. Hence, when applied in its presently dominant sense, the end-result of activation is likely to be, on the whole, a more deactivated society with a few isolated 'success cases' (where those who would get employed anyhow find jobs slightly more quickly than they would otherwise have done). With the ethical side of this paradigm so murky, it will moreover prove increasingly difficult for policy-makers, from the point of view of social justice, to endorse the orthodox activation paradigm. Due to the impersonal quality of most activation services delivered at public employment centres, their clientele is likely to grow increasingly frustrated and demoralized, the more coercive such services get.

Interestingly however, the empirical data presented in Chapters 5 and 6 of this book have demonstrated, through an analysis of 'accommodating' approaches to youth support, that it is possible to create genuine alternatives to activation which are based on voluntary participation. Such alternatives can be delivered through less impersonal means than standard activation functions in the West, and they hold out the promise of far greater effectiveness and better long-term outcomes. The next section recapitulates the two particular alternative support methodologies that arise from the cases of the Youth Independence Camp and the Youth Support Station. These methodologies are, needless to say, not completely unique to Japan, but they contain certain distinctive elements which have not been articulated before.

Emerging alternatives to 'activation' and promising theoretical threads

The ground-level youth support practices that were examined in Chapters 5 and 6 of this book contain a plethora of small innovations and important nuances that contribute to what I have called their 'activation strategies'. There are, as mentioned above, two more fundamental, though implicit, aspects to these practices which define them and which I would argue are to some extent transferable across different contexts (and therefore 'scalable'). To capture their sociological logic, I have referred to these as 'communities of recognition' and practices of 'exploring the user'. These two methodologies of youth support practice embody powerful alternatives to impersonal and short-termist kinds of labour market activation in our post-industrial societies. I present brief synopses of them here, followed by promising theoretical threads that can guide further research.

1) *Communities of recognition*: These, as exemplified by sites of youth support that adopt an 'accommodating' approach to their dealings with support-seekers, help restore the self-esteem of young people who have been labelled as deviant and denied recognition by mainstream society and its institutions. To achieve this, they employ various practices of recognition, beginning with giving youth space and time to 'be themselves' (which is the essential definition of *ibasho* in Japan) and the celebration of various small successes and accomplishments in a community setting. Rigid normative expectations, including those held by many parents, are negotiated and strong judgements about what a person 'should do' are suspended. Indeed, diverse criteria for evaluating successes and desirable outcomes are maintained, so that there is not one, but multiple valued outcomes. Strong links are built with local, national and even international collaborators, which means the boundary between the community and the outside world is

porous even as the former is required to guard its destigmatizing 'inner logic' against the logic of the surrounding society. Communities of recognition continue to provide social and sometimes material support even after a member finds a position within the wider society. Finally, such communities make efforts to change mainstream society through educating its leaders about the socio-economic issues it detects.

Theoretical threads: a large chunk of sociology (too large to fully review here) focuses on various aspects of community, from the classic work of Tönnies (1996) to the more contemporary research of Putnam (2000). Yet the chorus of recent research on community has been coloured by nostalgia, reflecting a longing for a 'warm' communality that has supposedly been defeated by an immoral, excessively individualistic type of modernity. Such research is deeply problematic and unable to deal with examples such as the Youth Independence Camps, which resemble familial *Gemeinschaft*-type collective arrangements that nevertheless respect individuality and vigorously interact with the outside world. Recent critiques, aired within Japan, of communities of recognition (sometimes referred to in Japanese as *shōnin no kyōdōtai*) as potentially inward-looking groups that tend to cool down the wider aspirations of their members through pleasant sociality also seem less than helpful here (see Furuichi 2010). Instead, a more promising concept may be that of the 'collaborative community' advanced by Paul Adler and Charles Heckscher within organizational sociology. They rightfully point out that 'it is the inability to conceptualize "post-modern" types of community that has led many observers into a nostalgia – sometimes enthusiastic, sometimes uncomfortable – for vanishing forms of social relationships' (Adler and Hecksher 2006:12). They point out that, beyond the *Gemeinschaft* ('community in the shadow of hierarchy') and *Gesellschaft* ('community in the shadow of the market') principles, there is a third collaborative form of organization that takes community itself as its dominant principle. This third form fuses collectivistic and individualistic elements, values interdependence and links the work community to a wider context on the local and global levels. The really fascinating aspect of collaborative communities – which can be productively studied through ethnographic methods at multiple sites, for example – is that their underlying principles seem to have relevance across various concrete types of communities, from groups of aspiring young entrepreneurs at living-room-like co-working spaces, to intra-company laboratories, to less work-focused communities of mutual support. It is an urgent task for sociology within and outside Japan to generate more research into these kinds of human organization that seem to be able to produce more complex, 'evolved' forms of collaboration by combining seemingly incompatible principles (independence and interdependence; individuality and collective practices; personal networks and transparency, etc.). We cannot, of course, presume that these kinds of collaborative communities will somehow arise 'automatically' or that they will always function smoothly, for they are likely to rely on a set of key conditions in order to thrive.

2) *Exploring the user*: This is a concept that denotes a search-based approach to youth support and social inclusion. Here, 'search' refers to a process where the active agent does not necessarily know what he/she is looking for at the outset, but recognizes it when he/she finds it (Stark 2009). Search, in the case of youth support, relies on youth workers, as individuals and as tightly interconnected teams, who accumulate 'thick', nuanced information on the supported youth, their parents, potential job opportunities and other related institutions. The four narratives presented in Chapter 6 demonstrate that it is absolutely vital to elicit case-specific information instead of relying on macro-data or general observations and recommendations. It is such case-specific information on related people and institutions that constitutes the key terrain in the process of support, the goal of which is to recombine these elements in a creative and mutually beneficial fashion (producing 'value' to all involved parties). Linear recipes to guide the support process, once again, cannot exist due to the tremendous complexity involved (which explains why the groups examined in this book have largely done away with step-by-step process guides, although they do offer these to outside inquirers who still tend to expect linearity in youth support). The most important technique of exploration, in the cases studied in this book, consists of long-term observation of a support-receiver by youth workers. This can be accomplished through following the individual as he/she engages in work training and other social activities (which is possibly the approach that generates most useful information) or through face-to-face interaction, including counselling activities. Both approaches can, of course, be combined in various forms. Exploration necessarily unfolds within communities of recognition (that need not comprise residential institutions, but that all rely on a spirit of mutual trust and egalitarianism) which provide secure and destigmatized spaces for exploration. The rich information that practices of exploring the user unearth exposes the biases in standard individual-level survey data that obscure fundamental interactions and links between complex factors of exclusion (Chapter 6). Exploration is a promising basis for 'reflexive policy-making' where, instead of attempting to solve social problems in a purely top-down manner (based on large, but methodologically problematic surveys), the complex information accumulated by front-line workers informs formal policy designs.

Theoretical threads: while various ethnographic, immersive studies of youth practices may provide relevant theoretical insights here, the work of David Stark (2009) on the significance of multiple evaluative principles within diverse work organizations is among the most promising conceptual reference in relation to processes of search. The 'orders of worth' highlighted by Boltanski and Chiapello (2007) in *The New Spirit of Capitalism* inform Stark's conceptual thinking, but the latter is far more optimistic regarding the creative potential inherent in the friction that emerges between contrasting evaluative criteria. The search for new kinds of value unfolds most potently at the very overlap of conflicting, alternative standards. Stark's conceptualization of 'search' is indebted to John Dewey's philosophical pragmatism.

Scaling up the alternatives: Towards a diversified future of work

In one of the first sections of this book, I sketched out the so-called post-industrial employment dilemma which, amid global financial markets, rapid technological change and growing service sector employment, confronts countries with two options: either permitting higher rates of unemployment or welcoming a higher volume of low-quality, insecure employment. This basic dilemma has proven particularly acute for countries such as Japan where social protection and indeed a person's social status, including the degree of recognition he/she receives, have been so intimately bound up with attachment to standard employment (Italy, Spain, Greece and South Korea face a broadly similar situation). In the absence of a sudden revival of high economic growth, it would appear that there are no truly satisfactory solutions to this trade-off between either high unemployment or proliferation of low-prospect jobs.

Yet we have just seen how Japan's youth support sector has addressed the difficult situation around young people's worklessness in many inventive ways, albeit on a micro scale. Although such youth support measures have so far come nowhere close to being able to counter monumental macro-level problems, they contain seeds for a more fruitful relationship between youth, policy and work. As captured by the two concepts of communities of recognition and exploring the user, they have created a new methodology of activation and inclusion. This methodology is founded on the conferral of recognition on young people who have not been recognized as valuable citizens by mainstream society. Based on this essential platform, they have guided youth to diverse forms of work and education through recombining existing resources and addressing a complex bundle of challenges through processes of search and exploration.

There is, in fact, a certain profound underlying logic to these sets of practices that speaks directly to the troubled employment system and discredited corporate-centred lifestyles that Japan is now known for. This is the logic of multiple evaluative criteria, whereby the outcome of a youth support process or indeed the 'success' of an individual in his/her life is judged multi-dimensionally. Such multi-dimensionality is the polar opposite of the 'one-size-must-fit-all' normative model dominant in Japan since at least the 1970s: it contests the ideal that successful men should work for long hours at large corporations – which function as *Gemeinschaft*-like hierarchical communities that 'own' their employees – and that successful women ought to become housewives and part-time workers. By the same token, it questions the character of the broader social welfare regime which strongly favours those who conform to the normative way of working and family formation (see Osawa 2011, for a state-of-the-art account on gender and social policy in Japan). Just as the Independence Camps and the Support Stations celebrate the various small and large successes of their members, and just as these groups endorse several alternative ways to achieve personal success, so can social norms and policies be reformed to value diverse ways of living and working. From the point of view of multiple evaluative criteria – a philosophical idea that resonates with the concept of social citizenship while having positive implications for innovation and the economy more broadly (see Stark 2009, regarding the latter) – multi-dimensionality should be built into various policy designs across the entire welfare state, from work-related policy to the measurement of national well-being. Incidentally, there is already a global movement towards diversified ways to appraise success at the personal, communal, national and indeed the international levels, one reflection of which is the questioning of gross domestic product (GDP) as the sole legitimate indicator of progress and the growing popularity of including happiness and quality of life indicators in this process.

Because wide-scale suffering, in today's advanced economies, relates not only to material deprivation but also to lack of active recognition from one's intimate others, peers, community, workplace and broader society, it is vitally important to consider how the degree and quality of recognition people enjoy can be increased. Introducing multiple evaluation criteria holds out great promise on this count, as it will help decouple an individual's formal employment status and the degree of respect that he/she generally enjoys. To not attempt such a decoupling, amid conditions of increasing labour market instability and polarization, would be hard to defend. At its core, the employment 'crisis' that exists in Japan and other advanced nations is not simply about skill deficits and the 'activation' of the non-employed into elusive standard employment positions. It is, rather, a crisis of an ideologically rigid, one-dimensional social model where the very worth of individuals and their families hinges on precarious labour markets amid unpredictable flows of finance and technology. In a recent account that discusses changing discourses around class and masculinity in Japan, Slater and Galbraith (2011) hit upon this very point as they interpret the media reporting on the Akihabara slayings of 2008. These slayings were committed by a male dispatch worker who repeatedly complained, in the blogosphere, about how he was denied the recognition and respect that members of the middle-class used to be able to expect in Japan. Despite the gruesome nature of his crime, comments regarding the perpetrator's unrecognized, unstable employment condition resonated strongly in the mainstream media, arousing considerable sympathy.

Unfortunately, for anyone wishing to promote a more multi-dimensional society where human worth is not allotted so arbitrarily based on one's employment position, there is one major problem: to change relevant policies is extremely hard, and changing entire policy models or regimes is yet harder. With the bulk of more senior voters still benefiting from the one-dimensional logic of the old employment system (in which they have a vested interest as well-protected 'insiders'), Japan, though not alone, has found reforming its employment and social security systems all but impossible. While there has indeed been some labour market deregulation, such reform has merely shrunk the scope of the traditional employment system, keeping its symbolically and institutionally protected core intact. The growing group of people occupying the periphery, in other words, is still judged by the normative standards of the core and are thus given little recognition. It would seem that the structural underpinnings of this situation are unlikely to change any time soon.

Is there, then, any viable way out of the post-industrial employment dilemma in practice? For those committed to existing frameworks and concepts, probably not. But a pragmatic solution is in sight for those willing to consider unconventional pathways of social change. The most strategically promising way forward, as far as I can see, is 'scaling up the alternatives under the radar'. Precisely because alternative ways of working and living, as well as more diverse standards of evaluation, are so vehemently resisted in the political sphere, they need to be expanded 'under the surface' and outside formal political channels at the grass-roots level. Despite the decreasing willingness to fund the welfare state, various financial, material and human resources still exist in great abundance in any advanced society, including Japan, and these may be harnessed to create more spaces where alternative activities are not only recognized but economically supported and even rewarded. The focus here needs to be not on blueprints but on experimental practices, some of which will grow into coherent prototypes. Prototypes, e.g. in the areas of employment support, local exchange schemes, social care, art promotion, ethical trade and so forth are in many ways more attractive than top-down policy designs because they embody practices that have been shown to work in a given context. In terms of the development and diffusion of significant prototypes, much depends on the ingenuity and resourcefulness of new leaders who may be called 'quiet mavericks' (qM) – tactful multi-talented actors who mediate between various parties to combine resources in new ways, informed by innovative ideas and distinctive personal philosophies (Toivonen, Norasakkunkit and Uchida 2011).

As the youth support programmes featured in this book demonstrate, it is not necessary for such 'quiet mavericks' (a group which includes many youth support managers) to fully dismantle the existing structures and elements that constitute their country's employment system, social security regime and economy. Instead, it is merely required that they creatively recombine these elements to serve new purposes and to accord with an evolved sociological logic. The possibilities are endless and certainly include even methods suited to rearranging the dominant employment system. Here, in order to gradually work towards systemic change, interested corporations and other work organizations can join hands with social entrepreneurs to formulate, for instance, alternative criteria for hiring and evaluating young workers. By then persuading more and more employers to join their ranks, they will be able to scale up these revised hiring and evaluation standards. In such large-scale projects, 'intrapreneurs' at government agencies and various corporations – individuals who are talented at identifying the particular pressure points on which larger shifts hinge – are likely to assume an important role also. Indeed, as the case of Japan's emerging youth policy demonstrates, this kind of search for new practices and alternative standards of success is precisely what is now underway in the shadow of a troubled mainstream society.

Appendix A

The central actors involved in developing Japan's first youth inclusion policies (Japan's youth policy community).

Name	Affiliation	Role
GENDA Yūji*	Professor, Institute of Social Science, Tokyo University	Leading policy entrepreneur; main advocate of *NEET*; central node in Japan's youth policy network
KOSUGI Reiko*	Chief Researcher, Japan Institute of Labour and Policy Training	Key policy entrepreneur; main freeter authority; coordinator of academic research on *NEETs*
MIYAMOTO Michiko*	Professor, University of the Air (Hōsō Daigaku)	Another key policy entrepreneur; chief advocate of the English Connexions Service in Japan
The 'INNOVATOR'	A former chief, the Career Development Support Office, MHLW	Key bureaucrat and architect of new inclusion policies (author of the Youth Support Station)
The 'SPONSOR'	A former Administrative Vice President and former Chief of the Occupational Security Bureau, MHLW	Most high-ranking youth policy advocate within the MHLW (inventor of the Youth Independence Camp)
KUDŌ Sadatsugu	Director, NPO Seishōnen Jiritsu Enjo Sentā (Youth Independence Support Centre)	Single most influential Japanese youth support 'veteran'; closely connected with central government
KUDŌ Kei	Director, NPO Sodate-age Netto	Son of Kudō Sadatsugu; most influential younger generation youth support leader and entrepreneur; the youngest member of youth policy deliberation meetings (*kenkyūkai*)

*Genda, Kosugi and Miyamoto are all members of the Youth Independence Camp Expert Committee (Wakamono Jiritsu Juku Senmon Iinkai).

Appendix B: List of interviews cited in this book

Listed below are the formal interviews that are directly cited in the present book with the exception of interviews with the staff at Yokohama Youth Support Station (which are placed in a separate appendix below). All the interviews were conducted in Japanese without the assistance of any interpreters or third parties.

I asked policy-makers both general questions about policy-making processes and specific questions regarding particular choices (such as the choice of policy models, providers and enrolment fees, etc.). All formal interviews with MHLW and Cabinet Office officials were recorded digitally and subsequently analysed with attention to specific language and terms used for describing and justifying policy. Other interviews were recorded by hand as this was considered more appropriate. Most of the interviews listed below were complemented by repeated discussions in casual settings.

Government officials

BABA Junro (Deputy Director for Policy on Youth Affairs) and MORI Nobuko (Counsellor for Policy on Youth Affairs), Office of Director-General for Policies on Cohesive Society, Cabinet Office, 21 March 2008.

Chief and two assistants, Career Development Support Office, MHLW, 30 May 2007.

Former chief (the 'innovator'), Career Development Support Office, MHLW, 4 July 2007; 13 September 2007; August 2008, several occasions.

Former Administrative Vice Minister and Chief of the Occupational Security Bureau (the 'sponsor'), MHLW, 26 November 2008.

Two officials in charge of running the Youth Independence Camp, Wakamono Jiritsu Juku Shien Sentā, Japan Productivity Centre for Socio-Economic Development, 17 April 2007.

Policy entrepreneurs / scholars

GENDA Yūji, Professor, University of Tokyo, several occasions between April 2007 and March 2008.

HONDA Yuki, Assistant Professor, Department of Education, University of Tokyo, 18 January 2008.

KOSUGI Reiko, Chief Researcher, the Japan Institute for Labour Policy and Training, 17 May 2007.

MIYAMOTO Michiko, Professor, University of the Air, Chairperson of the Committee on Comprehensive Independence Support Measures for Youth (Cabinet Office), 25 March 2008; and several occasions between September 2007 and April 2008.

SAKAGUCHI Junji, Professor, Rikkyo University, Chairman of the Youth Independence Camp Expert Committee, 17 March 2008.

Youth support experts

FUKUMORI Hirofumi, NPO CLCA, Youth Independence Camp Chief, 4 December 2007.

IWAMOTO Mami, K2 International Representative and Youth Independence Camp Chief, 11 May 2007; 1 April 2008; 28 August 2008, several occasions.

IWANAGA Makoto, Chief, Young Job Square Yokohama, 26 March 2008.

KANAMORI Katsuo, Advisor, K2 International and Columbus Academy, 14 December 2007.

KAWAMATA Nao, Director, NPO Peaceful House Hagurekumo, 15 June 2007.

KOBAYASHI, Representative, NPO Fermata, 13 February 2008.

KUDŌ Kei, Director, NPO Sodate-age Netto, 16 April 2007; and 27 August, several occasions.

KUDŌ Sadatsugu, Director, NPO Seishōnen Jiritsu Enjo Sentā (Youth Independence Support Centre), 22 April 2007.

Appendix C

Field visits to government-affiliated youth support sites (2007–8).*

Name of site	Times visited	Date / period of visit(s)
Yokohama YSS	20	April 2007–August 2008
K2 International YIC	19	May 2007–August 2008
Tachikawa YSS	2	April 2007 & 28 March 2008
CLCA YIC, Odawara	1	3–5 Dec 2007
'Peaceful House' Hagurekumo YIC, Toyama	1	12–15 June 2007
Cosmo Working School YIC, Mitaka, Tokyo	1	1 June 2007
Rōkyō YIC, Chiba	1	31 May 2007
Fermata YIC & YSS, Osaka	1	13 Feb 2008
Okinawa YSS	2	19 & 25 Feb 2008
New Start YIC	1	23 March 2008
Adachi YSS	1	25 March 2008
Kurume/Fukuoka YIC	1	31 October 2007
Chishin Gaku Juku YIC	1	1 November 2007
Fukuoka YSS	1	1 November 2007
Kyoto YSS	1	26 April 2008

*YSS: Youth Support Station
YIC: Youth Independence Camp

Appendix D: Fieldwork approaches and impressions ('the arrival story')

I arrived in Tokyo in late March 2007 just in time to attend the annual spring reception of Tokyo University's Institute of Social Science (Shakai Kagaku Kenkyūjo, or Shaken) that marks the beginning of a new academic year. It was at this convivial reception that I first met Genda Yūji (then Assistant Professor), a leading Japanese labour market economist and my official host at Tokyo University. A highly energetic and approachable scholar, he kindly offered a desk for my use at his cosy office. Located in a large building right by the university's famous Red Gate (Akamon), Genda's office would become my invaluable home base for the duration of the fieldwork conducted for this book.

Having Genda as my key 'insider' contact in the world of Japanese youth policy and youth support meant that my fieldwork got off to a flying start. In the first two weeks, I was introduced to other 'movers and shakers' in the youth field, including Kudo Kei (of the NPO Sodateage Netto), one of Japan's youngest and most dynamic support experts at the time. In what developed into a rapid snowballing pattern, Kei then introduced me to a number of other important contacts in the youth support community. Among these were Mr Iwanaga of the brand new Yokohama Youth Support Station as well as Ms Iwamoto of K2 International, also based in Yokohama. Although I did not yet know it at the time, these two organizations would become two of my main field sites from the autumn of 2007 onwards.

Since Genda had been closely involved with the government to hammer out new youth policies (he had, among other roles, served as the chair of a Cabinet Office youth committee in 2005, with Honda Yuki, among others, and continued to serve as a member of the Youth Independence Camp Expert Committee), he was also able to give me access to contacts within Japan's youth policy community. Among the first people within this community that I interviewed here were two young officials at the Japan Productivity Centre for Socio-Economic Development (a public corporation that closely collaborates with the government) who were in charge of overseeing the Youth Independence Camp at the national level. These officials kindly briefed me about the practical aspects of the scheme, helping me to grasp its operational target group (married women were not included because they were, in the officials' words, considered 'socially included' in Japan; long-term *NEETs* were given priority as the main target for support), while explaining some of the pressing challenges that the programme faced (most importantly, the Camps were having trouble with recruiting enough students). By May 2007, I was interviewing the leading youth policy bureaucrats at the Career Development Support Office (Kyaria Keisei Shienshitsu) of the Ministry of Health, Labour and Welfare. These bureaucrats spared no effort in trying to explain to me the government's reasons for having enacted the novel – and even in the Japanese context quite extraordinary – youth measures I happened to be investigating. Based on these early interviews I drafted an article that discussed Japan's changing youth policy through the prism of the Youth Independence Camp for *Sociologos*, a Tokyo University student journal. In the process of drafting this article, I was able to receive critical advice from Professor Miyamoto Michiko (University of the Air) who soon became another important mentor on my journey into the fascinating, yet deeply puzzling, world of Japanese activation policies for young people.

Towards the early summer of the same year, I came to understand that, rather than the three MHLW bureaucrats officially whom I had interviewed in May (and who were in charge of youth support programmes at the time), it was the former chief of their office who had played a critical role in youth policy development three years or so earlier. With help from Genda, I was able to arrange an interview with the past chief for early July, after which I realized that here was the single most important informant as far as the policy-making dimension of my project was concerned.

This key informant – to whom I refer simply as 'the innovator' in the book to recognize his central, creative role in the policy-making process – proved extremely receptive to my research project and promptly invited me for another meeting, this time at the top-floor restaurant of the MHLW. At this meeting we were joined by another equally talkative official (attached to the prestigious post of *shingikan*, or a policy adviser) whose favourite interests included debating capitalism and classic social theory. Over the year that followed, the spirited youth policy innovator invited me to three further restaurant gatherings (*nomikai*) with senior youth support leaders mainly from the voluntary NPO sector. Gatherings such as these, while not necessarily described explicitly in this book, greatly expanded my view of the field, of the many dilemmas it faced and the considerable tensions that existed between its participants (especially between those who were invited and those who were not!). I noticed in retrospect that, as we held more talks, I was able to receive much better and more delicate data from the key bureaucrat regarding the contested origins of the Independence Camp and the Support Station (see Chapter 4) and came to understand his background and values very well. Though I had many opportunities to learn about the conflicts and disagreements between various participants in the field, I was equally struck by the sheer passion of actors such as the innovator and their ability to nevertheless cooperate with diverse parties despite not always seeing things the same way.

In addition to meeting several other important officials, from Cabinet Office youth bureaucrats to the former top of the MHLW (the Administrative Vice Minister), I busied myself with visiting as many actual sites of youth support as possible. Although I could only carry out interviews and limited participant observation at most of the institutions I visited, I was invited to do three-day stays at the NPO Hagurekumo in rural Toyama prefecture as well as the Independence Camp of the NPO CLCA in Odawara (southern Kanagawa prefecture). In some ways, these stays were the most impressive and memorable part of my fieldwork as they taught me something important not only about just how comprehensive youth support could be, but also about how rejuvenating it could be *physically*.

To give one example, at the CLCA Independence Camp, located on the side of a mountain 40 minutes' drive from Odawara City, we were woken up in the morning by the sound of a *wakaiko*-drum at 6 am, after which mediation and recital of the founder's textbook followed. We then cleaned the front yard and the adjacent road of leaves and, after breakfast, headed out for 'job training' (*jobu-tore*) – which in this particular case consisted of picking tangerines. Lunch and dinner – always vegetarian *shōjin ryōri* – were served at the CLCA director Wada's house nearer to Odawara over friendly chatter. Both the students and the staff at CLCA were, I soon found, extraordinarily talkative and contemplative, which ensured that my three days would be both inspiring and positively exhausting. At the end of the three days, I returned to Tokyo feeling tired but also healthier than possibly ever before. In addition to any prior symptoms of stress, gone were my suspicions that all young people branded in Japan as *NEETs* or *hikikomori* might be quite reclusive or shy. Indeed, the students I had met at CLCA were some of the most talkative and inquisitive people I had met before in *any* educational institution in any country.

I should underline that the active cooperation and genuine friendliness of various youth supporters was absolutely crucial to my fieldwork and contributed tremendously to my understanding of youth exclusion and activation in Japan. Although I also socialized with over 100 supported youth at various Independence Camps and Support Stations as well as at a large joint camp event in Yokohama (which was, with plenty of self-irony, called the '*NEET* Summit' and is commemorated on the cover of this book), it was impossible to gain balanced access to all young people at a given site due to ethical reasons (many individuals were in a fragile state, so I made it a rule to be as discreet as well as non-intrusive as possible). Hence I realized that the best way to grasp the circumstances of supported youth was to consult extensively with staff. Staff were, of course, not without their biases but, holding discussions with several members at each support site that I observed continuously, I was able to elicit a great range of perceptions regarding the complex conditions and long-term trajectories of supported youth (see especially Chapter 6).

It was at first surprising how comfortable I, as a Finnish-born observer and later as a volunteer staff member, felt at my two main fieldwork sites, the

Yokohama Support Station and K2 International. Interestingly, it appeared that, for most users and staff (a few of which, I later found, spoke very good English), my presence was neither particularly odd nor unusual. Partly this was due to the fact that these centres frequently received both domestic and international observers. Yet I felt that another major reason was their generally open character: the fundamental philosophies of these institutions were based on accommodating those who, in the context of Japanese society, have 'non-standard' backgrounds and who, according to staff, are frequently treated as social minorities or outcasts in the broader world (see Chapter 7). This view is, of course open to some criticism, since it seems that many Support Station users come from families that are relatively well-to-do financially, but my genuine impression is that they are among some of the more tolerant communities one can encounter in today's Japan. They way in which they treated various kinds of 'difference' – suppressed in typical school and work contexts – painted a picture of an alternative society radically at variance with Japan's mainstream social institutions.

In addition to interviews and field visits to support sites, I attended over 30 youth support events in 2007 and 2008, from public forums to private conferences where government officials and support group leaders periodically convened to discuss issues of policy and practice (or to be more exact, where bureaucrats announced policy decisions and where supporters mainly engaged in mutual exchanges of opinion, with little consequence for the premeditated policy decisions!). Public forums served to expand my contacts and my general understanding of the youth field, while confirming the topicality of issues around young people's employment and activation at the time.

These forums ranged from large and highly formal, even ceremonial government events to small seminar-like discussions by 'dissidents' who criticized the government for 'coercing youth into independence' (which, with certain qualifications, accords with my analysis of the wider pattern of 'symbolic activation' which I set out in Chapter 1, though not with how youth support services have actually been carried out at most sites of support). On the other hand, the so-called Sui-yon-kai ('the fourth Wednesday club'), a monthly gathering of enterprising youth support leaders which was usually held at an *izakaya* in Shinjuku, offered a more informal channel for me to learn about the latest trends and important currents in the field. The Sui-yon-kai was also a prime example of the energetic networking activity that was going on at the time and that bound together different sites of support through their leaders' exchanges. (I later heard that, after 2008, these get-togethers grew less and less frequent, perhaps reflecting changes in the field and the emergence of new topics around which to organize networking meetings).

Although I do not explicitly discuss this in the main chapters, the emotional dimension of youth work became amply clear to me in the course of fieldwork. For one, through actually working as a youth supporter myself, I was able to personally experience the joy that the staff had said they felt each time a young person placed a request to consult them at a support centre. Often such 'consultations' consisted of discussions on the varied interests of the young man or woman in question, including music, languages, politics and movies. Yet, in many cases, the most important element of such meetings seemed to reside in the simple act of listening. Indeed, as someone who had the opportunity to meet dozens of support-seeking Japanese youth in person, it is difficult, in hindsight, to not agree that there seems to be a large unmet demand in the lives of many young people for a friend talk to, for having someone who is willing to just listen. Perhaps for this reason, some leading youth supporters such as Kudō Kei have begun to take a strong interest in the problem of loneliness in modern urban settings, possibly to turn this currently quiet form of suffering into a more tangible policy issue (I have recently noted similar trends and debates in my own country, Finland). In any case, the strong emotional side of youth support work is easily missed in writing up research results, and indeed most studies of 'activation' measures ignore it from the very beginning by not including this dimension in their research designs. I am not at all sure whether this book is able to sufficiently convey the less tangible but still crucial emotional aspects of organizing, giving and receiving support in today's Japan, but I would certainly encourage more scholarly attention to such matters. The brief discussion on 'recognition' in Chapter 7 may, at least for some readers, suggest an attractive way to bridge these emotional aspects of youth activation (and exclusion) with macro-level issues such as structural labour market change.

There is no doubt that the ethnographic elements of this study at least partly reflect my own background and characteristics, for the ethnographic researcher is required to use him/herself as the main research instrument. At the time of conducting my survey, I was a 27-year-old PhD student at the University of Oxford, with a relatively high fluency in speaking Japanese. Having previously undergone four years of university education in Japan proved a critical benefit as I was comfortably able to communicate in Japanese with those I met in the field, from bureaucrats at government offices down to supported young people at various Youth Independence Camps while taking baths or picking up tangerines. I do not, however, claim that my language and communication skills were perfect (I am a native speaker of Finnish) and it is well possible that I may have missed significant nuances and sub-texts present in various interactions. Nevertheless, I have strived to remain trans-parent in my description of key issues and events to minimize problems. On a related note, despite close affiliation with many youth workers and key decision-makers over the course of my fieldwork, I have also tried to remain as impartial as possible in my interpretation of the findings. Distancing myself from the field took considerable time, but after the lapsing of several years, I feel that I have become better able to see the 'larger picture' of what was going on during those hectic months of interviews and participant observa-tion in 2007 and 2008. I hope my informants understand that such distancing is indeed crucial for producing valuable scholarly work, despite the fact that some may find themselves represented in a somewhat strange light within the broad terrain of Japanese youth support.

As should be apparent from this short fieldwork description, a lot of 'invisible work' has gone into the preparation of this book and I have ultimately had no choice but to be selective in choosing what to include in my account and what to leave out. I therefore need to apologize to all those who have contributed to this project but who do not appear in person on the pages of this book (or whose contributions are not explicitly recognized). In any case, I have strived to 'over-report' as far as possible to allow the reader to reach his or her own conclusions based on rich data, and I have also tried to provide alternative explanations, where appropriate, to the same end.

Appendix E

The key features of the Youth Independence and Challenge Plan (2003) and the Youth Independence and Challenge Action Plan (2004).

Ministry of Economy, Trade and Industry

2003: Enactment of the Job Café; training of high-skilled human resources; support for business start-ups, provision of entrepreneurship education

2004: Execution of the high-skilled career plan at colleges and universities via industry-academia collaboration; promotion of the generational transfer of technical skills in key manufacturing sectors and IT; development of skills in strategic services; improving the responsiveness of university education in IT and technology management to industry needs; comprehensive support for young entrepreneurs; the Job Café

Ministry of Health, Labour and Welfare

2003: Career development and employment support to promote attachment to stable jobs (*shokuba teichaku*), dispatch of youth career consultants; introduction of the Japanese 'dual system'; optimisation of the youth labour market; cooperation on the Job Cafe

2004: Enactment of the Youth Independence Camp, the Young Job Spot and accelerated basic work skills courses (to cultivate the work motivation and confidence of freeters and non-employed youth); launch of the Job Passport scheme; provision of counselling and courses to promote stable attachment to jobs (*shokuba teichaku*); expansion of occupational training opportunities; promotion of youth's interest in monozukuri (high-skilled manufacturing and, engineering and handicrafts etc.); establishment of a trial employment system; running of the Japanese 'dual system' via subsidies to companies

Ministry of Education, Culture, Science and Technology

2003: The new career education plan; the high-skill career plan; re-education for freeters; development of the Japanese 'dual system' at vocational schools and colleges

2004: 'Workplace experience' programme (*shokuba taiken*) and internships for lower secondary school students; the dispatch of professionals to schools to discuss occupations, industry and the significance of work; the career search programme; the expansion of internship opportunities; the education of vocational specialists (*senmonteki shokugyōnin*)

Inter-ministerial

2004: 'The State-Society Movement to Improve the Human Competence of Youth' (*Wakamono no Ningenryoku wo Takameru tame no Koku-Min Undō*) to promote awareness regarding youth problems and new youth measures

Sources: The data for programmes and projects in 2003 follows the breakdown given in Yokoi (2006) while the 2004 data is from the official Youth Independence and Challenge Action Plan outline (Cabinet Office 2004).

Appendix F

The most influential articles and books that constructed the *NEET debate (2003–6)*.

Date	Author(s)	Publication
2003		
March	Kosugi, Reiko et al. (Japan Institute for Labour Policy and Training)	Shogaikoku no Wakamono Shūgyō Shien Seisaku no Tenkai: Igirisu to Suwēden wo Chūshin ni (Developments in Youth Employment Support Policy in Foreign Countries: A Focus on the UK and Sweden): a research report
March	Kosugi, Reiko and Yukii Hori (Japan Institute for Labour Policy and Training)	Gakkō kara Shokugyō e no Ikō wo Shien Suru Shokikan e no Hiaringu Chōsa Kekka: Nihon ni okeru *NEET* Mondai no Shozai to Taiō (Results from a Survey of Institutions that Support the School-to-Work Transition: The Nature of the *NEET* Problem in Japan and Relevant Responses): a research report
2004		
January	Genda, Yūji (Institute of Social Science, University of Tokyo)	'14-sai ni "ii otona" to deawaseyō: wakamono ga shitsugyōsha ni mo furītā ni mo narenai jidai ni' ('Let's make 14 year olds meet "good adults": an age when youth struggle even to become unemployed or freeter') Chūō Kōron, February 2004 (published in January of the same year): a general article
May 17	Kosugi, Reiko	'Hatarakanai wakamono "nīto", 10-nen de 1.6-bai shūgyō iyoku naku oya ni "kisei" ' (Non-working youth 'nīto' increase 1.6-fold in 10 years, have no will to work, sponge off parents), Sankei Shimbun: a newspaper article
July	Genda, Yūji (University of Tokyo) and Mie Maganuma (freelance writer)	Nīto: Furītā demo naku, Shitsugyōsha demonaku (Nīto: Neither Furītā nor Unemployed): a best-selling book for the general audience

Appendix F (continued)

Date	Author(s)	Publication
September	**Ministry of Health, Labour and Welfare**	Heisei 16-nen-ban Rōdō Keizai Hakusho (White Paper on the Labour Markets 2004): a government publication that found 520,000 'non-employed' youth
December	Kosugi, Reiko, Kudō Sadatsugu, Miyamoto Michiko, Hori Yukii and others (JILPT)	Wakamono Mugyō: Nīto (Youth Non-Employment: Nīto): a special issue of the academic journal Nihon Rōdō Kenkyū Zasshi (The Japan Labour Research Journal)

2005

Date	Author(s)	Publication
April	Kosugi, Reiko (ed.), Hori, Yukii & Michiko Miyamoto	Furītā to Nīto (Freeter and Nīto): an academic book
June	Futagami, Nōki (NPO New Start Jimukyoku)	Kibō no Nīto (Nīto of hope): a general interest book
July	Genda, Yūji & Reiko Kosugi (Japan Institute for Labour Policy and Training)	Kodomo ga Nīto ni Nattara (What to Do If Your Child Becomes a Nīto): a general interest book for parents
July	The Cabinet Office (Seisaku Tōkatsu-kan, Kyōsei Shakai Seisaku Tantō) & a research committee chaired by Genda Yūji	Seishōnen no Shūrō ni kan suru Kenkyū Chōsa (A Research Report on Youth Employment): the first government report regarding the 'NEET' issue
Summer	Ministry of Health, Labour and Welfare	Kōsei Rōdō Hakusho (White Paper on Health, Labour and Welfare): a government publication that employs the word nīto
October	Genda, Yūji	Hataraku Kajō: Otona no tame no Wakamono Dokusho (Excessive Work: A Youth Reader for Adults): a general interest volume
November	Kudō, Kei (NPO Sodate-age Netto)	'Nīto' Shien Manyuaru ('Nīto' Support Manual): a general book for practitioners and the public

2006

Date	Author(s)	Publication
January	Honda, Yuki (Tokyo University), Naitō, Asao & Kazutomo Gotō	'Nīto' tte Iu na (Don't you Dare to Use the Word 'Nīto'): a critique aimed at the general public

Appendix G

The development of the Youth Independence Camp and the Youth Support Station, 2001–8 (flow of key policy-making events).

Year	Month	Event	Key actor(s)	Stream/level
2001	June	Five Young Work Plazas open; a small number of Young Hello Work centres also appear	MHLW	Ministries
2002	September	Government deliberations regarding responses to youth unemployment and the freeter problem begin	The chief of Shokugyō Antei Kyoku	Ministries
	December	A proposal for a 'youngsters' independence camp' is rejected by the LDP in favour of measures for middle-aged workers laid off due to restructuring	The chief of Shokugyōou Antei Kyoku, the LDP	Ministries, MPs
2003	March	The Japan Institute for Labour publishes a comparative report on youth unemployment, introduces 'NEET' to Japan	Japan Institute of Labour, Kosugi Reiko	Experts
	April	The Job Café and the Young Job Spot are launched	MHLW, METI	Ministries
	June	Three ministries and the Cabinet Office issue the Youth Independence and Challenge Plan	MHLW, MEXT, METI, Cabinet Office	Ministries, MPs
2004	February	The chief of the Career Development Support Bureau is charged with overseeing the Youth Independence Camp	The chief of the Career Development Support Bureau	Ministries
	Spring	The Youth Independence Camp is promoted by two important policy committees; the admin. vice minister directly introduces it to the Chief Cabinet Secretary Fukuda	Rōdō Seisaku Suishin Giin Renmei, Seisaku Chōsakai (LDP), the MHLW admin. vice minister	Ministries, MPs

Year	Month	Event	Key actor(s)	Stream/level
	August	The Youth Independence Camp is included in the government's draft budget for fiscal 2005	MHLW, Ministry of Finance	Ministries
	Autumn	An expert committee is convened to deliberate on how to implement the Youth Independence Camp	Experts and practitioners	Ministries, experts
	December	The Youth Independence and Challenge Action Plan is issued; the YIC is incorporated into the scheme; a limited budget is approved	MHLW, MEXT, METI, Cabinet Office, Ministry of Finance	Ministries, MPs
2005	February	A key policy-maker presents a blueprint for the Youth Support Station after a request from the admin. vice minister, receives swift approval	Admin. vice minister, the chief of the Career Development Support Bureau	Ministries
	Summer	The Youth Independence Camp is implemented at 20 sites across Japan	20 private groups (incl. NPOs)	Ministries, practitioners
2006	April	Five more Youth Independence Camps opened	MHLW, private organisations	Ministries, practitioners
	Autumn	The first Youth Support Stations open; most Young Job Spots are abolished	MHLW, local governments and NPOs	Ministries, practitioners, localities
2007	April	The number of Youth Independence Camps is increased to 30 and that of Youth Support Stations to 50	MHLW, private organisations	Ministries, practitioners
2008	April	The Youth Support Station is changed from a 'pilot' to a 'regular' programme, a total of 77 centres are to be opened within the year	MHLW, private organisations	Ministries

Appendix H

The staff at the Yokohama Support Station as of fiscal year 2008 (citations in Chapter 6 are based on the staff positions indicated here)

Staff member position	Sex	Main duties	Background	Qualifications
Administrative staff (kanrishoku)				
Chief	F	Management (YPY board member)	Prior career at an IT consulting; marketing experience	Industrial counsellor
Assistant chief	M	Management (YPY board member)	Youth support work; school non-attendance and soc. withdrawal experience	MSc in sociology, research experience
Floor manager	M	Scheduling of appointments and events, counselling	Soc. withdrawal experience; a former supportee; support group founder	
Full-time staff				
Networker 1 (renkei)	F	Building and maintaining partner ships	Long experience in the welfare sector; a co-op staff; PR work	
Networker 2 (renkei)	M	Building and maintaining partner ships; sexual minorities representative	A former supportee (*tōjisha*)	
General services manager	F	The coordination of support services	Considerable youth support experience; a former staff of the Young Job Spot	
Mental counsellor	F	Mental counselling and group therapy; the planning of mental health service	PhD candidate in psychology at a prestigious university	Clinical psychologist (*rinshō shinrishi*)
Part-time staff (hijōkin shokuin)				
Educational planner	M	The planning of educational activities (*manabinaoshi*); career counselling; YPY board member	Human resource management at a major bank (laid off during company restructuring); dispatched to the YSS from Gurōbaru Saito, a for-profit company	Career consultant

Staff member position	Sex	Main duties	Background	Qualifications
Educational planner	F	The planning of educational activities incl. artwork; career counselling(NPO board member)	Career in business; school counselling; expert of the Steiner method	Career consultant
Planner for guardians' services 1	F	Activities for guardians (planning and delivery); career counselling	Former employee of the Ministry of Foreign Affairs, various other work experience, long stays abroad with husband	Career consultant (fluent English skills)
Planner for guardians' services 2	F	Activities for guardians (planning and delivery)	The mother of a former supportee; dispatched from a parents' group	
Planner for guardians' services 3	F	Activities for guardians (planning and delivery)	Business coaching, aroma therapy	
Professional counsellor 1	F	Mental counselling		Clinical psychologist
Professional counsellor 2	F	Mental counselling	Systems manager (10 years in the IT sector); past depression experience due to overwork	Mental health and welfare worker
Professional counsellor 3	F	Counselling, work camp representative	Dispatched from the youth work camp organisation NICE	
Professional counsellor 4	M	General and labour-related counselling	Dispatched from the Temp Workers' Union	
Receptionist	M	Reception duties (no counselling)	Former user of the Support Station	
Volunteers				
Volunteer receptionist	M	Assisting with reception duties (no counselling)	Former user of the Support Station	
Volunteer 1	M	Survey design, counselling	University lecturer	PhD, social science
Volunteer 2	F	Counselling	University lecturer	Clinical psychologist, senior industrial counsellor
Volunteer 3	M	International counselling	PhD candidate	

Appendix I

A chronological history of K2 International.

Year	Event
1989	'International Columbus Academy' is founded by Pacific Marine Project Co
1990	Three sailing boat voyages are carried out in Micronesia with 20 tōkōkyohi children
1991	The Academy is re-launched by Katsuo Kanamori as a voluntary organisation supported by parents and prestigious Yokohama psychiatrists
1992	The Academy opens a restaurant in Yokohama to generate income. Communal living is begun in nearby apartments to facilitate longer-term support
1993	'New Zealand Columbus Academy', a communal living facility and home stay programme in Auckland, NZ, is launched
1993–98	The organisation carries out six yacht voyages and four expedition tours
1994	'Columbus Academy NZ' is registered as a limited company in New Zealand
1996	'International Columbus Academy' is established as a joint-stock company in Japan
2000	'NPO Columbus Academy' is established with the active support of guardians
2003	A student with Asperger's syndrome dies at the Auckland facility on 26 February: 9 students are charged with assault and kidnapping; the Academy is forced to discontinue activities in New Zealand.** The group is re-organised under 'K2 International Japan Ltd'.*
2004	'K2 International Australia Ltd.' is launched in Sydney, Australia.* 4 male students are handed 3,5-year prison sentences for manslaughter by Auckland High Court. Five others charged with murder refuse to return to New Zealand from Japan and charges against them are dropped.**
2005	K2 International is entrusted with running a so-called 'Youth Independence Camp' as part of the government's new 'youth independence support' policy. Mami Iwamoto is appointed as the director.
2005–7	Low-profile activities are resumed in New Zealand. An affiliated food company and a welfare care home are founded in Japan. Mami Iwamoto is awarded a 'Woman of the Year' award by Nikkei Woman in 2007 for exemplary youth support, management and for increasing employment opportunities. K2's website announces it has trained more than 700 students over its history.

Sources: 1988–98 data from Kanamori 1999. *Shareki, K2 International (2007).
**New Zealand Herald Tribune (27 February 2003; July 4 2003; 3 December 2004).

Appendix J

A sample monthly schedule for Y-MAC students, October 2007.

Monday	Tuesday	Wednesday	Thursday	Friday	Saturday	Sunday
1 Am: break Pm: job seminar at ward office	2 Am: voice training Pm: writing interview articles	3 Volunteering day	4 Am: getting used to writing Pm: yoga	5 Sports day	6 Free	7 Free
8 National holiday	9 Am: drawing Pm: writing a CV	10 Volunteering day	11 Am: writing work histories Pm: business manners seminar	12 Am: first aid training Pm: sports	13 Y-MAC explanatory session, job-seeking seminar	14 Free
15 Farm work trial camp	16 Farm work trial camp	17 Farm work trial camp	18 Am: English class Pm: Yoga	19 Am: how to receive customers 1 Pm: festival preparation	20 Putting out a food stall at a festival	21 Free
22 Sports day	23 Am: Drawing Pm: job-seeking workshop at ward office	24 Volunteering day	25 Am: a nutrition workshop Pm: how to receive customers 2	26 Am: learning writings skills for work Pm: communicating without hurting the feelings of others	27 Y-MAC explanatory session, job-seeking seminar	28 Free
29 Sports day	30 Am: voice training Pm: business writing	3 Volunteering day				

Appendix K: On the establishment of the Yokohama Support Station and the chronic instability of youth work in Japan

As Chapter 4 of this book makes clear, the Job Café and the Young Job Spot were the two main employment-related (public) counselling centres for youth in Japan that predated the Support Station. While the Job Café was designed mainly for *freeters* and job-seeking students and did not differ from Hello Work in terms of its key functions (beyond the fact that it was customized for youth), the Young Job Spot was based on a concept that was distinctive compared to past programmes and constituted a clear step towards the Support Station. Since the presence of a Young Job Spot in Yokohama from July 2003 to March 2007 – at which point it was abruptly abolished – greatly influenced the development of the Yokohama Youth Support Station in that city, its history is sketched out here. This account will also help to clarify how the Young Job Spot differed from its follower.

First, as we saw before, the Young Job Spot was a MHLW-initiated programme, the overall management of which was contracted out to the government-affiliated, semi-autonomous Employment and Skills Development Organization of Japan (Dokuritsu Gyōusei Hōjin Koyō Nōryoku Kaihatsu Kikō; henceforth KNKK) based, incidentally, in Yokohama City. The Kanagawa subsidiary of this institution was the organ directly responsible for the Job Spot in Yokohama, but it in turn had delegated the day-to-day running of the service to an NPO with far-reaching roots by the name of Kusu no Ki Gakuen (The Camphor Tree School). The head of this NPO was Mutō Keiji (born in 1935), a retired elementary school teacher who had after a long teaching career opened a so-called 'free school' for children unable to attend normal public schools due to bullying or other difficulties (see Chapter 2). It was explained to me by some of the senior staff at the Yokohama Support Station that this 'veteran' of youth support was the true 'birth father' (*umi no oya*) of not only the NPO Yūsu Pōto Yokohama but also of another group known as Reload. The former of these was launched in 2006 to manage the Youth Support Station and the Young Job Square, the revived Young Job Spot. The latter of the two NPOs, Reload, emerged in 2005 to run the Chiiki Youth Plaza for mainly *hikikomori* and *futōkō* youth.

The first crucial thing about the Young Job Spot in Yokohama is that, like most of the other centres under the same scheme, it was run solely on public money flowing through the KNKK. This was the key reason for its high vulnerability to changes in policy as shall soon be seen. Second, although it was clear that the centre was primarily designed as an employment support service with an appropriate assortment of personal computers and job magazines available for free use, it was one with a relatively relaxed atmosphere and a welcoming air. The interior of the centre was colourful and there was a rest area as well as plenty of open space to facilitate free interaction. In addition to the formally qualified career counsellors who were dispatched by the KNKK, the 'shop floor' was occupied by six or seven 'attendants', mainly young people in their mid-to-late twenties, but also a few more senior staff. This was to render the service more accessible for young *freeters* who were thought to be uneasy about talking to more elderly advisers about their concerns. Strictly speaking, the attendants were not 'counsellors' as most had no formal qualifications to this end, but rather possessed varied backgrounds and career histories.[1] It was hoped that, from among this diverse team, the majority of visitors could find at least one (emotionally) compatible mentor. As for the target group, practically anyone aged between 15 and 30 who did not know what kind of work suited him or her – or what kind of job he or she wanted to seek – was welcomed to pay a visit and discuss their concerns (*nayami*). Improved 'self-understanding' and the clarification of a feasible future path, without compulsion or coercion, was the explicit goal of the Job Spot. This non-judgemental mode of counselling was later replicated by the Support Station. To stir interest both in specific careers and in working in general, strong emphasis was put on regular 'forums' where a diverse range of employees and professionals spoke about their experiences (Genda and Maganuma 2004:64–65).

So the Young Job Spot was characterized by peer support, some career counselling and motivation-building activities. Importantly, it did not incorporate mental health-related services that would later be given a central role in the Support Station scheme. The former chief conceded in an interview, moreover, that the Job Spot 'had not been a very organized service' as it did not keep rigorous records of its users or activities. Furthermore, its links to other (potentially) relevant institutions in the local community were non-extensive and limited mainly to cooperation with the public employment services (that referred a number of youth from the Hello Work centres to the Job Spot and vice versa). Disappointing, thus, the key policy-maker's wishes, the service had – at least in Yokohama – failed to reflect into practice the core concept of building a local network of youth support initiatives and related institutions. Instead, it tended to 'hoard' work that, as the bureaucrat who had designed the scheme insisted, should have rather been shared and coordinated more widely (Innovator, 30 August 2008). In terms of its target group, the Job Spot prioritized those who were able to work if provided with relatively little support – in short, *freeters* who were seen as having 'stumbled' temporarily – so there were no real efforts to reach out for those in the *hikikomori* category. Crucially, the *NEET* concept did not exist in Japan when the programme was first designed and neither policy-makers nor practitioners were yet acutely aware of youth who had more complex problems than many of the relatively advantaged young adults who could independently access the centre. Nevertheless, according to past staff members, the emergence of the Job Spot in Yokohama and at other locations marked the start of 'youth support' as it is currently known.

There is a third point about the Yokohama Young Job Spot that makes it particularly interesting a case: it had in fact not been set up by 'local' actors from Yokohama City (or the wider Kanagawa Prefecture) or the KNKK, but by the youth support veteran Kudō Sadatsugu's Youth Independence Assistance Centre (Seishōnen Jiritsu Enjo Sentā) that had been specially commissioned for the job. As already discussed in Chapter 4, it was Kudō himself who had actively lobbied the MHLW to build public youth support measures in the first place, and it was his original support network in Fussa, western Tokyo (in addition to a different centre in Chiba), that the central bureaucrat had drawn on when designing both the Young Job Spot and later the Youth Support Station.[2] So, since the Young Job Spot was the product of both Kudō and the MHLW, it was considered fitting to have the former set up a 'model case' among the 30 or so Job Spots plotted across Japan in 2003. However, in actuality, it was Kudō's son Kei (born in 1977) who directly oversaw the process and acted as the chief of the centre for the first six months. After half a year he handed over management to local staff (many of whom were affiliated with Kusu no Ki Gakuen) as he had 'grown tired of the long commute between Tachikawa and Yokohama' and felt that his participation was no longer crucial (Kudō Kei 26 March 2008). That the Kudō family was involved here not only illustrates its strong influence in the world of youth support in Japan, but also shows how the bureaucrat in charge tried to make sure that the specific support model he had identified would be formalized successfully via government policy.

During the period of Kudō's oversight, some of the users and staff at the Young Job Spot would unwittingly come to play a role in the social construction of '*NEET*' via their interviews published in *NEET: Shitsugyōsha demo naku, furītā demo naku* by Genda and Maganuma (2004:57–99). Portrayed as indulgent, globe-trotting adult children who chose to remain unemployed (or work as paid volunteers), even when presented with seemingly promising opportunities, their voices no doubt contributed to the public disparagement of *NEET*s at the time. According to former staff at the Job Spot, however, the interview accounts by Maganuma were blatantly biased and ignored the hundreds of youth who came to the centre suffering from extreme work-induced exhaustion and severe depression (Networker 1, 26 March 2008). Such youth had been employed as care workers, IT experts and restaurant staff, typically working very long hours under poor work conditions and with low salaries. No wonder, then, that the staff at the support centre – along with many other youth support workers across Japan – were infuriated by the writings of Genda and Maganuma, leading many to downgrade their appraisal of the former, previously lauded for his pro-youth analyses (see Genda 2001).[3]

Although the severe, complicated nature of the problems faced by youth at the Young Job Spot gradually became clearer to members of staff, according to one, exhortations were made by the KNKK to only report relatively 'lenient' cases to the outside world (i.e. to news reporters, writers and government officials).[4] As they were requested to conform to a premeditated image in this way, the staff felt as if the centre was there to serve the needs of the policy and its administrators rather than those of its clients (Networker 1, 1 April 2008). Although administrative requests of the above kind undoubtedly had limited coercive power, the situation had a certain resemblance to that of the 1960s when reporting on youth suicides – that were all too common among young workers of Japan's top companies and their subcontractors – was forbidden by officialdom (see Chapter 2).

Less than four years after the service had been enacted, it was reported by the Kanagawa version of *Tokyo Shimbun* on 8 March 2007 that the Yokohama Young Job Spot was to be closed down in the following month. This decision came abruptly and delivered a shock to the staff and many of the users, the latter who, it was claimed, had numbered as many as 13,000 per year.[5] It appeared to the staff that the abolition had been decided unilaterally by the MHLW, which refused to reconsider the decision despite desperate appeals by many of those directly affected. However, in strict terms, what unfolded was a process of restructuring rather than the outright shut-down of a popular service. An agreement had been made earlier between Yokohama City and the NPO Yūsu Pōto Yokohama regarding the opening of a new service – the Yokohama Youth Support Station – in the very same building in December 2006. Once the government discovered that the NPO Yūsu Pōto was closely affiliated with the NPO Kusu no Ki Gakuen (the organization that ran the Young Job Spot), it announced that it could not keep funding both initiatives. Clearly, endorsing two similar services run by essentially the same people in the same location was clearly a non-option from the government's point of view. Indeed, recalling the criticisms of the Young Job Spot as a waste of tax-payers' money (Chapter 4), the only legitimate choice available for the bureaucrats in charge was to direct funds to one of the two NPOs lest they risk severe public criticism. A further factor was that the KNKK itself was an embattled organization, and hence phasing out the Young Job Spot (in Yokohama and across Japan) in favour of a new scheme administered by the JPCSED was preferable from the point of view of the MHLW.

Interestingly, the policy expert who had originally introduced the Youth Support Station scheme to decision-makers and stakeholders in Yokohama was none other than Miyamoto Michiko, a senior professor at University of Air who has been one of the most ardent proponents of this new policy since its inception. She had chaired a Yokohama-based committee on the '*NEET*' problem and youth exclusion in Kanagawa Prefecture between the summer of 2005 and the spring of 2006, producing a report and persuading, in the process, Yokohama City to provide the necessary financial backing for the Support Station. As a result of the generosity and enthusiasm of the city administration that had in fact played a role in local *hikikomori* support for some time, a brand new Support Station was established in Yokohama in December 2006. The launch was a successful one, acknowledged by the extension of funding from the central government starting in April 2007.

In the spring of 2007, the Young Job Spot was inevitably closed down, partly as the unintended casualty of the new support plan that was pushed by both the local and national governments (it should be remembered, though, that the whole scheme was being phased out across Japan at this time). However, the staff of the discontinued centre rallied to find a new sponsor and managed to reopen their facility as the 'Young Job Square' just a few weeks after the Support Station had first opened its doors. This time the service was run under the umbrella of the NPO Yūsu Pōto Yokohama (instead of Kusu no Ki Gakuen) and without direct government involvement, which was a great source of vindication for the centre's chief who had apparently run into a grave personal conflict with the bureaucrat in charge at the MHLW (Iwanaga, 18 April 2007). Although the NPO Yūsu Pōto Yokohama retained a largely cooperative stance towards the local and national governments, the sudden abolition of the Young Job Spot had left its members deeply suspicious of the central government and its plans. They moreover came to see public support programmes as a highly precarious, even whimsical, source of funding that could not be relied on in the long term; hence, they are now becoming painfully aware of the need to diversify their support base.[6] Nevertheless, until local fund-raising capabilities improve and company sponsorships proliferate, government-sponsored services such as the Youth Support Station feel that they are operating on shaky ground and need to constantly worry about their sustainability.

Notes

Preface

1 See especially Rosenbaum, J. E. and Kariya, T. (1989) 'From high school to work: Market and institutional mechanisms in Japan', *American Journal of Sociology*, 94: 1334–65. Also see Brinton, M. (2011) *Lost in Transition: Youth, Work, and Instability in Postindustrial Japan*, Cambridge, Cambridge University Press.

2 We make this point in the following paper, stressing, unlike most Japanese sociologists, the astonishing resilience in Japan of preferences for the 'standard life-course' (moving through a 'good school' and 'good university' to a prestigious company and then to marriage, with married women becoming homemakers): Toivonen, T., Norasakkunkit, V. and Uchida, Y. (2011) 'Unable to conform, unwilling to rebel? Youth, globalization and motivation in Japan', *Frontiers in Cultural Psychology*, 2 (Article 207).

3 One of the first papers empirically to ground this point is Lee, S. (2011) 'The shift of labour market risks in deindustrializing Taiwan, Japan and Korea', *Perspectives on Global Development and Technology*, 10.

4 See pages 32–35 in Cave, P. (2007) *Primary School in Japan: Self, Individuality and Learning in Elementary Education*, Abingdon, Routledge. Also see Slater, D. (2010) 'The "new working class" of urban Japan: Socialization and contradiction from middle school to the labor market'. In: Ishida, H. and Slater, D. H. (eds) *Social Class in Contemporary Japan*, Abingdon, Routledge.

5 See the following two books: Yoneyama, S. (1999) *The Japanese High School: Silence and Resistance*, London, Routledge. Furuichi, N. (2011) *Zetsubo no Kuni no Shiawase na Wakamonotachi* (The Happy Youth of a Desperate Nation), Tokyo, Koudansha.

6 On delinquent youth, see Yoder, R. S. (2004) *Youth Deviance in Japan: Class Reproduction and Non-Conformity*, Melbourne, Trans Pacific Press. As for school-refusal, see Yamazaki, A. (1994) 'The medicalization and demedicalization of school refusal: Constructing an educational problem in Japan'. In: Best, J. (ed.) *Troubling Children: Studies of Children and Social Problems*, New York, Aldine de Gruyter.

7 The story of Totsuka is told in greater detail in the following sources on which I rely here: Miller, A. (2010) 'Taibatsu: "Corporal punishment" in Japanese socio-cultural context', *Japan Forum*, 21: 233–54; Miller, A. and Toivonen, T. (2010) 'To discipline or accommodate? On the rehabilitation of Japanese "problem youth"', *Asia-Pacific Journal*, 22 June; Miller, A. (2012) 'Taibatsu: From educational solution to social problem to marginalized non-issue'. In: Goodman, R., Imoto, Y. and Toivonen (eds) *A Sociology of Japanese Youth: From Returnees to NEETs*, Abingdon, Routledge.

8 See the documentary movie on Totsuka's career and training practices, *The Heisei Dilemma*, released in 2011.
9 See Goodman, R. (2012a) 'The "discovery" and "rediscovery" of child abuse (jidō gyakutai) in Japan'. In: Goodman, R., Imoto, Y. and Toivonen, T. (eds) *A Sociology of Japanese Youth: From Returnees to NEETs*, Abingdon, Routledge.
10 For example: Schoppa, L. (2006) *Race for the Exits: The Unraveling of Japan's System of Social Protection*, Ithaca, Cornell University Press; Brinton, M. (2011) *Lost in Transition: Youth, Work, and Instability in Postindustrial Japan*, Cambridge, Cambridge University Press.
11 See Toivonen, T. (2011b) 'Japanese youth after the triple disaster: How entrepreneurial students are overcoming barriers to volunteering and changing Japan', *Harvard Asian Quarterly*, Winter 2011, 8, 4: 53–62.
12 For authoritative sources on these concepts, see: Nicholls, A. (2006) *Social Entrepreneurship: New Models of Sustainable Social Change*, Oxford, Oxford University Press; Nicholls, A. and Murdock, A. (eds) (2012) *Social Innovation: Blurring Boundaries to Reconfigure Markets*, Basingstoke, Palgrave Macmillan.

1 Getting young adults back to work: A post-industrial dilemma in Japan

1 Without wishing to deny the significance of prior developments, in this era the country's GDP growth rate sank from 3.4 per cent in 1991 to a negative growth rate of two per cent in 1998, after which economic growth recovered only modestly (and eventually plunged again following the global financial crisis of 2008).
2 According to the Cabinet Office of Japan, non-standard workers earn roughly 85 per cent of what their standard worker contemporaries do in their early 20s, but only about 60 per cent in their early 40s (Cabinet Office 2008a). The former are, moreover, not usually covered by corporate pension plans or the government's unemployment insurance scheme.
3 The so-called 7-5-3 phenomenon, referring to the statistical fact that 70, 50 and 30 per cent, respectively, of middle school, high school and university graduates now quit their first jobs within the first three years, has received plenty of attention in Japan since the early 2000s.
4 At first glance, one might think that Japan was an 'enabling state' already well before the emergence of the Western activation paradigm, for it has tended to focus policy and welfare benefits on the productive elements of society. While this is in some respects true, suffice it to say here that Japan's prior productivism was nevertheless distinct from the 'neoliberal' activation paradigm discussed in this section in that it espoused Keynesian pump-priming to prop up labour demand instead of aggressively targeting formally inactive individuals to improve labour supply. Also, the Japanese labour markets contained several inefficient 'sheltered' sections, which contradict the neoliberal emphasis on efficiency.
5 Osawa (2011:148) hits on the same point as she notes that, in contrast to Japan, many Western countries have unemployment assistance or jobseekers' allowance schemes that do not depend on contributions (as Japan's employment insurance system does) and that are extended not only to older employees but also to new graduates as well as the self-employed.
6 This is not to say that politicians and parties have no role altogether – indeed, youth policy could not have been made without their endorsement – but bureaucrats do tend to assume more leadership in policy-making in Japan than is the case in many west European countries. Takegawa (2005), for instance, argues that all Japan's major welfare reforms were realized under strong leadership from the state bureaucracy (Takegawa 2005:177). Chalmers Johnson's classic account on the

'Japanese miracle' illustrates the bureaucracy's leading role in Japan's development (Johnson 1982). See Chapter 4 for more on the role of bureaucrats in policy-making.
7 I witnessed only a handful of instances where staff referred to supported youth as 'clients' (*kuraiento*); this was limited to only those staff with a career consulting background.
8 As of writing this, several large anti-nuclear demonstrations, some by specific youth groups, were being carried out in Tokyo and several other parts of Japan. Moreover, organizations such as Youth for 3.11. were seizing the opportunity to engage more young people in disaster relief activities with an eye to raising a new batch of civil society leaders (Toivonen 2011b).

2 The emergence of youth independence support policy

1 Japanese youth policy, viewed broadly, has for long had a dual character, comprising employment measures (overseen by labour bureaucrats) and youth development as well as anti-delinquency measures (spearheaded, currently, by the Cabinet Office and the Ministry of Justice). Educational policy is another interrelated domain. I have made a conscious choice, consistent with the nature of the *NEET* debate and symbolic activation, to focus predominantly on employment-oriented policy here. A study that examines youth development programmes such as the Ship for World Youth (*Sekai Seinen no Fune*), run by the Cabinet Office for purposes of international exchange and leadership training, would no doubt result in a highly interesting alternative account of 'Japanese youth policy'.
2 See Dower (1999) for an authoritative historical account of the conditions Japan faced after the war.
3 Occupational counselling came to be promoted, once again, as a central solution to youth employment issues in the 2000s, reflecting, at least in part, institutional continuities within the section of MHLW in charge of youth policy (see Chapter 6).
4 Sakaguchi is proud of his role as a 'founding father' of youth work in Japan and he continued to participate, as an adviser and patron, in the development of new youth support and staff training initiatives in the 2000s (see Chapters 4 and 5).
5 See Goodman, Imoto and Toivonen (2012) for a thorough review upon which this section draws.
6 Miyamoto (2002) discusses all these, while Kaneko provides an exhaustive account of the discourses surrounding the *hikikomori* (2006). Genda (2001/2005) offers an influential critique of *freeters* as well as of the *parasite single* 'phenomenon' invented originally by Yamada (1999). Also see Slater (2010), Kosugi (2008) and Smith (2006) for more on *freeters*.
7 See Yoneyama (1999) on the *tōkōkyohi*, Goodman (1990) on the *kikokushijo* and Goodman (2000) on child abuse, as well as Kinsella (2012) on compensated dating.
8 Distinct from the kinds of institutions discussed here, Goodman's (2000) authoritative account discusses how government child protection facilities (*yōgōshisetsu*) have catered to children whose parents have been deemed unfit to raise them (Goodman 2000). The so-called 'youth support homes' (*jiritsu enjo hōmu*), private after-care facilities which proliferated between the mid-1980s and the 1990s due to funding from local governments and the state, somewhat resemble the private initiatives described here, but differ in terms of their primary target group (Goodman 2000:134–36).
9 See Wada (1997) and Kudo and Sutajio Potto (1997).
10 It is indeed necessary to bear in mind that the practices of these kinds of 'accommodating' groups have indeed evolved over time, as the example of the increasingly safety-conscious K2 International (Chapter 5) demonstrates.
11 Tokyo Shure, established in 1985 by Okuchi Keiko, was the pioneering 'free school' in Japan (Yoneyama 1999:213). Although not a residential institution itself, its

204   *Notes*

egalitarian and tolerant ethos has clearly influenced the thought of many communal living-based support groups. According to a popular guidebook, there were at
least 116 – mainly non-residential – 'free schools' and 105 'support schools' for
futōkō youth as of 2007 (Manabi Rinku 2007).

12 One promising way to test this assumption would be to design a comparative study
that evaluates levels of institutionalization, the nature and frequency of youth
problem 'panics', and the ownership and funding of youth support institutions.

13 The *ikiru chikara* ('competence for living') educational vision that was sketched by
a government advisory council in 1996 made individuality a salient concept in the
policy world. This vision advocated the development, in children, of both 'traditional' qualities such as consideration for others and cooperation, as well as newer
ones, such as creative, individual and independent thinking (Cave 2007:18).

14 See Cave (2007) for a comprehensive review of debates on individuality in Japanese
education (Cave 2007:13–51). It should be noted here that individualism (*kojin-
shugi*) and individuality (*kosei*) have been quite clearly distinguished in the
Japanese language, with the former carrying negative connotations of selfishness
and immaturity while the latter recognizes individual differences in a more positive
sense (Hendry 1992:56).

15 Interestingly, the now much criticized concept of self-responsibility was first
applied during the Koizumi era in the financial realm, from where it later leaped to
the domain of social policy and became a more general rhetorical device.

16 Such trends have since developed further, leading to the 'From-Welfare-to-Work'
Five-Year Promotion Plan incorporated in 2007 in the government's Strategy for
Raising Economic Growth Potential 2007 (MHLW 2008:237).

17 'Independence support' has been a major theme in the domain of homeless people's support in the 2000s as well, though it is beneficial to note that the concept of
'independence' came to be constructed and interpreted very differently in this
sphere compared to the field of youth support.

18 This is not to say that the Plan was the first instance of cross-ministry cooperation
in social policy. The Angel Plans of the 1990s that aimed to increase the provision
of childcare also comprised such cooperation (Roberts 2002), as did many old
people's policies in the 1980s (Campbell 1992). Ambaras (2006) also mentions past
anti-delinquency campaigns that brought together several ministries and other key
social institutions.

19 MHLW's data show that the youth employment budget leaped from 3.6 billion yen
in 2002 to around 33 billion in 2009.

20 Yamada Masahiro also claimed to have become concerned about rising poverty
among youth (despite having earlier promoted the morally laden *parasite single*
discourse), pointing out that the poverty rate of 18- to 24-year-olds leaped to
15.1 per cent in 2002 from just 7 per cent in 1987. At the same time he observed that,
since so many live with their parents, youth poverty may remain largely concealed
in commonly used household-based statistics (Yamada 2006:35, 42–44, 53).

21 It was stressed that youth services should get 'closer' to young people so as to
better reach this group and be more effective. The name Job Café – apparently
conjured up by Prime Minister Koizumi himself – was part and parcel of such a
more-youth-centred orientation (the conscious 'branding' of youth programmes has
since become a real trend across the government and the civil society, yielding
gems such as Young Job Square, *Jobu-tore*, after 'job training', and *Mane-kone*,
'money connection').

22 In the absence of direct brokering rights, Job Cafés cooperate with adjacent Hello
Work centres, e.g. by accompanying users during visits and consultations to provide
emotional support.

23 It is possible to view the Youth Support Station – that was assigned much laxer
performance criteria – as an eventual response to this dilemma.

24 During my fieldwork, it was not uncommon to hear government and civil society actors alike speak in terms of 'preventing *NEETs*' (*nīto yobō wo suru*) before they could emerge, almost as if such youth were a disease of some sort. Such a conceptualization easily links up with views that posit parents as responsible for 'breeding *NEETs*', a connotation that is evident in books that target parents such as Genda and Kosugi's Kodomo ga Nīto ni Nattara ('What to do if your child becomes a *NEET*'; Genda and Kosugi 2005).

25 It has been argued by educationalists such as LeTendre that varieties of 'guidance' – including academic and living guidance – form the very foundation of Japanese school education (LeTendre 1996). It would be interesting to investigate whether new paradigms are replacing such types of guidance in a similar way as 'career education' is now replacing 'career guidance'.

26 Cave (2007) makes the same comment about the educational discourses of individuality and *ikiru chikara*, the influence of which he himself studies empirically through participant observation at Japanese elementary schools (Cave 2007).

27 This view was expressed by professor Ichikawa of Tokyo University during one of the meetings of the executive council for the 'State-Society Movement to Raise the Human Competence of Youth'.

28 Here, 'human competence' is a rough translation by the author of *ningenryoku*, described as the 'integrated competences of being able to interact with others in society, to cooperate, and to live vigorously as an independent human being' (MHLW 2006:234). In the sense that it synthesizes demands for both interdependence and independence, this concept bears close resemblance to the education policy discourse of *ikiru chikara* ('competence for living') as outlined in Chapter 1.

29 'State-society movement' has a peculiar meaning in its contemporary Japanese context. One is tempted to translate it into English as 'national movement' since the word *kokumin* usually refers to 'nationals' of a given country. However, beginning with the *Shin-Seikatsu Undō* of the 1950s (that aimed to urgently suppress fertility), such 'movements' have been initiated by the state to elicit cooperation from various sectors of society. *Kan-Min Undō*, 'a movement of government officials and various private actors', would thus surely be a more fitting name. One early example of a youth-related movement is the Bright Society Campaign of 1951 that engaged 'a wide range of government agencies, welfare organizations, and community groups in order to prevent crime and delinquency' (Ambaras 2006:193).

30 See the campaign's website at www.mhlw.go.jp/bunya/koyou/wakachalle/index.html.

31 Such symposia typically consisted of speeches and panel discussions by various 'experts' such as Genda Yuji, Kosugi Reiko, Kojima Takako and Miyamoto Michiko, with limited time for audience questions, although some adopted more participatory formats.

3 *NEET*: Creating a target for activation

1 I wish to remind the reader here that I do not endorse any discriminatory usages of *NEET*. Nor do I deny the experience of tangible pressures and pain among youth without work in contemporary Japan. For purposes of inquiry, I adopt what is a detached analytical approach here. The reader will therefore have to wait until Chapters 5, 6 and 7 to read more about the possibly harmful, or otherwise problematic, consequences of the *NEET* category on real young people.

2 This section draws extensively on Toivonen (2011), an article previously published in *Japan Forum*.

3 The Home Office did not like 'Status Zer0' as it was seen to lack these qualities (Howard Williamson, phone interview, 23 April 2009). 'NEET' was criticised again in the 2000s as promoting a 'deficiency model' of youth and for biasing policies

towards simply getting youth to 'exit' this category without concern for their long-term careers or well-being (see, e.g., Yates and Payne 2006).

4 Genda (2004) did strive to bring attention to the poor employment opportunities enjoyed by those youth who did not enter or graduate high school, but this never became more than a footnote in the mainstream *NEET* debate.

5 There was never any real disagreement over the exclusion of married men and women from the *NEET* category, as marriage tends to be taken as evidence of 'social inclusion' in Japan (Toivonen 2008).

6 In contrast to Britain, for instance, it is vital to note that 'housework' in this context was not assumed to include child-rearing, owing to the fact that only married women are expected to have children in Japan (see, e.g., Hertog 2008). There is, moreover, a separate policy category for single parents, which partly explains why lone carers never featured in the Japanese *NEET* debate.

7 The dearth of publicly accessible longitudinal panel data on youth certainly contributed to this latter omission.

8 Immediately after the publication of his article in *Chuō Kōron*, Genda addressed a combined study council of the ruling and opposition parties at the Japanese Diet, which raised the salience of non-employed youth among politicians to the point of prompting the opposition Democratic Party of Japan (DPJ) to incorporate '*NEET* counter-measures' in its Upper House election Manifesto (Asahi Shimbun 2004b).

9 She first discussed the issue in an interview that was published in a *Sankei Shimbun* article on 17 May 2004 with the title, 'Non-working youth "nīto" increase 1.6-fold in 10 years, have no will to work, sponge off parents'. Summarizing the findings of an interview survey, Kosugi was one of the first to identify distinctive sub-categories within *NEETs* in an effort to explain the underpinnings of this phenomenon that many found perplexing and shocking (see below).

10 Miyamoto (2004:24) stresses the arbitrariness of the decision to separate *NEETs* conceptually from the unemployed in light of the highly 'narrow' definition of unemployment in Japan (most employment surveys consider only activities in the final week of the relevant survey month).

11 The first major forum took place in November 2004 under the title 'Wakamono Mugyōsha no Jitsujō to Shiensaku wo Kangaeru' ('Thinking about the Current Situation of Non-employed Youth and Support Measures'). Its proceedings were speedily published by JIL in its academic journal *Rōdō Kenkyū* in December 2004, and this provides a comprehensive synopsis of policy debates on *NEETs* at the time.

12 This and other *NEET* books are part of a wider, older body of literature on youth problems and rehabilitation authored by practitioners such as Kudō Sadatsugu, Wada Shigehiro and the Totsuka Hiroshi (of the Totsuka Yacht School).

13 I have regrettably not yet heard of any studies that have systematically scrutinized TV representations of *NEETs* (or of other recent youth labels); if one was conducted, it would undoubtedly make highly fascinating reading. My own understanding is that, in many cases, TV youth problem coverage is essentially 'staged': the media recruits young people and compensates them for playing, for example, the role of a *NEET* or the role of a teenage prostitute (see Kinsella 2012), according to a premeditated script and pandering to established stereotypes.

14 This study (reported in Toivonen 2009) analysed all articles carried by the Tokyo morning edition of *Asahi Shimbun* that discussed the issue of *NEETs* (as opposed to just mentioning the term) between 12 September 2004 – the date that the first article on *NEETs* appeared – and 9 September 2005, amounting to 27 articles in total. The focus was put on the critical first year of reporting to observe initial claims-making and definitional efforts.

15 There were some efforts to quantify the economic effects of *NEETs*. Also, *NEET* was cited in connection with specific criminal acts even on the pages of *Asahi Shimbun*. The word 'poverty' (*hinkon*) was, however, almost never used in connection with

NEETs by claim-makers such as Genda or Kosugi, let alone the conservative government, in the key period of 2004 to 2006.

16 However, the categorization of subsequent youth initiatives as 'employment measures' led to a dilemma: employment-related achievement targets became the sole indicators of programme performance. As Chapters 5 and 6 point out, this was rather out of sync with many support-seekers' lived realities, and youth support leaders indeed argue for a more diverse set of performance indicators.

17 Kingdon (2003) posits that policy entrepreneurs may be driven by the promotion of personal interests, the wish to advance certain values or affect the shape of policy, and the sheer enjoyment of advocacy (Kingdon 2003:123). In other words, policy actors may be motivated by a desire to guard their jobs or to expand the clout of their agency/agencies, as well as to develop personal careers; by a broad ideological vision; or alternatively, by the enjoyment derived from various forms of participation. All of these motivations were, arguably, present in the Japanese *NEET* campaign, though it is also possible to stress empathy as a relevant motivational driver.

18 This is true virtually by definition: if youth were not a muted group and were instead able to shape the framing of social issues and policy campaigns, they would surely not wish to problematize themselves (they would have been more likely to call attention to young people's needs and demands rather than to youth problem labels; see Toivonen and Imoto 2012).

19 By contrast, NPOs and other private youth support groups have had a financial interest in the *NEET* debate and in new government policies, but their representatives were not in a position to frame the debate (although the likes of Kudō Kei and Futagami Nōki subsequently strived to influence it).

20 I do not directly discuss *parasite singles* here, since this category has mainly denoted young people who are in employment and overwhelmingly female; it did not, for these reasons, play a direct role in the construction of the *NEET* category. However, it is possible to view *parasite singles* as essentially belonging to the wider discourse on *freeters* (see Genda 2001/2005).

21 Even though Genda was unarguably central to disseminating this new language, it is impossible to establish with certainty which ideas were originally his and which came from other sources. This is why I do not try to trace the origins of every single concept here but instead strive to map out the central themes around which youth were debated within the youth policy and support communities in 2004–08, based on key publications and immersive participant observation.

22 Naitō was not the only one to point out that Genda, despite being a labour market economist, had not written in any length about the role of the labour markets and companies when discussing *NEETs* in 2004 (see Honda *et al.* 2006:163).

23 The idea of 'social exclusion' has its origins in France (Beland 2007), where it originally referred to groups that were neglected by the Bismarckian social insurance system (Duffy 1997). The concept migrated to Japan through the UK context where it substituted for 'poverty' until the accession of New Labour that defined it primarily as 'multiple deprivation' (Hills and Stewart 2005:9). Education (for youth) and paid work (for adults) were emphasized as the best forms of inclusion during New Labour's rule. Levitas identifies three distinctive social exclusion discourses that imply different causes and solutions (2005:3). In Japanese academic discussions, social exclusion is typically associated with long-term unemployment, *freeters*, '*NEETs*', single mothers, the homeless, the disabled and the working poor, as well as with the expansion of social disparities, or *kakusa* (Fukuhara (ed.) 2007:1; also see Iwata and Nishizawa 2005). This is peculiar and important because it shows that popular social categories – rather than, say, the idea of multiple deprivation or robust conceptualizations of exclusion – strongly shape how social exclusion is thought of in Japan.

24 Kosugi (2004).

4 Crafting policy: Sympathetic bureaucrats in a hostile climate

1 This is not to say that youth policy bureaucrats did not have a hand in prompting the *NEET* debate itself. As Chapter 3 documents, it was the MHLW's Career Development Support Section that had commissioned JILPT to compile the initial policy reports through which *NEET* was first 'imported' into Japanese discourse.
2 The US Job Corp is a federally funded programme that was launched in the 1960s as part of the Johnson administration's War on Poverty. It annually trained 70,000 youth – most of whom came from poor backgrounds – in its heyday in the 1970s (Levitan and Johnston 1975). Although the number of enrollees has since fluctuated and decreased overall, the Job Corps remains an important historical example of residential youth training. It should be noted that Job Corps enrollees receive a monthly allowance and are not required to pay any fees. On the other hand, the Okinawa Sangyō Kaihatsu Seinen Kyōkai was originally established by the Japanese construction ministry in the early 1950s. Two groups with similar pedigrees were identified in Miyazaki and Kumamoto prefectures.
3 Neither of the two key policy-makers ever mentioned ethnic or poor youth as significant target groups for the Youth Independence Camp. This is consistent with the basic middle-class, ethnically Japanese orientation of the programme framework.
4 See Foreword. Also see Yoneyama (1999) for a critical account on violence and deadly incidents at Japanese schools as well as special training facilities such as Totsuka's.
5 Since the Totsuka Yacht School incidents are well known across Japan and have given private residential training a rather bad reputation, the bureaucrat in charge probably also wanted to disassociate the scheme he was designing from suspicious and widely criticized disciplinarian initiatives.
6 In the autumn of 2007, the maximum regular fee charged across all Youth Independence Camps was 444,000 yen in contrast to a minimum fee of 180,000 yen; lowered fees ranged from 315,000 yen to 105,000 yen. As a rule, the government pays a subsidy that equals the regular participation fee and a higher subsidy per each enrollee from a household earning less than 4 million yen per annum (although not all the camps have a lowered fee system in place). See Japan Productivity Centre for Socio-Economic Development (JPCSED 2007a).
7 Since the launch of the Independence Camp many have wondered why it offered training for only three months. While the scant budget set obvious limits to the scope of the programme, the key policy-maker had in fact thought that anything longer than three months might actually discourage many youth from applying: three months offered a 'soft landing', so to speak, and did not appear to require too much of a commitment from either youth or their guardians (the latter who may prefer a clear time frame for their offspring to finish training and, ideally, move into independent living). However, Chapter 5 will demonstrate that, in reality, some enrollees have the choice of continuing their training for as long as two years provided they shoulder the attendant fees.
8 Both of the pioneering officials moreover regretted that new youth policies had not been enacted any earlier, pointing out that Japan had for too long been preoccupied with elderly people's policies.
9 However, the initial budget for this programme was negotiated by the administrative vice minister, consistent with his role as the prime youth policy patron.
10 The three key MHLW officials I interviewed in late May 2007 as well as the Cabinet Office bureaucrats I interviewed in March 2008 all stated that the Connexions models had been 'consulted' (*sankō ni shita*) by policy-makers – their predecessors – as they enacted the Support Station. The exception among youth support practitioners was the particular 'veteran' whose training scheme, as this chapter finds, influenced the Youth Support Station. This veteran has frequently boasted about having had a hand in this new programme (see below).

11 Miyamoto was not the only scholar to recommend the creation of 'comprehensive' youth responses of some kind. For instance, Kosugi Reiko also called for 'diverse services for a diverse layer' of youth, to be delivered at a 'one-stop' centre or via a network (Kosugi 2004:13–14). There was a broad agreement between key policy entrepreneurs, thus, on the broad outlines of desirable programmes, but disagreement on specific principles.
12 Reports compiled by the Japan Institute of Labour (in particular, Kosugi and Hori 2003) strengthened the bureaucrat's awareness of existing support measures in Japan that were run by private groups.
13 Interestingly, the successor of the innovator (at the Career Development Support Bureau of the MHLW) mentioned in a speech that it would have, in his mind, been more appropriate had the Support Station been enacted before the Independence Camp and not the other way around (Wakamono Jiritsu Juku Renraku Kaigi, September 2007). In terms of policy-making strategy, however, it may have in fact been a wise move to introduce a more peripheral scheme first: this way policy-makers could effectively defuse some of the most intense criticisms before pushing through a more important programme (in this case, the Youth Support Station).
14 Interview, three leading bureaucrats, Career Development Support Bureau, MHLW, 30 May 2007.
15 There are a great number of grassroots-level organizations and NPOs who specialize in visiting the homes of the so-called *hikikomori*, which indicates that a certain demand for such measures exist. The NPO New Start's 'Rental Big Sister' (*Rentaru Onēsan*) scheme is one of the best-known of these. Such schemes are employed by parents as a 'means of last resort' for prompting their offspring to overcome social withdrawal, albeit no doubt with mixed success. The most salient risks associated with 'home visits' include the risk of negative outcomes where an 'overly' coercive approach is taken, or where the withdrawn youth develops a strong emotional attachment to his or her visitor (violent reactions to visitors is also an acknowledged concern).
16 This middle-class focus is consistent with the class aspects of the *NEET* when it was first defined: non-employed youth were viewed predominantly as the lazy offspring of affluent families who had no financial pressure for working or doing much else besides enjoying their lives (see Chapter 3).

5 The Youth Independence Camp: Communities of recognition?

1 As documented in Chapter 4, eligible applicants are those 15- to 34-year-olds who have completed compulsory education and have been out of work, schooling and training continuously for over a year without (formally) seeking jobs in this period. Moreover, applicants must have past job-seeking experience and they should be unmarried (JPCSED 2007a).
2 Main selection conditions are set out in a four-page government document that also specifies, among other things, that delivery organizations must have the status of a legal person; sufficient youth support know-how and achievements (*jisseki*); formal approval from the prefectural government; 'sufficient' staff; a clear curriculum; and plans for job-seeking support even after students have completed the programme. They should also provide comprehensive information about their activities, management and finances during audits.
3 This choice of name was influenced directly by the 'Modern Apprenticeship' training programme that started in the UK in the 1990s.
4 This chapter relies mainly on participant observation and interviews for its data. At K2, Iwamoto (in charge of the Youth Independence Camp programme) was the main contact. I held three formal interviews with her in addition to dozens of

informal talks. I also interviewed Kanamori, K2's founder, and held discussions with the other ten or so staff members. Made into an official volunteer member, I observed various workshops, took part in sports events, attended one larger three-day camp and facilitated group discussions, adding up to a total of 16 visits between the spring of 2007 and the summer of 2008.

5 For Kanamori, the former is linked to cultivating emotional breadth and the latter to intellectual study and experiencing the outside world while learning its rules. Despite the gendered terms, Kanamori does not think that 'maternal' upbringing can only be provided by the mother and vice versa.

6 According to Kanamori, foreclosing the option of returning to the parental home in such a radical way requires and ensures a high level of determination (*kakugo*) on the part of parents and participants. The parents usually commit to K2's programme since they view it as a 'means of last resort' after having been 'let down' by schools, counsellors, hospitals and other institutions.

7 K2 students are reported to attend language schools, high schools and universities in these countries, though Kanamori emphasizes that priority is put on restoring mental and physical health. The fact that many former 'school-refusers' graduate university abroad is a great source of pride for K2, vindicating its view that it is indeed Japanese society, not the youth themselves, that leads young people to feel ill, refuse school and withdraw socially.

8 K2 maintains a rather comprehensive, upbeat website, complete with photographs and frequently updated blogs (URL: www.k2-inter.com).

9 A slightly lower fee for households earning less than 4 million yen annually is available for the initial three months (Youth Independence Camp Y-MAC fee schedule, K2 International 2007; by contrast, younger students who join the Columbus Academy programme instead must pay 630,000 yen for their initial three months and are thereafter charged 105,000 yen per month). See Chapter 4 on why a significant participation fee was attached to the Youth Independence Camp despite it being a government-subsidized scheme.

10 Regular training events are also organized for staff, sometimes by other youth support experts, on topics such as safety in support practice, or by mental health professionals and city administrators.

11 As of 2007 and 2008, K2 operated two small *okonomiyaki* restaurants and one sports café, each of which provided training and part-time work opportunities to current and former students.

6 The Youth Support Station: Exploring the user

1 Along with having strong financial backing, the Yokohama Support Station received the highest number of users out of all Support Stations across Japan in fiscal 2006.

2 '*Yokohama de no shūrōshien no iriguchi*'.

3 '*Ima made mietekonakatta sō ga dan-dan to mietekita*' (17 December 2007).

4 Individual care and counselling have been largely downplayed in the post-war era by Japanese social and medical services as well as within systematic therapies such as Naikan (see Ozawa-de Silva 2006). This is true of the youth support sector before the emergence of the Youth Support Station as well.

5 The Support Station's first annual report mentions the drafting of 'personal plans', but these are not generally made any more. The reason, according to the clinical psychologist, is that planning ahead systematically is simply too difficult for most users due to the complicated nature of their problems and especially due to the instability of the labour markets. In such a context, drafting overly rigid plans and timetables would cause many support-receivers to feel undue pressure and fear over possible failure to progress accordingly.

8 The use of Social Skills Training is not yet established in the realm of Japanese youth support, but it has been employed widely in psychiatric training. As the name suggests, this type of training aims to prepare those who feel confounded or insecure in social situations to interact with others more confidently. In the Japanese context, this may comprise learning how to bow or greet correctly with the right timing, use correct language (including honorifics), respond to questions and engage in small talk during breaks (YYSS 2008:134). Such training can be especially important for individuals suffering from conditions such as autism that make it difficult for them to comprehend various social cues and situations without conscious practice.

9 A total of 90 per cent of training places, at this point, were at small non-profit organizations belonging to the Workers' Collective Association (which has over 200 members in Kanagawa prefecture). These comprised elderly day care centres, recycle shops, small food preparation and delivery businesses, and bakeries. The other types of workplaces that cooperated in 2007 included a restaurant, a data-inputting business and a cleaning service (YYSS 2008: 132). Subsequently, 18 youth were hired by Workers' Collective member organizations and five others by other catering and welfare organizations.

10 See Chapters 3 and 4 regarding persisting social expectations regarding parental responsibility over the problems of socially excluded young adults.

11 These two groups – housewives and pensioners – have been the drivers of much of civil society in Japan from the environmental and consumer movements of the 1970s to the support of socially excluded youth, although more young adults have joined in since the great earthquake that shook Kobe in 1995 (the Great Hanshin-Awaji Earthquake; see Chapter 1).

12 Another commonly given explanation is that those who have themselves experienced social exclusion or withdrawal and have since recovered are able to understand the predicaments of supported youth well and are thus good supporters. This argument is often criticized by many practitioners who are themselves not *tōjisha*. However, compared to those with no personal experience or direct knowledge of social exclusion, there is no doubt that many *tōjisha* have a strong ability to empathize with other supported youth.

13 The staff are acutely aware of – and indeed resent – the strict line drawn between 'regular' and 'irregular' workers at many companies, witnessing first hand the negative effects of this division on the youth who consult them.

14 Parents, on the other hand, appeared to her as much less likely to achieve change.

15 The pressure was keenly felt also at the Tachikawa Support Station in western Tokyo at the time of my second visit there in March 2008: this centre had, with a sense of resignation, decided to acquiesce and make sure all staff acquired a recognized qualification by the summer of the same year.

16 To elicit relevant data, I asked staff at the Yokohama Youth Support Centre direct questions about the use and non-use of *NEET* in the first series of interviews, discussed it with various users, and took note whenever the term was cited.

17 One reason for this may be that younger support-seekers tend to be directed to the city-run Seishōnen Sōdan Sentā located only a couple of train stations away. Another bigger reason is, however, the general tendency in Japan to postpone the seeking of outside help until a higher age, even as statistics show that a high proportion of fresh upper-secondary school graduates fall into the *NEET* category.

18 This discourse is also quite distinctive from the more pedagogical and philosophical (sometimes dogmatic) discourses of residential youth support institutions which are predominantly created by strongmen leaders, or 'veterans', who are not as interested in social structural issues (see Chapter 5).

19 On the worldwide diffusion of American diagnostic criteria (and of 'ways of going crazy'), see Watters (2010).

20 All names in this account have been changed to guard the privacy of the youth.
21 The interview survey of *NEETs* on which Kosugi bases her culturalist categorizations (Kosugi 2004; see Chapter 3) provides a classic example of the dangers of such research.
22 It remained difficult, in the absence of longitudinal data, to evaluate the 'performance' of the Support Station in relation to formal employment outcomes at this point. At the Yokohama centre, about a fourth of users were said to have found employment with assistance from the Support Station in my fieldwork years. The difficulty of gauging the performance of this scheme may, however, be a blessing rather than a curse, for it prompts various stakeholders to evaluate the worth of youth support from numerous contrasting angles. This may protect the initiative against political attacks based on that fact that it isn't getting enough young adults 'back to work'.

7 Beyond symbolic activation: Scaling up the alternatives

1 Esping-Andersen's account on the 'incomplete revolution' around women, social policy and work is a highly welcome exception on this count (Esping-Andersen 2009).

Appendix K: On the establishment of the Yokohama Support Station and the chronic instability of youth work in Japan

1 Kudō Kei, the founding chief of the Young Job Spot in Yokohama, explained at the time that he favoured those with 'unusual' career histories; those who had no pressing need to seek formal employment at the time of application; and those of a type that was not yet represented among his team (Genda and Maganuma 2004:63).
2 Adachi (2006) confirms this flow of events. However, although Kudō is often found to boast that he was the one who 'designed' the Young Job Spot, the bureaucrat in charge insists that this is not accurate, since it was the latter who fully conceptualized the scheme (see Chapter 4).
3 Genda duly responded to many of these criticisms in his next book, *Hataraku Kajō* (2005) which focused squarely on excessive work and included discussions on depression as well as the role of counselling (Genda 2005a).
4 Only those cases where youth were physically and mentally healthy but 'confounded' over the choice of a job (*genki dakedo shigoto ni nayandeiru wakamono*) were to be reported on (Networker 1, 1 April 2008).
5 The chief of the service wrote later in a greeting as the chief of the Young Job Square that the Job Spot had been visited by 13,000 youth yearly. However, if this figure is to be taken as accurate at all, it must rather refer to the number of *visits* rather than the total number of individual *users*. The real number of individual users is likely to have been closer to 1,000.
6 Paradoxically, it could be argued that this sense of insecurity was largely consistent with the government's wishes, as it hopes that local sources of funding can largely replace its own outlays in the near future.

References

Adachi, N. (2006) *Oya to Hanarete 'Hito' to Naru* (*Parting with Parents, Becoming a 'Person'*), Tokyo, NHK Shuppan.

Adler, P. and Hecksher, C. (2006) 'Towards collaborative community'. In: Hecksher, C. and Adler, P. (eds) *The Firm as a Collaborative Community: Reconstructing Trust in the Knowledge Economy*. Oxford, Oxford University Press.

Allison, A. (2009) 'The cool brand, affective activism and Japanese youth', *Theory, Culture and Society*, 26, 2–3: 89–111.

Ambaras, D. R. (2006) *Bad Youth: Juvenile Delinquency and the Politics of Everyday Life in Modern Japan*, Berkeley, University of California Press.

Arnett, J. J. (2004) *Emerging Adulthood: The Winding Road from the Late Teens through the Twenties*, Oxford, Oxford University Press.

Asahi Shimbun (2004a) 'Nīto kyūzō ga tou mono' ('Questions raised by the rapid increase of NEETs') (2 October), *Asahi Shimbun*.

——(2004b) 'Shūgaku sezu hatarakanu wakamono "nīto", 6 nen go 100-man-nin, Dai-Ichi Seimei-ken shisan' ('Dai-Ichi Seimei Research estimates: "NEETs", youth who do not study or work, will increase to one million in six years') (22 October), *Asahi Shimbun*.

——(2005a) '"Nīto" 84-man 7000-nin, Naikaku-fu 02-nen suikei, 15–34-sai no 2.5%' ('Cabinet Office estimate finds 847,000 "NEETs" in 2002, adding up to 2.5% of 15–34 year olds') (24 March), *Asahi Shimbun*.

——(2005b) '"Shigoto" meguri jikken jugyō: Nīto taisaku, zaikai noridasu, Seisansei Honbu ('Experimental classes about "work": The business world gets involved in NEET measures says Productivity Centre') (6 March 2005), *Asahi Shimbun*.

——(2005c) 'Wakamono no jiritsu: Saisho no ippo wo sasaeyō' ('Let's support youth in their first steps towards independence') (5 August), *Asahi Shimbun*.

Asai, J. and Morimoto, W. (2005) *Nīto to Iwareru Hitobito: Jibun no Kodomo wo Nīto ni Sasenai Hōhō* (*People Called Nīto: The Way to Prevent Your Child from Becoming a Nīto*), Tokyo, Takarajima-sha.

Avenell, S. (2010) 'Facilitating spontaneity: The state and independent volunteering in contemporary Japan', *Social Science Japan Journal*, 13, 1: 69–93.

Bandura, A. (1997) *Self-Efficacy: The Exercise of Control*, New York, W. H. Freeman.

Beland, D. (2007) 'The social exclusion discourse: Ideas and policy change', *Policy and Politics*, 35, 1: 123–39.

Bell, D. (1973) *The Coming of Post-Industrial Society: A Venture in Social Forecasting*, New York, Basic Books.

Best, J. (1989) *Images of Issues*, New York, Walter de Gruyter.

Betzelt, S. and Bothfeld, S. (eds) (2011) *Activation and Labour Market Reforms in Europe: Challenges to Social Citizenship*, Basingstoke, Palgrave Macmillan.

Boltanski, L. and Chiapello, E. (2007) *The New Spirit of Capitalism*, London, Verso.

Borovoy, A. (2010) 'What color is your parachute? The post-pedigree society'. In: Ishida, H. and Slater, D. H. (eds) *Social Class in Contemporary Japan*. Abingdon, Routledge.

Brinton, M. C. (2001) 'Social capital in the Japanese youth labour market: Labor market policy, schools, and norms', *Policy Sciences*, 33: 289–306.

——(2011) *Lost in Transition: Youth, Work, and Instability in Postindustrial Japan*, Cambridge, Cambridge University Press.

Cabinet Office (2003) *Wakamono Jiritsu Chōsen Puran* (*Youth Independence and Challenge Plan*), Tokyo, Cabinet Office (Wakamono Jiritsu Chōsen Senryaku Kaigi), the Government of Japan.

——(2004) *Wakamono Jiritsu Chōsen Akushon Puran* (*Youth Independence and Challenge Action Plan*), Tokyo, Cabinet Office (Wakamono Jiritsu Chōsen Senryaku Kaigi), the Government of Japan.

——(2008a) *Kokumin Seikatsu ni kansuru Yoron-Chōsa* (*A Survey on the Life of the Nation*), Tokyo, Cabinet Office, (Wakamono Jiritsu Chōsen Senryaku Kaigi), the Government of Japan.

——(2008b) *Yūsu Adobaizā Yōsei Puroguramu* (*Youth Adviser Training Programme*) [*outline*], Tokyo, Cabinet Office, (Wakamono Jiritsu Chōsen Senryaku Kaigi), the Government of Japan. URL: www8.cao.go.jp/youth/model/h20/iinkai/k-1/pdf/s-4.pdf.

Campbell, J. C. (1992) *How Policies Change: The Japanese Government and the Aging Society*, Princeton, NJ; Oxford, Princeton University Press.

——(1996) 'Media and policy change in Japan'. In: Pharr, S. J. and Krauss, E. S. (eds) *Media and Politics in Japan*. Honolulu, University of Hawaii Press.

Cassegard, C. (2010) 'Lek och bemäktigande – de alternativa rummens roll i sociala rörelser' ('Play and empowerment: The role of alternative space in social movements'), *Sociologisk forskning*, 47, 2: 49–72.

Cave, P. (2007) *Primary School in Japan: Self, Individuality and Learning in Elementary Education*, Abingdon, Routledge.

Chiavacci, D. (2005) 'Transition from university to work under transformation: The changing role of institutional and alumni networks in contemporary Japan', *Social Science Japan Journal*, 8, 1: 19–41.

Dahrendorf, R. (1958) 'Toward a theory of social conflict', *The Journal of Conflict Resolution*, 2, 2: 170–83.

Dower, J. W. (1999) *Embracing Defeat: Japan in the Aftermath of World War II*, London, Allen Lane.

Duffy, K. (1997) *Review of the International Dimension of the Thematic Priority on Social Integration and Exclusion*, Report to the Economic and Social Research Council. Swindon, ESRC.

Emmenegger, P., Hausermann, S., Palier, B. and Seeleib-Kaiser, M. (2012) *The Age of Dualization: The Changing Face of Inequality in Deindustrializing Societies*, Oxford, Oxford University Press.

Esping-Andersen, G. (ed.) (1996) *Welfare States in Transition: National Adaptations in Global Economies*, London, UNRISD/Sage Publications.

——(1999) *Social Foundations of Postindustrial Economies*, Oxford, Oxford University Press.

——(2009) *The Incomplete Revolution: Adapting to Women's New Roles*, Cambridge, Polity Press.

Estevez-Abe, M. (2003) 'State-society partnerships in the Japanese welfare state'. In: Schwartz, F. J. and Pharr, S. J. (eds) *The State of Civil Society in Japan*. Cambridge, Cambridge University Press.

Fukuhara, H. (ed.) (2007) *Shakaiteki Haijo, Hōsetsu to Shakai Seisaku (Social Exclusion, Inclusion and Social Policy)*, Kyoto, Hōritsu Bunkasha.

Furlong, A. (2006) 'Not a very NEET solution: Representing problematic labour market transitions among early school leavers', *Work, Employment and Society*, 20: 553–69.

Furlong, A. and Cartmel, F. (1997) *Young People and Social Change: Individualization and Risk in Late Modernity*, Buckingham, Open University Press.

Furuichi, N. (2010) *Kibō Nanmin go-Ikkō-sama: Peace Boat to 'Shōnin no Kyōdōtai' Gensō (Hope Refugees: Peace Boat and the Illusion of 'Communities of Recognition')*, Tokyo, Kōbunsha Shinsho.

——(2011) *Zetsubō no Kuni no Shiawase na Wakamonotachi (The Happy Youth of a Desperate Nation)*, Tokyo, Kōdansha.

Futagami, N. (2005) *Kibō no Nīto: Genba kara no Messeji (The NEETs of Hope: A Message from the Field)*, Tokyo, Tōyō Keizai Shinpōsha.

Genda, Y. (2001) *Shigoto no Naka no Aimai na Fuan*, Tokyo, Chūō Koron Shinsha.

——(2001/2005) *A Nagging Sense of Job Insecurity: The New Reality Facing Japanese Youth*, Tokyo, International House Press.

——(2004) '14-sai ni "ii otona" to deawasey(om)', *Chūō Kōron*, February, 162–19.

——(2005a) *Hataraku Kajō: Otona no tame no Wakamono Tokuhon (Excessive Work: A Youth Reader for Adults)*, Tokyo, NTT Shuppan.

——(2005b) 'Jyakunen mugyōsha no jijyō' ('The situation of non-employed youth'). In: Cabinet Office (ed.) *Seishōnen no Shūrō ni kan suru Kenkyū Chōsa (A Research Report regarding Young People's Employment)*. Tokyo, Cabinet Office (Seisaku Tōkatsukan, Kyōsei Shakai Seisaku Tantō), the Government of Japan.

——(2007) 'Jobless youths and the NEET problem in Japan', *Social Science Japan Journal*, 10, 1: 23–40.

Genda, Y. and Maganuma, M. (2004) *NEET: Furītā demo naku, Shitsugyōsha demo naku (NEET: Neither Freeter nor Unemployed)*, Tokyo, Gentōsha.

Genda, Y. and Kosugi, R. (2005) *Kodomo ga NEET ni Nattara (What to Do if Your Child Becomes a NEET)*, Tokyo, NHK Press.

Gilbert, N. (2002) *Transformation of the Welfare State: The Silent Surrender of Public Responsibility*, Oxford, Oxford University Press.

Goodman, R. (1990) *Japan's 'International Youth': The Emergence of a New Class of Schoolchildren*, Oxford, Clarendon Press.

——(2000) *Children of the Japanese State: The Changing Role of Child Protection Institutions in Contemporary Japan*, Oxford, Oxford University Press.

——(ed.) (2002a) *Family and Social Policy in Japan: Anthropological Approaches*, Cambridge, Cambridge University Press.

——(2012a) 'The "discovery" and "rediscovery" of child abuse (*jidō gyakutai*) in Japan'. In: Goodman, R., Imoto, Y. and Toivonen, T. (eds) *A Sociology of Japanese Youth: From Returnees to NEETs*. Abingdon, Routledge.

——(2012b) 'Shifting landscapes: The social context of youth problems in an ageing nation'. In: Goodman, R., Imoto, Y. and Toivonen, T. (eds) *A Sociology of Japanese Youth: From Returnees to NEETs*. Abingdon, Routledge, 159–173.

Goodman, R. and Peng, I. (1996) 'The East Asian welfare states: Peripatetic learning, adaptive change, and nation-building'. In: Esping-Andersen, G. (ed.) *Welfare States in Transition: National Adaptations in Global Economies.* London, UNRISD/Sage Publications.

Goodman, R., Hatakenaka, S. and Kim, T. (2009) *The Changing Status of Vocational Higher Education in Contemporary Japan and the Republic of Korea (UNESCO-UNEVOC Discussion Paper),* Bonn, UNESCO-UNEVOC International Centre.

Goodman, R., Imoto, Y. and Toivonen, T. (eds) (2012) *A Sociology of Japanese Youth: From Returnees to NEETs,* Abingdon, Routledge.

Gottfried, H. (2008) 'Pathways to economic security: Gender and nonstandard employment in contemporary Japan', *Social Indicators Research,* 88, 1: 179–96.

Hall, P. (1993) 'Policy paradigms, social learning, and the state: The case of economic policymaking in Britain', *Comparative Politics,* 25, 3: 275–96.

Hendry, J. (1992) 'Individualism and individuality: Entry into a social world'. In: Goodman, R. and Refsing, K. (eds) *Ideology and Practice in Modern Japan.* London, Routledge.

Hertog, E. (2008) 'The worst abuse against a child is the absence of a parent: How Japanese unwed mothers evaluate their decision to have a child outside wedlock', *Japan Forum,* 20, 2: 193–217.

Higuchi, A. (2007) 'Nihon ni okeru wakamono mondai to shakaiteki haijo: "Tekisetsu na shigoto", "kasseika", "tagenteki katsudou" wo megutte' ('Youth problems and social exclusion in Japan: Regarding "decent work", "activation" and "multi-activity"'). In: Fukuhara, H. (ed.) *Shakaiteki Haijo, Hōsetsu to Shakai Seisaku (Social Exclusion, Inclusion and Social Policy).* Kyoto, Hōritsu Bunkasha.

Hilgartner, S. and Bosk, C. (1988) 'The rise and fall of social problems: A public arenas model', *American Journal of Sociology,* 94, 1: 53–78.

Hills, J. and Stewart, K. (2005), *A More Equal Society? New Labour, Poverty, Inequality and Exclusion,* Bristol, Policy.

Holmqvist, M. (2009) *The Disabling State of an Active Society,* Surrey, Ashgate Publishing.

Honda, Y. (2004) 'The formation and transformation of the Japanese system of transition from school to work', *Social Science Japan Journal,* 7, 1: 103–15.

——(2005) *Wakamono to Shigoto: 'Gakkō Keiyu no Shūshoku' wo Koete,* Tokyo, Tokyo University Press.

——(ed.) (2007) *Wakamono no Rōdō to Seikatsu Sekai: Karera wa Donna Genjitsu wo Ikiteiru ka (Youth Labour and Life Worlds: What Kind of a Reality Are They Living?),* Tokyo, Ōtsuki Shoten.

——(2009) *Kyōiku no Shokugyōteki Igi: Wakamono, Gakkō, Shakai wo Tsunagu,* Tokyo, Chikuma Shobō.

Honda, Y., Naitō, A. and Gotō, K. (2006) *'Nīto'tte Iu na!,* Tokyo, Kōbunsha.

Hook, G. and Takeda, H. (2007) '"Self-responsibility" and the nature of the postwar Japanese state: Risk through the looking glass', *The Journal of Japanese Studies,* 33, 1: 93–123.

Horiguchi, S. (2011) 'Coping with hikikomori: Socially withdrawn youth and the Japanese family'. In: Ronald, R. and Alexy, A. (eds) *Home and Family in Japan: Continuity and Transformation.* Abingdon, Routledge.

——(2012) 'Hikikomori: How private isolation caught the public eye'. In: Goodman, R., Imoto, Y. and Toivonen, T. (eds) *A Sociology of Japanese Youth: From Returnees to NEETs.* Abingdon, Routledge.

Instance, D., Rees, G. and Williamson, H. (1994) *Young People Not in Education, Training or Employment in South Glamorgan*, Cardiff, South Glamorgan Training and Enterprise Council.

Inui, A. (1999) 'Wakamono-tachi no "gakkō kara shakai e" wo sasaeru kōkyō system' ('The public system that supports youth in moving from "school to socieity"'), *Gakkō seikatsu shidō*, 140.

Ishikawa, R. (2007) *Hikikomori no Gōru: 'Shūrō' demo naku, 'Taijin Kankei' demo naku (The Goal of Withdrawn Youth: Neither 'Work' nor 'Social Relationships')*, Tokyo, Seikyūsha.

Iwata, M. and Nishizawa, A. (eds) (2005) *Hinkon to Shakaiteki Haijo: Fukushi Shakai wo Mushibamu Mono (Poverty and Social Exclusion: Eating Away at the Welfare Society)*, Kyoto, Minerva Shobō.

Johnson, C. A. (1982) *MITI and the Japanese Miracle: The Growth of Industrial Policy, 1925–1975*, Stanford, CA, Stanford University Press.

Jones, G. and Wallace, C. (1992) *Youth, Family and Citizenship*, Buckingham, Open University Press.

JPCSED (2007a) *Wakamono Jiritsu Juku Shien Sentā (Youth Independence Camp Support Centre)*, Tokyo, Japan Productivity Centre for Socio-Economic Development. URL: <www.jiritsu-juku.jp> (accessed in September 2007).

——(2007b) *Special Survey on Non-Employed Youth at Sites of Youth Employment Support*, Tokyo, Japan Productivity Centre for Socio-Economic Development.

——(2009) *Wakamono Jiritsu Juku Shien Sentā (Youth Independence Camp Support Centre)*, Tokyo, Japan Productivity Centre for Socio-Economic Development. URL: <www.jiritsu-juku.jp> (accessed in March 2009).

Kalisch, D. (1991) 'The active society', *Social Security Journal*, August 1991.

Kanamori, K. (1999) 'Koronbusu Daikōkai: Intānashonaru Koronbusu Akademī no Ayumi' ('The Great Columbus Voyage: The course charted by the International Columbus Academy'), *Gekkan Shōnen Ikusei*, 514: 8–15.

Kaneko, S. (2006) *Hikikomori and Cultural Debates about Japanese Personhood: An Anthropological Study of Japan's So-Called 'Socially-Withdrawn Youth'*, University of Oxford DPhil thesis.

Kariya, T. (2011) 'Credential inflation and employment in "universal" higher education: Enrolment, expansion and (in)equity via privatisation in Japan', *Journal of Education and Work*, 24, 1: 69–94.

Kariya, T. and Honda, Y. (eds) (2010) *Dai-Sotsu Shūshoku no Shakaigaku: Dēta kara Miru Henka (English title: The Sociology of Transition from University to Work: Empirical Studies of the Changing Mechanisms of Contemporary Japan)* Tokyo, Tokyo University Press.

Kariya, T., Sugayama, S. and Ishida, H. (eds) (2000) *Gakkō, Shokuan to Rōdō Shijō (School, Public Employment Security Offices and Labour Markets)*, Tokyo, Tokyo University Press.

Kasza, G. J. (2006) *One World of Welfare: Japan in Comparative Perspective*, Ithaca, NY, Cornell University Press.

Kemp, P. (2006) 'Young people and unemployment: From welfare to workfare?'. In: Barry, M. (ed.) *Youth Policy and Social Inclusion: Critical Debates with Young People*. Abingdon, Routledge.

King, D. and Wickham-Jones, M. (1999) 'From Clinton to Blair: The Democratic (Party) origins of welfare to work', *The Political Quarterly*, 70, 1: 62–74.

Kingdon, J. W. (2003) *Agendas, Alternatives, and Public Policies*, New York, Longman.

Kinsella, S. (1998) 'Japanese subculture in the 1990s: Otaku and the amateur manga movement', *The Journal of Japanese Studies*, 24: 289–316.

——(2012) 'Narratives and statistics: How compensated dating (*enjo kōsai*) was sold'. In: Goodman, R., Imoto, Y. and Toivonen, T. (eds) *A Sociology of Japanese Youth: From Returnees to NEETs.* Abingdon, Routledge.

Kosugi, R. (ed.) (2003) *Shogaikoku no Wakamono Shūgyō Shien Seisaku no Tenkai: Igirisu to Suwēden wo Chūshin ni* (*Developments in Youth Employment Support Policy in Foreign Countries: A Focus on the UK and Sweden*), Tokyo, Japan Institute for Labour Policy and Training.

——(2004) 'Jyakunen mugyōsha zōka no jittai to haikei' ('The current situation with and the background to the increase in non-employed youth'), *Nihon Rōdō Kenkyū Zasshi*, 533, 12: 4–16.

——(ed.) (2005) *Freeter to NEET (Freeters and NEETs)*, Tokyo, Keisō Shobō.

——(2008) *Escape from Work: Freelancing Youth and the Challenge to Corporate Japan*, Melbourne, Trans Pacific Press.

Kosugi, R. and Hori, Y. (2003) *Gakkō kara Shokugyō e no Ikō wo Shien Suru Shokikan e no Hiaringu Chōsa Kekka: Nihon ni okeru NEET Mondai no Shozai to Taiō* (*Results from a Survey of Institutions that Support the School-to-Work Transition: The Nature of the NEET Problem in Japan and Relevant Responses*), JIL Discussion Paper Series 03–001, Japan Institute for Labour Policy and Training.

Kudō, K. (2005) *'Nīto' shien manyuaru* (*A NEET Support Manual*), Tokyo, PHP Shuppan.

(2006) *Sodate-Age Netto: Wakamono no Jiritsu wo Shien Suru* (*Sodate-Age Net: Supporting the Independence of Young People*), Tokyo, Surugadai Shuppan.

Kudō, S. and Sutajio Potto (1997) *ōi Hikikomori, Sorosoro Soto e Detemiyōze* (*Hey Hikikomori, It's About Time We Try and Go Out*), Tokyo, Potto Shuppan.

Lähteenmaa, J. (2010) 'Nuoret työttömät ja taistelu toimijuudesta' ('The young unemployed and the struggle for agency'), *Työvoimapoliittinen aikakausikirja* (*Finnish Labour Review*), 4/2010: 51–63.

Lee, S. (2011) 'The shift of labour market risks in deindustrializing Taiwan, Japan and Korea', *Perspectives on Global Development and Technology*, 10, 2.

Leheny, D. (2006) *Think Global, Fear Local: Sex, Violence, and Anxiety in Contemporary Japan*, Ithaca, NY, Cornell University Press.

LeTendre, G. (1996) 'Shidō: The concept of guidance'. In: Rohlen, T. and LeTendre, G. (eds) *Teaching and Learning in Japan.* Cambridge, Cambridge University Press.

Levitan, S. A. and Johnston, B. (1975) *The Job Corps: A Social Experiment That Works*, Baltimore, Johns Hopkins University Press.

Levitas, R. (2005) *The Inclusive Society? Social Exclusion and New Labour*, Basingstoke, Macmillan.

Lunsing, W. (2003) '"Parasite" and "non-parasite" singles: Japanese journalists and scholars taking positions', *Social Science Japan Journal*, 6, 2: 261–65.

MacDonald, R. (ed.) (1997) *Youth, The 'Underclass' and Social Exclusion*, London, Routledge.

Manabi Rinku (2007) *Zenkoku Furīsukūru Gaido 2007–2008-nenban: Shōchūkō Futō-kōsei no Ibasho Sagashi* (*A Guide to Free Schools across Japan in 2007–2008: The Search of School-Refusers from Elementary, Secondary and Upper Secondary Schools for a Place of Their Own*), Tokyo, Līfu Shuppan.

Marshall, T. H. (1950) *Citizenship and Social Class*, Cambridge, Cambridge University Press.

Mathews, G. (2004) 'Seeking a career, finding a job: How young people enter and resist the Japanese world of work'. In: Mathews, G. and White, B. (eds) *Japan's Changing Generations: Are Young People Creating a New Society?* London, RoutledgeCurzon.

METI (2004) *'Wakamono no tame no Wan-Sutoppu Sābisu Sentā (Tsūshō Jobu Kafe)' Jigyō no Moderu Chīki no Sentei ni tsuite (Regarding the Selection of Pilot Regions for the 'One-Stop Service Centre for Youth (Job Cafe)' [press release]*), Tokyo, Ministry of Economy, Trade and Industry, the Government of Japan.

——(2008) *Jobu Kafe Jigyō no Heisei 19-nendo Jigyō Hyōka, Heisei 20-nendo Jigyō Mokuhyō (Zenkoku Torimatome) (Job Cafe Programme Evaluation for 2007 and Programme Goals for 2008)*, Tokyo, Ministry of Economy, Trade and Industry, the Government of Japan.

MEXT (1999) *Shotō Chūtō Kyōiku to Kōtō Kyōiku to no Setsuzoku no Kaizen ni tsuite (Regarding the Improvement of the Connection between Primary and Secondary Education and Higher Education)*, Tokyo, MEXT (Chūō Kyōiku Shingikai), the Government of Japan.

——(2006) *Kyaria Kyōiku no Suishin no Tebiki (A Handbook Regarding the Promotion of Career Education)*, Tokyo, MEXT, the Government of Japan.

MHLW (2002) *Teishotokusha no Aratana Seikatsu Shien Shisutemu Kentō Purojekuto Hōkokusho (Report: A Deliberative Project Regarding a New Livelihood Support System for Low-Income People)*, Tokyo, Ministry of Health, Labour and Welfare, the Government of Japan.

——(2004) *Heisei 16-nen-ban Rōdō Keizai Bunseki (The 2004 White Paper on the Labour Markets)*, Tokyo, MHLW, the Government of Japan.

——(2005a) *Health, Labour and Welfare White Paper*, Tokyo, Ministry of Health, Labour and Welfare, the Government of Japan.

——(2005b) *Heisei 17-nen-ban Rōdō Keizai Bunseki (The 2005 White Paper on the Labour Markets)*, Tokyo, MHLW, the Government of Japan.

——(2006) *Health, Labour and Welfare White Paper*, Tokyo, Ministry of Health, Labour and Welfare, the Government of Japan.

——(2007a) *Heisei 19-nen-ban Rōdō Keizai Bunseki (The 2007 White Paper on the Labour Markets)*, Tokyo, Government of Japan.

——(2007b) *Kimi no Chikara, Mirai no Chikara: Wakamono Shien Genba kara no Messēji (Your Power – the Power of the Future: Messages from the Frontlines of Youth Support)*, The Office of the State-Private Sector Movement to Raise the Human Competence of Youth, Employment Security Bureau, MHLW, the Government of Japan.

——(2008) *Health, Labour and Welfare White Paper*, Tokyo, Ministry of Health, Labour and Welfare, the Government of Japan.

Miller, A. (2010) 'Taibatsu: "Corporal punishment" in Japanese socio-cultural context', *Japan Forum*, 21, 2: 233–54.

——(2012) 'Taibatsu: From educational solution to social problem to marginalized non-issue'. In: Goodman, R., Imoto, Y. and Toivonen (eds) *A Sociology of Japanese Youth: From Returnees to NEETs*. Abingdon, Routledge.

Miller, A. and Toivonen, T. (2010) 'To discipline or accommodate? On the rehabilitation of Japanese "problem youth"', (22 June) *Asia-Pacific Journal*.

Miyamoto, M. (2002) *Wakamono ga Shakaiteki Jyakusha ni Tenraku Suru (The Emergence of Youth as a Socially Disadvantaged Class)*, Tokyo, Yōsensha.

——(2004) 'Shakaiteki haijo to jyakunen mugyō: Igirisu, Suwēden no taiō' ('Social exclusion and youth non-employment: Responses in England and Sweden'), *Nihon Rōdō Kenkyū Zasshi*, 533, 12: 17–26.

——(2005) 'Prolonged transitional period and policy', *Japan Labour Review*, 2, 3: 73–91.

New Zealand Herald Tribune (2003a) 'School Director Charged in Relation to Student's Death' (27 February), *New Zealand Herald Tribune*.

——(2003b) 'Academy Where Japanese Man Died is Closing' (4 July), *New Zealand Herald Tribune*.

——(2004) 'Four Men Jailed 3.5 Years for Beating Student to Death' (3 December), *New Zealand Herald Tribune*.

Nicholls, A. (2006) *Social Entrepreneurship: New Models of Sustainable Social Change*, Oxford, Oxford University Press.

Nicholls, A. and Murdock, A. (eds) (2012) *Social Innovation: Blurring Boundaries to Reconfigure Markets*, Basingstoke, Palgrave Macmillan.

OECD (1989) 'Editorial: The path to full employment: Structural adjustments for an active society', *Employment Outlook*, Paris, OECD.

——(2008) *Jobs for Youth: Japan*, Paris, OECD.

Office for National Statistics / Department for Education and Skills (2003) *Statistical Release SFR 31/2003*, London, Department of Education and Skills.

Okita, T. (2003) 'Kyōiku kara Shokugyō e no Ikō no Gaikan to Sūsei' ('School-to-Work Transition: Overview and Trends'). In: Kosugi, R. (ed.) *Shogaikoku no Wakamono Shūgyō Shien Seisaku no Tenkai: Igirisu to Suwēden wo Chūshin ni* (*Developments in Youth Employment Support Policy in Foreign Countries: A Focus on the UK and Sweden*). Tokyo, Japan Institute for Labour Policy and Training.

Osawa, M. (2011) *Social Security in Contemporary Japan*, Abingdon, Routledge.

Ozawa-de Silva, C. (2006) *Psychotherapy and Religion in Japan: The Japanese Introspection Practice of Naikan*, London, Routledge.

Peck, J. and Theodore, N. (2000) 'Beyond "employability"', *Cambridge Journal of Economics*, 24: 729–49.

Pekkanen, R. (2003) 'Molding Japanese civil society: State-structured incentives and the patterning of civil society'. In: Schwartz, F. J. and Pharr, S. J. (eds) *The State of Civil Society in Japan*. Cambridge, Cambridge University Press.

——(2006) *Japan's Dual Civil Society: Members without Advocates*, Stanford, CA, Stanford University Press.

——(2004) 'Postindustrial pressures, political regime shifts, and social policy reform in Japan and South Korea', *Journal of East Asian Studies*, 4: 389–425.

Pierson, P. (1998) 'Irresistible forces, immovable objects: Post-industrial welfare states confront permanent austerity', *Journal of European Public Policy*, 5, 4: 539–60.

Putnam, R. D. (2000) *Bowling Alone: The Collapse and Revival of American Community*, New York, Simon and Schuster.

Rebick, M. (2005) *The Japanese Employment System: Adapting to a New Economic Environment*, Oxford, Oxford University Press.

Roberts, G. (2002) 'Pinning hopes on angels: Reflections from an aging Japan's urban landscape'. In: Goodman, R. (ed.) *Family and Social Policy in Japan: Anthropological Approaches*. Cambridge, Cambridge University Press.

Rosenbaum, J. E. and Kariya, T. (1989) 'From high school to work: Market and institutional mechanisms in Japan', *American Journal of Sociology*, 94, 6: 1334–65.

Sakaguchi, J. (2007) '"Yūsu wāku to Kirisuto-kyō kyōiku": Wakamono no kyōiku, fukushi to rōdō' ('"Youth work and Christian education": The education, welfare and labour of youth'), *Studies on Christian Education* (*Japan Institute of Christian Education at Rikkyo University*), 24.

Sankei Shimbun (2004) 'Hatarakanai wakamono "nīto", 10-nen de 1.6-bai shūgyō iyoku naku oya ni "kisei"' ('Non-working youth "nīto" increase 1.6-fold in 10 years, have no will to work, sponge off parents') (17 May), *Sankei Shimbun*.

Schneider, A. and Ingram, H. (1993) 'Social construction of target populations: Implications for politics and policy', *American Political Science Review*, 87, 2: 334–47.

——(eds) (2005) *Deserving and Entitled: Social Constructions and Public Policy*, Albany, State University of New York.

——(2008) 'Social constructions in the study of public policy'. In: Hostein, J. A. and Gubrium, J. F. (eds) *Handbook of Constructionist Research*. New York, Guilford Press.

Schoppa, L. (2006) *Race for the Exits: The Unraveling of Japan's System of Social Protection*, Ithaca, NY, Cornell University Press.

Schwartz, F. J. (2003) 'Introduction: Recognizing civil society in Japan'. In: Schwartz, F. J. and Pharr, S. J. (eds) *The State of Civil Society in Japan*. Cambridge, Cambridge University Press.

Slater, D. (2010) 'The "new working class" of urban Japan: Socialization and contradiction from middle school to the labor market'. In: Ishida, H. and Slater, D. H. (eds) *Social Class in Contemporary Japan*. Abingdon, Routledge.

Slater, D. and Galbraith, P. W. (2011) 'Re-narrating social class and masculinity in neoliberal Japan: An examination of the media coverage of the "Akihabara Incident" of 2008', *Electronic Journal of Contemporary Japanese Studies*, September 30, 2011.

Smith, C. S. 2006. *After Affluence: Freeters and the Limits of New Middle Class Japan*. Yale University PhD Dissertation.

Social Exclusion Unit (1999) *Bridging the Gap: New Opportunities for 16–18 Year Olds Not in Education, Employment or Training*, London, Cabinet Office, the Government of the United Kingdom.

Spector, M. and Kitsuse, J. (1977) *Constructing Social Problems*, Menlo Park, CA, Cummings Publishing Company.

Standing, G. (2009) *Work After Globalization: Building Occupational Citizenship*, Cheltenham, Edward Elgar.

Stark, D. (2009) *The Sense of Dissonance: Accounts of Worth in Economic Life*, Princeton, NJ, Princeton University Press.

——(2011) *Labor Force Survey (long-term time series data)*, Tokyo, Ministry of Internal Affairs and Communications, the Government of Japan. URL: <www.e-stat.go.jp/SG1/estat/List.do?bid=000001007702andcycode=0> (accessed 5 May 2011).

Takahashi, Y. (2005) 'Jichitai ni yoru Shūgyō Shien toshite no "Jobu Kafe" no Genjō' ('The current situation of "Job Cafe" as a local government employment support measure'), *Nihon Rōdō Kenkyū Zasshi*, 539: 56–67.

Takegawa, S. (2005) 'Japan's welfare-state regime: Welfare politics, provider and regulator', *Development and Society*, 34, 2: 169–90.

Thoits, P. A. (2011) 'Resisting the stigma of mental illness', *Social Psychology Quarterly*, 74, 1: 6–28.

Toivonen, T. (2008) 'Introducing the Youth Independence Camp: How a new social policy is reconfiguring the public-private boundaries of social provision in Japan', *Sociologos*, 32: 40–57.

——(2009) *Explaining Social Inclusion and Activation Policy for Youth in 21st Century Japan*, A University of Oxford PhD thesis.

——(2011a) '"Don't let your child become a NEET": The strategic foundations of a Japanese youth scare', *Japan Forum*, 23, 3: 407–29.

——(2011b) 'Japanese youth after the triple disaster: How entrepreneurial students are overcoming barriers to volunteering and changing Japan', *Harvard Asian Quarterly*, Winter 2011, 8, 4:53–62.

Toivonen, T. and Imoto, Y. (2012) 'Making sense of youth problems'. In: Goodman, R., Imoto, Y. and Toivonen, T. (eds) *A Sociology of Japanese Youth: From Returnees to NEETs*. Abingdon, Routledge.

Toivonen, T and Imoto, Y (forthcoming) 'Transcending labels & panics: The logic of Japanese youth problems', Contemporary Japan.

Toivonen, T., Norasakkunkit, V. and Uchida, Y. (2011) 'Unable to conform, unwilling to rebel? Youth, globalization and motivation in Japan', *Frontiers in Cultural Psychology*, 2 (Article 207).

Tönnies, F. (1996) *Community and Society (Gemeinshaft und Gesellschaft)*, New Brunswick, Transaction Publishers.

Turner, V. (1975) 'Symbolic studies', *Annual Review of Anthropology*, 4: 145–61.

Wada, S. (1997) *'Kan' wo Sodateru: Ikizumaranai Kyōiku (Fostering 'Sensibility': Education That Does not Come Against Dead-Ends)*, Tokyo, Jiyūsha.

Walther, A. and Pohl, A. (2005) *Thematic Study on Policy Measures Concerning Disadvantaged Youth. Study Commissioned by the European Commission: Final Report*, Tubingen, IRIS.

Watters, E. (2010) *Crazy Like Us: The Globalization of the American Psyche*, London, Free Press.

Weathers, C. (2001) 'Changing white–collar workplaces and female temporary workers in Japan', *Social Science Japan Journal*, 4, 2: 201–18.

Weathers, C. and North, S. (2009) 'Overtime activists take on corporate titans: Toyota, McDonald's and Japan's work hour controversy', *Pacific Affairs*, 82, 4: 615–36.

Wedel, J. R., Shore, C., Feldman, G. and Lathrop, S. (2005) 'Toward an anthropology of public policy', *The Annals of the American Academy*, 600, July 2005: 30–51.

White, M. (1987) *The Japanese Educational Challenge: A Commitment to Children*, New York, The Free Press.

Williamson, H. (1997) 'Status zero youth and the underclass: Some considerations'. In: MacDonald, R. (ed.) *Youth, The 'Underclass' and Social Exclusion.* London, Routledge, 70–82.

World Bank (2010) *World Development Indicators*, Washington, World Bank. URL: 121212 (accessed 1 September 2009 and 1 September 2010).

Yamada, A. (2006) *Shin-Byōdō Shakai: Kibō Kakusa wo Koete (The New Equal Society: Overcoming the Disparities of Hope)*, Tokyo, Bungei Shunjū.

Yamaguchi, M. (1970) 'Kinrō Seishōnen Fukukushi-hō Seitei no Haikei to sono Gaiyō' ('The enactment of the Working Youth's Welfare Law: Background and overview'), *Sanji Keizai Kenkyūjo Shohō*, 6: 3–15.

——(1972) *Ashita wo Hiraku Kinrō Seishōnen: Rōdō to Yoka no Chōwa no tame ni (The Working Youth Who Create the Future: Harmonising Work and Leisure)*, Tokyo, Dai-ichi Hōki Shuppan.

Yamazaki, A. (1994) 'The medicalization and demedicalization of school refusal: Constructing an educational problem in Japan'. In: Best, J. (ed.) *Troubling Children: Studies of Children and Social Problems.* New York, Aldine de Gruyter.

Yates, S. and Payne, M. (2006) 'Not so NEET? A critique of the use of "NEET" in setting targets for interventions with young people', *Journal of Youth Studies*, 9, 329–44.

Yoder, R. S. (2004) *Youth Deviance in Japan: Class Reproduction and Non-Conformity*, Melbourne, Trans Pacific Press.

Yokohama Youth Support Station (YYSS) (2007) *Empowerment (Annual Report)*, Yokohama, Yokohama Youth Support Station.

——(2008) *Empowerment (Annual Report)*, Yokohama, Yokohama Youth Support Station.

Yokoi, T. (2006) 'Wakamono jiritsu shien seisaku kara fuhenteki shitizunshippu e: Posuto Fōdizumu ni okeru wakamono no shinro to shien jissen no tenbō' ('From youth independence support policy to universal social citizenship: The prospects of youth careers and support practices in a post-Fordist context'), *Japanese Journal of Educational Research*, 73, 4: 432–43.

Yoneyama, S. (1999) *The Japanese High School: Silence and Resistance*, London, Routledge.

Youth Independence Camp Handbook Committee (2007) *Wakamono Jiritsu Juku Handobukku (Youth Independence Camp Handbook)*, Tokyo, Japan Productivity Centre for Socio-Economic Development.

Yuasa, M. (2008) *Hanhinkon: 'Suberidai' Shakai kara no Dasshutsu (Anti-poverty: Overcoming 'Slide-to-the-Bottom' Society)*, Tokyo, Iwanami Shinsho.

Index